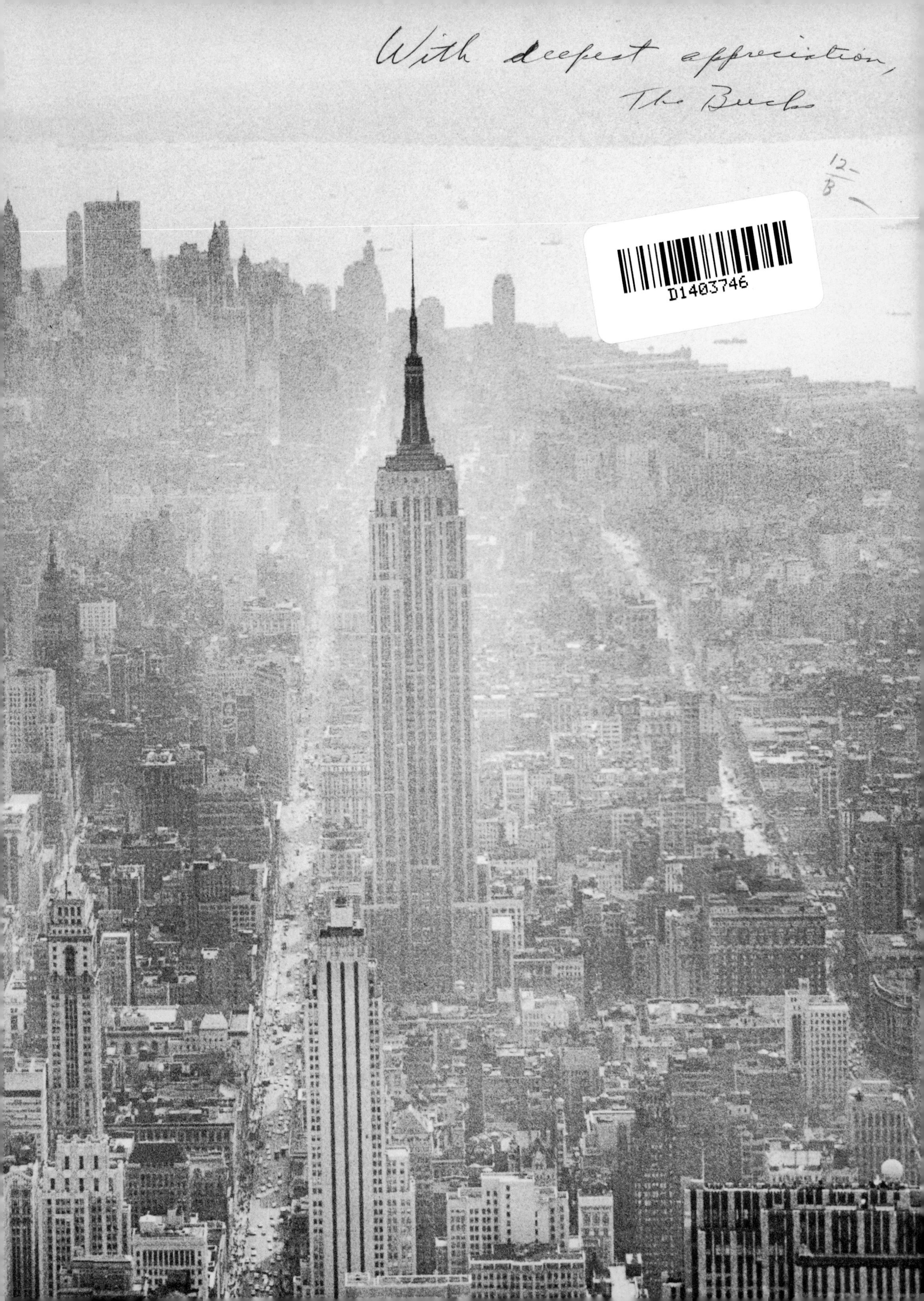

With deepest appreciation,
The Bucks

12-B

NEW YORK:
TRUE NORTH

Madison Square Garden; the National Horse Show.
For the Rangers, the customers wear cigars.

Photographs by SAM FALK

NEW YORK: TRUE NORTH

By GILBERT MILLSTEIN

DOUBLEDAY & COMPANY, INC., GARDEN CITY, NEW YORK

*A spire of
St. Patrick's Cathedral
between towers of
Rockefeller Center.*

For my wife,
Patricia Kip Millstein,
and my sons,
Ezra, Joshua and Jonathan

———

For my wife, Anne Falk

The ornamental star on the half-title page is actually a bolt with which iron rods supporting the floors and walls of many old New York buildings were fastened. Some of the material in Chapters 1, 2, and 4 through 10 appeared in somewhat different form in The New York Times. *Several paragraphs in the chapter, "Anarchy on Wheels," were published first in* Time *magazine. A number of Mr. Falk's photographs have appeared in* The New York Times.

First Edition

Designed by Joseph P. Ascherl

Madison Square Garden; stewards at the National Horse Show.
These are the relicts of Mrs. Astor, Ward McAllister, and Harry Lehr.

East Harlem; summertime.
The graciousness of the municipality
toward the downtrodden is notorious.

CONTENTS

466½ Pearl Street. Look for it in vain. It was torn down in 1962 after a century and a quarter of life and was replaced by a high-rise slab called an apartment house.

EDWARD ADLER
Author of the novel, Notes from a Dark Street

Let me get down to the bone. New York is a place on earth impossible to maintain any objectivity about. It is two distinct things to me. I look at it as a writer and I look at it as a city creature trying to make a living, and sometimes both pursuits fuse. This city is the fount of all my art, a source depthless deep, in which all forms are contained, foul and beautiful, dead and living – all effort; all things boil in this city, and, for me, it is the most terrible place on earth, in the gravest use of the word. The city is dying. In terms of my work, I might be Juvenal looking at Rome after the Republic died. The city is the Republic dying. It's unfortunate that we don't have the poets around to record it, a realist and a satirist like Juvenal to get the city down the way he got Rome, and an epigrammatist, like Tacitus.

Living in this city, in which I was born, causes my emotions to swing from moments of sheer aesthetic refinement, on the one hand, to terror, on the other. I saw something the other night that really threw me. I was crossing the Brooklyn Bridge. On the Brooklyn side, I saw a bird come to rest, in the afterglow of dusk, perched for a moment on a suspension cable. The bird imposed against the mechanical artifice – this is the city as nature to me. Swing the cycle over. I was driving slowly up Fourth Avenue at about one o'clock in the morning – I push a hack to help keep me writing – and there was a distinguished-looking, gray-haired man standing stark naked in front of Bible House. Stark naked. Not an instant's attention was paid to him. People passed him by as he stood slapping at his ribs for warmth. The terror is that a city like this can absorb an event so astonishing without a change. It was another proof for me that the Republic is dying, that we have reached a point of dissolution which cannot be reversed.

Nevertheless, I love the city with a passion. People always complain that what they face in this city is indifference. I don't believe that to be true. New Yorkers aren't indifferent; it's impossible for them to be, purely because they *have* to respond to the weight of the external city through which they move. I love it so *because* it is an external city – in the Miltonic sense. It is a phantasmagoria, ever shifting, its atmosphere made brilliant by the contention of all its elements. We sometimes mistake terror for indifference. The reason people pass this naked man by is, God knows, only some happy trick of circumstance that has deprived *them* of the opportunity to stand naked before Bible House. To the man whose instincts require nakedness before Bible House, the city will give the need expression. It is one of the conditions of life in this city, just as the bird on the bridge is.

The city represents the final state of anarchy. We have all the degradation here that Rome had when the Republic died. The parallels of vice are astonishing; patriotism is dead. The city is so damned human, and, like anything human, it must die. It's dying right before my eyes, but it's dying with a vigor that the world has never before seen.

WILLIAM B. ZECKENDORF
Real estate operator and builder

You've asked me what New York means to me. I've never thought of that before, so that anything I have to say is entirely extemporaneous and unrehearsed. I prefer to have it that way. New York has many facets that have a profound effect upon me. I have to include what I have received from New York, my impressions of where New York is going, and what I think of New York in the light of historical perspective. There are other aspects, but, you understand, *I'm* not writing a book, *you* are, and I am just one of dozens of others who are giving you their impressions. Go ahead – put that in there.

I have received, first, my livelihood from New York. Webb & Knapp, the real estate company, is, as you know, the instrumentality through which I work and survive. Secondly, the city has given me my education in the true sense of the word. And, third, it has given me a sense of *joie de vivre*. I'm a great believer in education coming from doing, from challenge, from emulation. The spirit of emulation arises from challenge and exposure to people, and New York, being the only true cosmopolitan city in the United States, in my opinion, has privileged me to know at first hand many of the outstanding leaders of our time in every field of endeavor. Through knowing them, I have learned to understand their thinking and, in many cases, to exchange challenges and parries and thrusts with them. This has a tendency to sharpen one's wits and increase one's need for ingenuity. It also broadens one's horizons. For better or worse, the end result of my efforts and deeds could never have been derived from a lesser city than New York.

I say this city has given me a sense of *joie de vivre* because it is the most sophisticated city in the United States and has offered me exposure to all extremes. Having been more fortunate than many others, my reaction to my victories, defeats, and stalemates has been to give me an understanding and love of life and the game of living that New York uniquely provides.

Fire escapes and terraces at Sixty-fifth Street and Third Avenue. Soot democratically covers rich and poor alike.

I think New York is the greatest brain center in the world or in the history of the world – absolutely and relatively. Both. Therefore, I must conclude that New York will take its place among the timeless cities of history. It is in the formative stage presently. I cannot estimate the date of its decline – I assume all cities must decline – but I would say that right now it is where Rome was in its ascendancy, possibly three quarters of the way to its peak. Likewise, Rome's predecessor, Athens, at the same point in *its* history. They're comparable, all right. I think the jury is out as to whether New York will make the full grade. That depends on a lot of things over which New York has no control: atomic warfare, the city's relative position against others competing for pre-eminence in the United States. Will it continue to grow as the seat of a world government? Will its various forms of art continue to expand? Or is it possible that it will be overcome and thwarted and frustrated by excessive materialism?

I feel that what we are doing at Webb & Knapp can be called enlightened materialism. With full knowledge and forewarning, we are prepared to venture into the hazardous fields of modern design, such as Kips Bay Plaza, an apartment development which was very, very speculative, in terms of both unknown costs

Park Avenue, west side, looking south from the plaza of the Seagram Building. In these acres of bright, blind glass, the tree has the reality of a potted palm in a hotel lobby.

and unknown acceptance. Such an effort is in the nature of primary aestheticism; we build other buildings without that as a leading motivation in order to be able to afford the luxury of the former. I would say that New York has gained less from us proportionately than other cities in this country directly, in the aesthetic sense; but, indirectly, New York has been the heir and beneficiary of a tremendous upgrading of general aestheticism, which was forced upon other builders by us — for reasons of emulation — so that our efforts have been beneficial out of all proportion to what we have built.

New York moves me in every way — and that notwithstanding I am aware of many of its deficiencies. The deficiencies, in relationship to the ensemble, are minuscule.

GREGORY CORSO
A poet

I was born on Bleecker Street, right across from the San Remo. I've lived on the Lower East Side, I've lived in Harlem, I've lived in Brooklyn, I've lived in the Bronx – Jewish neighborhoods, Italian neighborhoods, Irish neighborhoods, Negro neighborhoods. I know all the roofs of Manhattan; I used to fly pigeons from the roof when I was a kid, and when I lost a bird, I had to go up to the other roofs where they'd caught it. I knew the roofs that way and also by sleeping on them in the summertime. In the wintertime, I slept on the subways. So I think I have a right to be nationalistic about New York. I always say, "My City."

Since I got off the boat, of all the cities I've been to in the last four years in Europe, none of them can compare with this one. Londoners are not really city people. Berlin is a shell of a city and I believe the Jews took it with them. When Ben-Gurion suggested the Jews go back to Israel, I broke up laughing. If all the Jews left New York, it would be as corny as Berlin is today. Paris was beset by the Algerian thing and their sophistication has become very moody. The great Paris and the idea of the great Parisian is finished. I don't think it's any longer the mother city. The art world they had is in New York; the jazz world is in New York; the poetry world is in New York. And so, it seems, the world is in New York and I'm very happy to be in the world.

I don't feel it like a Broadway musical – none of this "New York, New York, it's a wonderful town" – but the city really makes me look at the people and see that they're almost a community. You go to a barbershop, they don't talk *low,* and everybody understands everything. I went in for a shave. The man said, "You need a haircut." I said, "I don't *think* I need one." "Well," he told me, "if you don't need a haircut, you don't need a shave, either," and everyone in the shop heard this and they all broke up laughing. I broke up too. I said, "Great." Everyone's on the ball in their consciousness, you see, and New York really is not square at all. In other words, you can be real crazy and not be thought of as merely an eccentric. Everybody is kind of batty in a way, anyway.

Whenever I met anybody in Europe who was very intelligent, and if they hadn't been to New York, I would feel something lacking in their intelligence. Then I got back and met some people here who have been putting New York down. I said, "What you have to do to appreciate the city is go out of it." Coming back on the boat was great – six in the morning, the sun was breaking through. Everybody rushed to look at the Statue of Liberty on the left-hand side. I stayed on the right-hand side and gazed at the parachute jump at Coney Island, and I said, "Ah, America's Eiffel Tower." And looked at the old Half Moon Hotel, it used to be, and I said, "Ah, Abie Reles." New York is a good place for a poet, because it is high class and a poet is high class. It's wonderful to be born a poet in the greatest country in the world, and to be born a poet in the greatest city in the greatest country in the world is the greatest blessing.

I have a mystique about New York. Maybe it makes no sense at all, but anywhere I walk, there is an experience in which I can realize myself. I believe in a sort of sensuality of the self and also in an aesthetic of the self, and since I'm only going to live this life once, I feel I have an obligation to do it right the first time. New York alone can do this for me. I would die in the suburbs. My idea of what Dante's hell was all about – the last circle – is Scarsdale. I have a fantasy that Scarsdale will be my personal hell and my punishment this: I'll get on the train every morning and leave for New York, intending to go to the Museum of Art, to eat in a place in Chinatown, or a small bistro I have the arrogance to feel only I know about. What happens? I step off the train and I'm in Roslyn.

I'm a great walker in New York. In my last year of high school, I remember walking into a secondhand bookstore on Fourth Avenue and picking up a Shakespeare & Co. edition of *Ulysses* for four dollars. Oh, that tremendous feeling of walking into that store, talking about that book, and walking away with it. I was a hundred feet tall. I'm not quite that tall any more, but at least a sense of what it was like comes back to me over and over. New York has a feeling for me like the Madeleine must have had for Proust. As a matter of fact, various authors, in their relation to a city, will help explain my feeling about New York. Compare Joyce and Dublin to Kafka and Prague. Kafka had a sense of estrangement from Prague; it was a necessary condition for him, and he did not experience Prague in the same sensual way that Leopold Bloom did Dublin, the way Joyce did. It's unfortunate that a man capable of so much feeling did not really feel his city; it was not an expression of his life experience. You compare this with Joyce and Dublin. There is an act of love between the two, the act of love – even the arrogance – of a man who says, "This is my city above all cities in the world." This is the way I feel about New York.

I do something similar to what Joyce does in *Finnegans Wake*. He speaks of the hithering and thithering waters of night. I have known the hithering and thithering streets of New York. Love Lane. Corlears Hook. Coenties Slip. Orange Street. Pineapple Street. Willow Street. Murray Hill. Mott Haven. Morrisania. The streets, the streets, like so many fruits that came off the sailing ships. I don't believe New York will disintegrate. I believe the life experience in it will be a function of who you are. Things disappear, it's true, but I can look back a long way and while my children won't have just exactly the experiences I did, I can give them a sense of continuity, of what it was like. If I can communicate to them my sense of excitement, they will look for their own life experience. Both will be valid and vital.

I have shown them how to look, how to experience, and I hope I have given them what my father gave me – the ability to go to something as an act of love. I'm lucky. He did give me that. He could not really read or write, you know, but he told me about Dante. I heard about Ariosto from him, about *Orlando Furioso*. When I read Spenser for the first time, I was in a rage – I felt Spenser had stolen the *Faerie Queene* from my father. There was an old Dutchman across the street from where we lived. He introduced me to the Brooklyn Dodgers. The point I'm making is that he, like my father, gave me the feeling that there was something to really care about. There was always next year – a feeling, a knowledge of transcendence, if you will – and that, I hope, is what I've given my kids.

Call it optimism, call it anything you want, but do you know something? We've become a kind of penny-dreadful cynic without the wit of Oscar Wilde. Malraux said somewhere that ours is the only age that has been deprived of transcendence. I see it in some of my patients and I've seen it in kids, especially in the early Fifties, in the so-called rebels without causes. They were always running to barricades, only nobody had a banner to tell them why they were fighting. Well, that's not caring. I feel I can give my children something to care about. I'm fighting the bastards off; I'm putting my *heart* in the dike. There *is* a sense of history here. Gide wrote something to the effect that not to know our parents is a call to valor. In other words, Gide felt that each generation ought to be a new one, cut off from the past and parental influence. I don't go with that. I don't think our time is a bastard on both sides of the blanket.

I've known many people all over New York – I'm a dedicated seeker-out of people – and all of them have a life experience. If you will allow them the excitement of their experience, it will live for you too. Before I became an analyst I

Greeley Square; holiday shoppers. Buy, push, curse, sweat, swear, give. Pay.

worked in a place where the janitor had been a major figure in the Irish Republican Army. We would sit down after hours and he would tell me about Easter Sunday and the General Post Office. It was a beautiful, fantastic recital. Such talk! Of Mick Collins, a wild and free and savage spirit so that lost causes should not be lost. And one day he crossed a bridge, he crossed a street, he crossed a death: they keened over their "laughing boy" and breathed a sigh of relief that blew out the penny-candle lies they lit for him. Where does a city find a row house of sameness enough to cause such a man to be the same as "the others"? My time and my city shall not do this to me and mine – each morning we leave No. 11 Eccles Street, throw our hearts down the street, and chase after them: what else is a street, a heart, and a metaphor for?

We no longer decorate our homes with the richest fabrics obtainable. People are like that. I'm a romantic, all right, but this is the way my romanticism works for me: I don't have to take the colors off the canvas to see things objectively; I don't have to transmute them into black and white. If you know and care who you are, this town leaves enough room between you and beat to live and love: desire is not a streetcar line in another town.

Manhattan, midtown to the Battery.
X number of realities carried to the nth power.

GRAFFITI

Not long ago, having looked at New York on a clear late winter afternoon from the glass-enclosed observatory on the one hundred and second floor of the Empire State Building (1250 feet above the spotted black ribbon of Fifth Avenue), a French trucking contractor named Louis Riguet made a small, ineffectual attempt to reduce to meaning a phenomenon for which nothing in his experience (neither more nor less than that of any fairly prosperous European; he had seen a bit of the world, but this was his first time in America) had prepared him. Asked by a companion, a New Yorker, what he thought of what he had seen, Riguet flung his arms outward and said, almost in exasperation, *"Gigantesque!"* A sense of anticlimax made him smile at himself, after which he fell silent and seemed tired, or, at any rate, deflated.

Mott Street near Broome; graffiti on a store window. Single stories at a single moment, they will all be written over.

Riguet's acquaintance nodded sympathetically and the two men took the elevator down to the eighty-sixth-floor observatory. (The indicator lights on that one show feet, not floors: 1225, 1200, 1165, 1135, 1100, 1075, 1050.) There, Riguet recovered something of his aplomb with a frankfurter and a soft drink at the snack bar. The two men then descended to the street, the elevator taking them down (like the one that had taken them up) traveling at a speed of 1200 feet a minute. The Frenchman's *"Gigantesque!"* was a reflex of a kind often followed by a second: faced with the ungraspable, a man is likely to try to impress himself upon it somehow, to become part of it. Thus, the tourist, shaken by eternity at Chartres, cuts his initials profanely into the reredos of the cathedral. On top of the Empire State Building, vertiginous with height, glutted, confused, and exhilarated by the unimaginable bulk of New York City and by distance (as far, under the right atmospheric conditions, as Massachusetts, Pennsylvania, Connecticut, New Jersey, and upstate New York), he scratches *graffiti* on the thick, unbreakable windows of the upper observatory and is appeased.

Hundreds of these notations scratched in the glass contend with each other and are incised one over another. On a pane to the southeast (Brooklyn, Manhattan, and Williamsburg bridges; the Chase Manhattan Bank, Union Square, and the tower and clock of the Metropolitan Life Insurance Building), can be read, "Khin & LL − of Burma." Over the LL −, someone had scratched, in forthright despair, *"Lonely."* Nearby, in space if not in time, were "L.A.D., C.A.D., K.R.M. Bolivia." An east pane (Kennedy Airport, the sprawl of Brooklyn and Queens; Bellevue and the new Veterans' Hospital, Peter Cooper Village, Stuyvesant Town, and the forbidding housing projects that hug the East River glowed a dull red in a late sun) recorded "D. Musty and D. E. Anstey (R.A.F.) From England. 18/6/57." To the northeast (Chrysler Building, Seagram Building, the octagonal

Pan Am Building pressing down on Grand Central Terminal before it; the Queensborough Bridge at Fifty-ninth Street, the Triborough at 125th, and, beyond, the long reach of the Bronx to Westchester County and Connecticut) was indited, "Viva Chile." Elsewhere were to be found "Neal Wickham, Georgia, '53," and "Leon Band, Tallahassee, Florida" – whoever, from wherever, owning an instrument sharp enough to mark glass and having the inclination to memorialize himself.

To read these, the eye must shorten its focus deliberately and pick them out; otherwise, they seem quite literally to vanish in the tremendous vistas they would like to interrupt for the purpose of calling attention to themselves. That is the metaphor of New York: the *idea* of the city (*Gigantesque!*) overwhelms the *graffiti,* the accounts of it. The irony is that even if they are not ignored (the New Yorker's ignorance of the city's past is monumental and his notion of its present not much more than gossip), they will not explain New York, however assiduously read, for, with the best will, the sharpest intelligence, the clearest eye, they refute each other.

Essentially, therefore, this book is a collection of *graffiti.* Each of its photographs is a single story at a single moment. Nobody can say when the story will be different. It contains what the writer calls the testimony of fifty-six witnesses to New York, as well as his own. These, too, are single stories at single moments. The objects in the photographs will change. The witnesses, from anthropologist, madam, philosopher, narcotics addict, and stockbroker to attorney, garage mechanic, teacher, and housewife, will, if only through the passage of time, change their testimony. They will stay or move away and they will die. Their *graffiti* are all they will leave and those, too, will be written over. To the writer, the testimony, his own and the rest, made clear at least two things: a typical New Yorker does not exist and yet, in his infinite variety, he is distinct from any other urban man; and all New Yorkers are bound tighter by the city (whether in love or hatred) than are the citizens of any other place.

WITNESS · A SURGEON

Professionally, one can take a very cynical and hard view of New York and call it a great city to learn medicine in because the slums, while deplorable, offer you the opportunity to sharpen and perfect your skills. It is the people who inhabit such slums who are your clinic population. All large cities have some such pool to draw on, but I think New York is unique in that it has continual waves of immigrants – by immigrants, these days, I mean, of course, Puerto Ricans, and Negroes coming from the South – who really provide you with the finest sort of clinical material. They are ignorant and unquestioning, and, having come from pretty backward places, they have a profound faith in the medical profession. Many second- and third-generation descendants of immigrants are schooled enough now to know that doctors are human beings with faults.

20

Above: The Brooklyn Bridge, from the Franklin D. Roosevelt Drive. If the George Washington Bridge is noble, the Brooklyn Bridge is a masterpiece.

Below: Housing projects; the new slums. Who will answer, when, for these prisons?

Citizens of New York.
Their strength is beyond belief.

Immigration today; displaced persons arriving aboard a military transport. Their numbers are circumscribed; as ever, their hopes are not.

Very well. These immigrants are the people on whom interns and residents train in everything from how to perform surgery to delivering babies and psychoanalysis. We can turn their minds and their bodies inside out because they come to us as charity patients, and while we do render them the care they need, we can also engage in some peripheral but still perfectly ethical practices with them in terms of sometimes subtle and sometimes fairly overt investigations of other bodily functions besides those they come to us for. Anything we ask of them in the way of obtaining permission to use experimental drugs or new surgical techniques is always granted to us. They are, in fact, grateful for any attention they get. Also, they're not aware, in most instances, that the people who are taking immediate charge of them are interns or residents who are actually no more than on-the-job trainees.

That is what makes New York a great medical center. New Yorkers aren't any smarter than anybody else; it's just that we have this immense pool of clinical material. By the very nature of things, we see more varieties of disease, more exotic diseases, more often; we get a larger experience of dealing with every kind of illness. So, if we aren't any smarter, we are more sophisticated. And that is what brings students to the city. A surgeon, for example, is interested in material to operate on. It's perfectly obvious that in small towns, or in middle-sized towns which are highly industrialized, union and health-insurance contracts permit most workers to have their own private physicians; residents don't get much to do. There's no clinic population. When you come here, where so many people aren't covered by fringe benefits, when you get this mass of people pouring into your hoppers who are, so to speak, at the mercy of interns and residents, you have a vein of raw material that will never get worked out.

So much for this town as a place to learn in. Now New York, being a very wealthy city, offers immense opportunities for someone with talent and diligence to build-up a huge practice and make large sums of money. However, there are 16,000 physicians in this city, which means you're in very intense competition. Human nature being what it is, some of these 16,000 want to make money faster than others, and they engage in unethical practices – fee splitting, unnecessary surgery, and the like – and the temptation to get into such practices is very great; I would say the temptation *and* the practices are greater in New York than anywhere else. Don't forget that by the time a man's finished his residency and armed-forces service and begun private practice he's in his mid-thirties. It takes at least ten years – in an entirely ethical way – before he can begin to get ahead, not just meet expenses.

That's a long time to wait. The men he's graduated from college with, who went into advertising or business, are already established and have families and have been putting away money for a long time. He gets angry and frustrated and it's no wonder a lot of young doctors cut corners, particularly in this town. I've been approached; I've been offered as much as five to ten thousand a year to play ball with some general practitioner and I've turned it down every time – but every time I turned something down I wondered whether it was because I was afraid of being found out or had high moral standards. I'm not prepared to say I know.

There's one other aspect of private practice here. Your patients are wealthy, perhaps, or at least they can usually afford private care, but they're a cynical lot, an unbelieving lot. They've read the lay journals and medical articles in popular magazines and they approach you with a damned wary eye. A mistake in New York City can be extremely costly. The moment it happens, these people rush off to their lawyers screaming malpractice and the first thing you know you're hit with a summons. As a result, malpractice insurance rates are the second highest in the country – California's first; you might expect that. The group I've been talking about, the get-rich-quick boys, are ruining things for us. They're always getting in trouble and up go the rates. I absorb those increases. No company likes to carry malpractice insurance and every year or two the County Medical Society switches its carrier because nobody wants the business. The only reason they take it on is that they hope doctors will insure with them for other things – autos, life, that sort of thing. They lose on malpractice, even at their astronomical rates.

I hate New York; I detest it; it's filthy; it's too big; it's anonymous; it's faceless. You would think medicine was a respected profession. But the attitude of New Yorkers – I exclude the immigrants, as I said – is distrustful and disrespectful. My father was a doctor and it wasn't that way in his time. Me, I'm just another worker in a service area. New York has diminished me. It's continually diminishing me. In private practice, I don't get any feeling of rendering any important service. When you've got 16,000 men in a city who can do the same thing as you almost as well or better, you're just not the pillar of the community you might be in a small town. I'd go away if I could, but I like teaching and I'd never get that opportunity in a smaller town; I'd be confined to private practice.

I know all about the marvelous opportunities New York offers in other areas – restaurants, theaters, art galleries, concerts – but I'm not impressed by them, nor do I attend them very often. I long for a quieter, less hectic existence, and, having had all these so-called advantages, I'm blasé about them. I did live for a couple of years in a small town and I enjoyed it immensely, but leaving New York now would mean too much of a financial sacrifice to me. And, as I pointed out, there *is* the teaching.

WITNESS

DR. MARGARET MEAD
An anthropologist

New York is a chief city that is not a capital and I think that that is one of the most striking things about it. London or Paris or any of the great cities of the world have always been capitals. They have had the imprimatur of court and government and people have been proud of them because they symbolized the national identity. New York is somehow anomalous from that point of view. The American people, on the whole, aren't proud of it. They think of it as separate from the rest of the country. They don't play any part in its upkeep – one is a by-product of the other – and they think New Yorkers look down on them.

There is a resentment against Washington, too: it's trying to throw its weight around, telling people what to do. "They don't understand us down there." But it isn't the same as the attitude toward New York. This city is seen as a kind of concentrate of un-American specialization; it is not like any other American city;

The American Museum of Natural History; a gallery of heads of prehistoric men. Margaret Mead works on the top floor.

it is extraordinarily sophisticated. I think it is felt that New York drains the rest of the country in a way that the capital doesn't. On the other hand, I can regard New York as the very epitome of the provincial in the sense that it has no responsibility to the rest of the country. People here tend to forget the country, to treat it as the "back blocks," as the Australians say, the sticks, "the old lady from Dubuque."

New York has a great deal of power, but I don't believe it has any responsibility.

Whom does New York represent? What we've done actually is to dislocate both our capital and our greatest city. We treat the capital as though it were in the middle of the Atlantic – it's nowhere and it has no cultural or intellectual or financial leadership – and then we take our greatest city and remove it from any formal responsibility. There seems to be a possible trend in the world toward the separation of the capital from the old, strong, dominating city, which is unfortunate. The city, in spite of what anyone says, *has* great power – financial and industrial, leadership in all the communications fields. When it is separated from government, two things happen – there are no sanctions to make the great city behave and the capital city is emasculated.

The phenomenon used to be dramatized in Australia – the legislators all went home on Friday and came back on Monday; there was nothing to stay in Canberra for over the weekend. What's happening in the United States is that, somehow, in the last quarter of a century or so, the philistine aspects of our Congress have been centered in Washington. We have no real national theater, no money for the arts and so on. At the same time, those same congressmen are approving orchestras, art galleries, and all sorts of things for their home cities. Washington is a place where people simply won't vote for the arts and the sciences, while in New York they're unmanageable.

New York is, essentially, one of the most unmanageable units in the world. The location of the citizenry is so peculiar, in that people who work here and exercise the greatest influence – at one level – live somewhere else. And then we have our very archaic laws, through which only the owner of property plays a significant role in what can happen. There is simply no role for people who don't own property, and, furthermore, Columbia University, say, is not the same kind of landlord as someone who owns one four-story house – they have different interests. Generally, though, this is a city of renters, and workers who live somewhere else. Ownership of a house and car is the national style today; living in an apartment and taking a taxi or the subway or a bus is the New York style.

Nevertheless, I don't want to live anywhere else. New York is the most interesting place in the world to live today. It moves fast and there is such a tremendous variety of things and institutions and peoples and ideas. I remember a play given back in the Twenties, written by one of the Capek brothers. A whole lifetime happened in twenty-four hours. There was a big clock at the back of the stage speeding things on. Babies grew up like that; war was declared at ten-ten and peace was made at ten-twenty. People were horrified at the idea. I liked it. After all, in the course of a day I may do a broadcast, arrange to write an article, have a discussion with a publisher, give a lecture in any one of a dozen colleges or universities, go up to Sterling Forest to discuss the development of research communities in New York State, go down to Princeton, or go somewhere else in New Jersey to see a small teachers' college suddenly turned into a state university.

I can eat any food in the world here. I can find someone who speaks almost any language. Oh, it makes a New Yorker absolutely wild if you talk a language he can't recognize. Sit on a subway sometime and talk a South Seas language to a European and the passengers'll boil with rage, because they *expect* to be *able* to recognize any language in the world. They're cosmopolitan as far as the rest of the world is concerned and only provincial toward the United States. You can have more fun here on less spare money, too, than you can in any city in the country. Rents are high, doctor bills are high, but if you have got your basic living expenses, there are more things to do and people don't go to sleep and something's happening all night. (Compare this, for example, with my home city of Philadelphia.) You can go into houses that are exactly as they were a hundred years ago, down to the last stick of furniture, and you can go a few steps and find the most modern apartments. You can go from poverty to wealth, from sophistication to stuffiness, in a couple of blocks. And you can change worlds. You can belong to twenty different circles in New York that don't overlap or you can belong to the one group of people who know all the same people all around the world.

It's an exciting city and it's a barbarously dangerous one, too, a frightful place to bring up children, nearly impossible to bring up more than one – that's for millionaires only. It's a city that's in disarray; it's disorderly, it's abominably run and falling to pieces. It's the only city in the world where you wake up in the morning and listen on the radio for announcements of what's broken down now, what's flooded now. It could get worse. But I'm not sure I want a rational city, either. I think that's the trouble with what we've been doing since the war – creating rational areas instead of living areas. We make great bleak areas where there are nothing but dwellings and great bleak areas where there are nothing but offices; areas that are unused a good part of the time, and, therefore, dangerous, and we've lost the sort of intricate interweaving of life which is still found in places like Greenwich Village. Which, I should add, is being absolutely destroyed.

The thing that really annoys me is the people who live in New York as though it were a small town. There are hundreds of thousands of such people who live here exactly as though they were in small towns thousands of miles away. They would be better off living in one – better air and better schools for their children, gossip with the neighbors and more comfort. They could watch television just as well somewhere else, go home and go to bed every night.

ROZLYNNE M———   WITNESS
A madam and former call girl

It offers everything and it takes something away. From me, it takes my youth and a lot of other things – but you can't blame the city alone for that. I was twenty when I came here to stay. I'd been in New York before that. I left my husband. He was fourteen years older than I was. He was a good man. I can't knock him today. He *did* take me out of The Life – I got in it young – and marry me. Why I came here and went back into the business was I couldn't like put all my energy into something else, or listen to one person that would guide me, so I stayed with my own way of thinking and that was The Life. I could change only if I went into some solid business or got married again with a man who'd understand. But that's something else.

The Life has changed, all right, and so has New York. All the glitter is gone. That doesn't mean I like it any the less. I go along with it. The financial end, the money, is different. People don't throw their money around like they used to and I learned the value of a dollar. If you go out now, you don't see the racket people, the fast-spending money; you see the legitimate businessman out in the clubs – if you see anyone in the clubs at all. Everything's gone down to a different level from that standpoint. It's funny, it's gone up in another – the buildings, things like that. When I see those buildings, I know what they're trying to say – they're light, they're airy, they're the greatest – but I'm not completely caught. Two years ago, I went looking for an apartment. They were new, pretty, beautiful, but no body or character to them. If you flushed the toilet, if you walked across the floor, everyone could hear you.

The business used to be a little bit slower-paced, a little bit more casual. Everything was. In the old days – I'm thirty-nine now – it was night work and maybe one in a night and it was dinner and a club, or a lot of clubs, and *then* a party. Now it's mostly day hours and never later than eleven o'clock at night and maybe half a dozen quick tricks instead of just one. What's changed that is the legitimate businessman took control. No more dawn patrol, no more kicks. A businessman'll go right into the bedroom, get it over with, and come out smiling. He's happy and he's gone. Maybe he'll bring two or three of his friends with him – it's convenient for all of them. He won't even stop and have a drink. A few will, that's true, but they're mostly Europeans.

Also, a girl in this business is like a barometer of business in general. She *survives* on the businessman and she knows when the stock market is up or down. I've noticed this particularly. When a man's had a real bad day, the first thought is he'd like to have a girl. It relieves them of the tension and they call me up – I've got two girls working for me – and they have a quick one before they go home or catch that train to the suburbs. I'm as commercial as they are. I go along with it. They just don't have time. They're in a hurry and it's in and out. In the old days, you could have that phone ringing till four, five, or six in the morning. Today, it's like they walk into a shop, they like this or that, buy it and get out. How long does it take a man if that's all he's got on his mind?

Once, you could say every day of the week was good. That's changed. Now it's Mondays and Fridays. You know why? Friday, they've got to face the wife for the weekend and Monday they've had it. Another thing – today's racket guys. They're punks. They don't have the class the older group had. They're on an entirely different level. The older ones are either legit businessmen now, out of the country, or dead. These new ones, I couldn't have anything to do with them. They frighten me. They don't use their heads. It's more difficult for a girl to work than it used to be, too. First, things aren't organized the way they were, but I'm glad of that, in a way. Second, the girl has to be a little bit smarter. She can't look so glamorous any more, with the furs and this and that, because even the squares know what that means. I tell my girls, "Be inconspicuous in the way you dress, very casual, don't draw too much attention to yourself. Play it down, you're much better off that way."

The change in the girls is fantastic. They're mostly homosexuals now – lesbians – and they're not nearly as good-looking, and if they're not homosexuals, they're sick some way or other. The change in the men is just as great. They're more depraved today. Their demands are greater. There are a lot more homosexuals among the men, too. Like some out-of-towners'll come to see one of my girls for three or four visits and then they'll lay a story on her, they'll say casually, "Oh, by the way, I'd like to try a boy, just for a change." And we know that's what they wanted all the time. I take care of them – I've got contacts – but that's something they wouldn't have asked me for twenty years ago.

It hasn't exactly disillusioned me, because I can accept it. I can still get a kick when a businessman calls me up, he's bugged about something in his office in the middle of the afternoon, and he asks me in like the code we have – we all have one of some kind – "Roz, what're you doing?" I'll say, "I've got a hole in the ceiling." He'll say to me, "Well, I'll need a couple of helpers to fix it." That means he wants two girls, and I'll tell him, "You've got it."

DAVID SUSSKIND
Television producer

To me, the city is the ultimate excitement, you know. It's got a rhythm, it's got a challenge; there is a brilliance to it. Maybe it's one part unpredictable climate, one part physical, one part some fierce, frenetic energy in the air. But it's also many other things that matter to me. It seems to be the nexus of life. So many worlds congregate in New York, overlapping and affecting each other. Unlike almost all other cities I have known in this country, it's not parochial in any way. It's relevant to the whole earth and to the human race. For me, it begins every day with *The New York Times* – not a day late, not the City Edition, but the final, well-proofread, Late City Edition, bringing the whole universe to my morning coffee.

It serves to give you a very accurate appraisal of your own place in life. If you begin the day in New York with the *Times,* you cannot take yourself too seriously. It buttresses your sense of humor and gives you some perspective on your relative importance. When you read about the Congo, Vietnam, Berlin, you realize your own efforts and your own dedications are kind of small. Contrast this with Hollywood, where the dailies and the trades make it seem that show biz is the be-all and end-all of the universe.

Then you go to work, set out in the streets, and there is a fascinating pulse, a hurry and an anxiety of people to go somewhere and do something with their day and with their lives. For me, the competitiveness of New York is enormously exciting. I'm a born competitor and here is – not only literally – the Yankee Stadium – but figuratively – the Stadium in all of public life, in everything, everything, everything. The rest of the country, compared to New York, is like whatever stadium they have in Birmingham or Altoona compared to the Yankee Stadium. The best is here, the quickest is here, the most aspiring are here.

New York has the most intense kind of pressure, but I absorb it; it's the very thing I love and thrive on. It excites me, it drives me and it thrills me. The very special, blistering pace shortens the life span – I'm guessing – but I would rather live this way, the way New York connotes, than any other kind of way longer. I feel enriched by this city. In my profession, particularly, New York is the hub of the universe. The theater is here; television – the kind of television that interests and excites me – is here. I am consecrated to the idea that motion pictures can and should be made here. We have the richest vein of talent in all areas – in acting, writing, and directing – and we have the marvelous tempo of New York in which creation becomes less the way to a pay check than a crusade.

I have made pictures and done television programs and produced plays in other cities and they are relatively barren of New York's magic and New York's inspiration. It is a very special treasure. There are so many creative juices here in all fields that contribute so largely to the country and the world. I am appalled at that kind of prejudice beyond New York which resents its pre-eminence. I cannot understand why my feelings about it and its absolute essentiality to everything meaningful in American life are not appreciated and honored and respected sufficiently. Too often, you discover in other cities open hostility, ugly prejudice, or a silly derogation. I don't believe the ancient bromide that something worth while in New York will not be comprehended west of the Hudson River. There are no hicks beyond Newark; there are Americans awaiting New York's contribution. It has been proven from time immemorial that they want it as we do.

Oh, there is a lot of New York today that is depressing in very real ways. There's a layer of dirt over the city; the traffic congestion, the gaping slum areas, the inadequacy of police protection are appalling. We are, all of us, apathetic, or seem to be, and we live under an irresponsible local government. I see the growing horror of Broadway and Times Square, the ghastly, tinny carnival aspect it has taken on, but even these ugly truths can't strip away or diminish the soul of New York, or the size of New York, or the electricity of New York. These are ugly blemishes that a good skin doctor could cure – or a good mayor. I love this city and I'm proud of it and I intend to live my life here and die in it.

Times Square. The frame of mind that made the Square what it is is probably best expressed this way: It contains statues to George M. Cohan and Father Duffy, but only a plaque in a shoestore window to Eugene O'Neill, who was born on the Square.

THE GREAT CITY

Beyond all others in history, New York is the most desirable and the most difficult of cities in which to live, a city both riven and joined by this and an infinity of paradoxes. It is one which, having touched a man, mauled or rewarded him, will thereafter, without his quite knowing why, exert on him forever the same unearthly fascination as the circus of Dr. Lao for the townspeople of Abalone, Arizona. "Oh, we've spared no pains," cries the little Chinese Barnum of Charles G. Finney's exquisite novel, "and we've spared no dough;/And we've dug at the secrets of long ago;/And we've risen to Heaven and plunged below,/For we wanted to make it one hell of a show./And the things you'll see in your brains will glow/Long past the time when the winter snow/Has frozen the summer's furbe-low."

New York is the endless celebration of everything. Nowhere else in the world will money, when tapped, be transmuted into as much poetry and as much dross; as much music, painting, writing and drama; as much history and as much rumor; as much kindness, cruelty, triviality, excitement, boredom, uprightness, skul-duggery, prophecy, cant, lies, and truth. Its facts, really, are untranslatable, al-though the babble of interpretation, of commendation, of condemnation never stops and is taken up, with insane confidence, by everybody from taxicab drivers to teams of scholars minutely measuring the extent of mental disturbance in a midtown Manhattan neighborhood. Nobody is in any better case than Joyce's washerwomen bawling incomprehensibly at each other across the Liffey. The facts of New York are as mysterious as Stonehenge; they are concepts like the light-year – convenient for figuration, for the purpose of making a comparison, awesome, verifiable, even, but not quite real. They are, like the reality of New York, x number of realities carried to the nth power.

The city is as contradictory as a skyscraper with a mansard roof and dormer windows and no other city has as many such skyscrapers or harbors as many contradictions. It is a city in which, with pain and care, the remains of five medieval European cloisters can be set down, stone by stone, in a hilly park in northern Manhattan to serve art and permit meditation in the midst of chaos; one also in which no new legitimate theater has been built since the Ethel Barrymore was opened on December 31, 1928; as well as one in which the slam of the wrecker's steel ball and the nattering of the pneumatic drill will never stop, so that meditation takes on the proportions of heroism. And yet New Yorkers achieve it with an act of will that would shame a yogi. It is not uncommon for a man reading a paperback edition of Plato to walk absently into a pimpled youth slowly turning the pages of a girlie magazine in front of a Broadway

John F. Kennedy International Airport; the TWA terminal. The identifying letters on a baggage tag are a form of cachet.

Lexington Avenue and Fifty-third Street, subway escalator on a weekday morning. Resurrection is recurrent, rapid, and rumpled.

The SS France, *outward bound past the Empire State Building. Arriving or departing, hers is a presence to reckon with.*

record shop with a doorway amplifier, from which is emanating the protracted, harsh, repetitive, and monotonous clamor of a new hit, and for the two to look up, turn aside, and continue on without having heard either apology or abuse. (There is an anti-noise ordinance, but it is enforced with a terrifying whimsicality.)

The citizens so little focus their attention that the passage of a law and the daily handing out of summonses will not deter them from walking anyhow across an intersection (in meditation) when a sign flashes "Don't Walk." (This law, too, is enforced erratically. The city has hired three and fired two traffic commissioners in a little above a decade; all of them have found themselves caught, beyond hope, in divided authority and politics. The attitude of the police is, "Traffic wants to make the rules? Let Traffic enforce 'em." The commissioner then proposes bold changes; he is called down to City Hall and told, sometimes not courteously, to lay off. Besides, his department never gets enough money to do what he would like to do, even if anyone gave him the right to do it.) But it is, nevertheless, a city straining so hard to hear that the scratch of a pen on Oscar Niemeyer's drafting board in Rio de Janeiro will make architect Wallace Harrison look up in Rockefeller Center and the rustle of heavy silk in the corridors of the House of Dior will halt traffic altogether in Seventh Avenue. Conversely, a tremor in Wall Street sets off a seismograph in Moscow. A joke made in Lindy's at midnight will be heard in the Beverly Hills Brown Derby the following lunch hour. It will be retold over the telephone from Hollywood to a television producer on Madison Avenue at four o'clock in the afternoon. He will hear it out politely, but without much enthusiasm, because he was in Lindy's when a press agent created it; furthermore, he will be in a hurry – before catching the train to Westport (three Scotches on the rocks out of Grand Central Terminal), he wants to get in a golf lesson, which he will take in a wildly improbable location: in a school on the fourth floor of an office building at the northeast corner of Broadway and Forty-second Street. (There is a motor-parts dealer in Mexico City who breaks his regular flights to Israel for the sole purpose of sharpening up his game at this school so that, a few days later, he may confound the three other members of his foursome at Israel's only country club, in Caesarea.)

New York City is the *true north* of the world, the focal point of industry and finance, art and entertainment and communications, an accumulation of things, people, and meanings so vast and compelling that any degree of sophistication, innocence or love or hatred, any frame of reference, is too inadequate and too narrow to scale it to size. New York has to be grasped humbly, exultantly, even with dislike, simply as a series of the most personal particularities, contingent on time, place, emotional and physical climate, and all of the tastes, sounds, sights, textures, pressures, and easements known to man. It is the pulse by which the heartbeat of the world is measured. The pulse is so insistent that it commands the attention of the most distracted and compels the belief, however unwilling, of the least committed. A lapidary adjusting his loupe in a loft on West Forty-seventh Street, the center of the diamond market, will hasten the steps of a miner in South Africa's Rand diggings, bring a brief, small smile of satisfaction to the otherwise impassive face of the gentleman from De Beers in London, and, in Antwerp, gladden the heart and steady the hand of a dealer in cut stones.

The diamond scrutinized on West Forty-seventh Street may be presented triumphantly to a lady in Dallas, but it will have been bought on Fifth Avenue. It may refract light from a crystal chandelier in a home on Coldwater Canyon in Beverly Hills, but the chances are the chandelier was purchased from an antiques dealer on Madison Avenue on the advice of an interior decorator in the East Fifties. The chances are no less that the popular music making the lady wearing the diamond breathe more quickly (creating more refractions) was composed in the Brill Building (on Broadway) or some other ambiguous warren nearby, heard first in a musical comedy (on Broadway), and recorded in a former church on the East Side, the acoustics of which have been found to be ideal (with some secular renovations) for recording. To the musicians playing this music, New York is The Apple, the world, and all other jobs elsewhere are just "gigs."

Rockefeller Plaza. Vichyssoise in summer and skater's waltzes in winter.

The Yankee Stadium. Much more often than not, the outcome is a foregone conclusion.

(It is no coincidence that the sense of the title of an avant-garde off-Broadway play, *The Apple,* is the world.) The jazz musician's Apple is the lyricist's "New York, New York, it's a hell of a town." In the faint, faint undertone of amused exasperation in the lyric (that of someone faced with the preposterous need to put calipers on the incalculable), there may be read as profound an expression as may be imagined of love and respect and awe. However expressed – on a stock ticker, a bill of lading, or an airlines baggage tag (IDL); in a letter of introduction, a clothing label, or a cheap iron miniature of the Statue of Liberty (possibly manufactured in Japan) – the yearning for the city is fierce and uncompromising. People will go to extravagant lengths to – there is no other way of describing the act – *achieve* New York.

"I want the best of everything. The best fruits, the best clothes, the best underwear, even if I'm the only one who knows I'm wearing it," an actress named Julie Newmar told an interviewer once. She is an exceptionally tall girl from California, blonde and theatrical, a celebrity in a small way. "That's why I came to New York," she added. "Because, if you make it here, you make it anywhere." The throb of conviction in her tone was unabashedly rich, nakedly sentimental as the *vox humana* of the organ in the Radio City Music Hall. She is a New Yorker, transfixed by the city. By the same token, a young drug addict reached the tormented conclusion that he, too, could not leave New York. He had tried California; he had tried Maine, the Adirondacks, the Catskills, but New York, as he put it, was the only scene he could make. He had been hooked in New York, he had kicked it in New York and been hooked there again, and in New York, he knew, was the only dependable source of the heroin that kept him at once alive and dead – no matter how many kilos of uncut junk the federals turned up in Brooklyn or the Bronx and no matter how often.

The best of everything that Miss Newmar wants is the business of New York, but it would, without doubt, bore her to learn how it is run. As the sociologist Daniel Bell has described it (the simile is a hackneyed one, but eternally useful), "In economic terms, New York is an iceberg. The visible portions are the theaters, art galleries, museums, universities, publishing houses, restaurants, nightclubs, *espresso* cafés, smart stores – all the activities that give the city its peculiarly glittering place as the metropolis of America." She might be mildly surprised to learn that, in all probability, most of the clothing she wears and the lingerie only she knows she has on is no longer manufactured in the city, although it is still, in terms of what the economists call "national-market activities," the largest manufactory in the world.

The city began life as a seaport. It has always had, through immigration – whether it was the torrential inpouring from Europe in the late nineteenth and early twentieth centuries, or the later migration of Negroes from the South and Puerto Ricans from their island commonwealth – a huge labor force. (Ironically, it has been shown that the wages of this force are, by and large, lower than those to be found in cities not a tenth the magnitude of New York.) Half a century or more has passed since heavy industry could feasibly remain inside the city's limits – it could not afford to, and, besides, the increase in the volume and speed of transportation was so great as to make it unnecessary. New York became, as Bell calls it, "a bazaar," the hallmarks of whose services were "speed, variety and specialization."

The Metropolitan Opera House; the Golden Horseshoe. Parvenu Vanderbilts built a "new yellow brewery on Broadway" to spite the proud Belmonts and their Academy of Music.

Industries were individually small – plastics, printing, electronics – or they did their creating in New York – publishing, the garment industry – and their manufacturing elsewhere. All were heavily dependent on a congeries of elements they could not themselves carry as overhead: financial agencies of one kind or another, "designers to the trade," fabricators of "little things." But the city has entered a new phase since the end of the Second World War. It is becoming a headquarters city, one in which a company *shows itself off* rather than makes something, and there is an ominous quality in the phenomenon.

Just as the rationalization of industry everywhere has made it impossible for people to lay their hands on the exact choice of their hearts – what the literary critic John Aldridge has termed "the right shade of blue" – so has it brought about a series of headquarters in which the buildings, the inhabitants, and the functions performed in them have come to resemble the awful visions of Fritz Lang's early motion picture, *Metropolis,* or Karel Capek's play, *R.U.R.* (It must be observed that both paled before the horror of their imaginings: both fell back and provided bad, unbelievable happy endings for their accounts of the mechanization of mankind.)

The buildings are a series of glass façades, glaring yet sightless, menacing and virtually undifferentiated. There are no elevator operators; elevators click, cough, vomit music of a kind as unspecific as the sound of air conditioning, and induce hysteria in highly impressionable people. There is no permanence in an office; an office is simply a collection of partitions that can be pulled down, stacked and moved away with breath-taking speed. So are the rational appointments of one of these. The man who puts a photograph of his wife and children on his desk is indulging a forlorn hope. The workers in these buildings are all engaged in some anomalous function of "service" so far removed from raw material or product that they, too, are no more differentiated than the buildings they perform their services in. They have no readily discernible crotchet, stance, or habit to set them apart from each other. (Only the psychiatrist can set one apart from a second and not always.) Once in a while the suppressed human being goes berserk – he throws all of his papers out of the window and sometimes follows them out; he holes up, in relief pathetic to imagine, in a run-down rooming house, but one that, he can tell, does not look exactly like all the others; he screams in the subway or exposes himself; or he punches his wife. Here are not rich eccentricities; here are aberrations and this man is, in fact, less easily distinguishable as an individual than even the unfortunate on an assembly line in Detroit. He, too, has been rationalized.

An additional piece of evidence exists to show the "headquarterization" of New York City. (The word was actually used in a discussion of the subject by two of today's Romans over dinner at the Four Seasons Restaurant.) That is the sudden building of a dozen hotels and motels (in New York, the meaning of "motel" is, in reality, a hotel whose stripped efficiency and clean but bare appointments keep the price of a room down) between 1960 and 1963, together with the frightened haste with which a dozen or so older hotels of the first rank began to spend $100,000,000 to remain in competition. The latter are anywhere from three decades to sixty-odd years old and they have developed two outstanding characteristics: high prices and an arrogant contempt for such amenities as decent food or enough towels. But the competition among the hotels is not so much for the rental of rooms, fundamental though this might seem to be, as for the convention and banquet business, which are the distressing acccompaniments to the headquarterization of a city.

The construction of two new first-class hotels is the most noticeable symptom; they are, in effect, the largest warts on the wart hog. The hotels are the Americana, another (as their publicity people like to say every time they build something new) "jewel" in the "crown" of the Tisch family (Loew's theaters, the Americana in Miami Beach, and so on), and the New York Hilton, exemplifying "the confidence of three men in a future bright with the promise of greatness for New York and the nation. . . ." (The three confident men were identified as Conrad Hilton, Laurance Rockefeller, and Percy Uris.) Their "emergence," as the New York *Times* phrased it, "and their ability to book 200 conventions that were formerly too big for the existing hotels . . . means that an estimated additional $50,000,000 will be spent annually in town."

Statistics can do neither hotel the justice required of their splendors. They now have the largest ballrooms and banqueting facilities in the city, so large that they caused the sober Commodore, Biltmore, and Roosevelt to merge theirs to bring in large conventions. Rather, it is in the odd, peripheral refinements that the story is best told. Both, for example, have installed elevators capable of carrying fully loaded trucks from the street to exhibition rooms. Both have gone in for a full panoply of electronic facilities that, in all probability, may frighten rather than edify guests: lights that tell people when there is a message for them at the Americana, a device at the Hilton permitting a person to dial on his telephone a number corresponding to the time he wants to be awakened. At a signal, he dutifully gives his name and room number; in the morning, he is awakened. He is untouched by human hands, unmoved by human voices. The Hilton can clean 30,000 pieces of silver daily by sound; the Americana provides remote-control stereophonic color television, "with an extra channel for closed-circuit telecasts."

For the Hilton, the decorator, William Pahlmann, created a "unique street of culinary dreams" and the press agents christened it the "Rue des Gourmets." On this *rue,* running the entire length of the Fifty-third Street lobby, are the Old Bourbon House (New Orleans), Valencia, (Spain), the Place Lautrec, including a simulation of the Place du Tertre, the Seven Hills (Rome), and the Kismet (the Far East), "echoing the fabled city of Byzantium in [its] decorative scheme." The Americana can counter with the Royal Box, La Ronde, the Golden Spur, the Columbian Coffee House, and, it should live so long, the Wooden Indian. Mention should be made, as well, of the Hilton's "Hospitality Suites," or small banquet rooms, named for "authors prominently associated with the New York Scene: Franklin P. Adams, Robert Benchley, Don Marquis, Damon Runyon, Lorenz Hart, Scott Fitzgerald and others." The décor of each is said to be "woven" around "memorabilia" of these "distinguished literary figures," not excluding Hart, who wrote lyrics for popular songs.

For some, New York is to be sniffed in the reek of continuity, although it is not a very old city. They find continuity in something as pure as the City Hall and the Greek Revival of Washington Square North, in such oddments as a nineteenth-century – early nineteenth-century – brick building on the south side of Spring Street, between West Broadway and Wooster Street, that has been cut exactly in half, cut in half right up to half the pediment (making half an attic) three floors up. (The owners run a restaurant, a dark brown, pleasant, cheap place on the ground floor; the building was bought by their family in 1891 and it was half a building then. They know no more than that and they do not much care.) For others, it is something as beguilingly bogus as brownstone buildings (the Connecticut Valley to this day has large deposits of the Triassic rock which is the source of this dark sandstone) resembling pieces of the Farnese Palace and storage warehouses like Inigo Jones's Banqueting House. For still others, it is the odd, polite opposition of Stanford White's Racquet and Tennis Club on Park Avenue, in its self-satisfied classicism, to the somber bronze modernity of Mies van der Rohe's Seagram Building directly across the avenue, or Gordon Bunshaft's light, gay Lever House, a block north of the Racquet and Tennis.

In the preface to the second volume of her long *History of the City of New York: Its Origin, Rise and Progress* (1877), Mrs. Martha Lamb wrote that the magnitude of her undertaking was such that "the structure became a matter of growth instead of architecture," and she was, in effect, as much confessing the historian's inadequacy as describing the outbreak of metropolis. Almost 800 pages later, she had come firmly to terms with the impossible, setting down: "Various landmarks have passed away; and property has changed hands and risen in value, in a ratio, which, if fully described, would seem like the vagaries of imagination." The only permanence that can be counted on is that of change. An entire generation knows nothing of the Third Avenue El (much less the Second Avenue) that turned light into lattices north from the Battery, through the Bowery to the Bronx, or the Sixth that headed west on Fifty-third Street, joining the Ninth to run north to the Polo Grounds, where the Mets, the new National League baseball team, created in 1961, played just long enough to wait out the building of a new stadium for them in Queens. In 1907 the artist John Sloan painted a picture of the Haymarket, an infamous, juicy dance hall in the old Tenderloin, an area that was a sink of corruption from about the close of the Civil War to the end of the century. (The way it got its name has taken on the patina of legend. Innumerable policemen preyed on its whores, madams, pimps, murderers, and gamblers and some became millionaires. Upon being transferred there in 1876, Captain Alexander S. Williams remarked to a friend, "I've had nothing but chuck steak for a long time, and now I'm going to get a little of the tenderloin.") A hamburger and hero-sandwich store stands on the site of the Haymarket today, at the southeast corner of Sixth Avenue and Thirtieth Street, an indubitable triumph for morality and a doubtful one for cuisine. The city's wholesale flower market, taking up both sides of Sixth from Twenty-seventh to Twenty-ninth streets, has long since replaced the deadfalls and cony snares in which flowers of another kind were peddled.

"I say to Booth's Theater farewell!" cried Helena Modjeska on the night of April 30, 1883, upon disengaging herself gracefully from the body of Maurice Barrymore's Romeo to arise from Juliet's bier. Hers were the last words spoken on the stage of Edwin Booth's temple, seven blocks south of the Haymarket. It had been built for Booth a short fifteen years before, of timeless granite, in the timeless Renaissance manner, by James Renwick, the architect of Grace Church. A lumpish and unlovely building to house McCreery's Department Store replaced it; McCreery's moved on, went out of business, and left behind the graceless pile that has been divided up into offices and floors for light manufacturing. Less than a mile up the avenue, the Rockefellers gave their Center Theater a surprising twenty-two years – from the bottom of the Depression (1932) to the height of prosperity (1954). What replaced the Center, a skyscraper matching others in the Center, is not ugly, but it brings in much more money. (Fiorello LaGuardia changed the name of the street, but it is characteristic of New Yorkers, in their haste and devotion to numbers, that they will not tolerate a mouthful like "The Avenue of the Americas," and go right on calling it Sixth Avenue.)

The ruthlessness with which any money society ultimately casts out all considerations other than money when its loose, shifting confederation of leaders wants something (the poultices of social reform notwithstanding) is most sharply recognizable in the United States, and, in this country, New York City, because of its size and power. No New Yorker needs to be told, for example, that the tremendous proliferation of building, both domestic and commercial, since the end of the Second World War was not undertaken for his welfare; in his cynical way,

Fort Tryon Park; the Cloisters. Stone by stone, icon by icon, five medieval monasteries were set down in New York, which can barely wait to tear down what it puts up itself.

he understands that very well. Far worse, though, is that, with the exception of tiny, exhausting revolts, the toll of which always exceeds the ground won, he passively permits himself and his city to be desecrated. A group of mothers on Central Park West forced Robert Moses to give up the notion of wrecking a few wretched square feet of asphalt playground to enlarge a parking lot for a nightclub in the park. For years the residents of Greenwich Village fought him and the city when he decided to widen a road through Washington Square to link up Fifth Avenue and West Broadway, principally for the benefit of the occupants of a luxury housing development he also helped engineer into being. Other examples could be adduced but not very many and not very successful. By and large, the New Yorker either keeps his mouth shut, fulminates in living rooms, or subsides with a squeaky letter to the editor.

In many ways Charles Follen McKim's Pennsylvania Station was ridiculous – a replica of the Baths of Caracalla supported on a steel skyscraper frame – but it *was* a great monument and good to look at, inside and out. Its owners, having succeeded in despoiling it inside, then sold it to developers. They planned to slap down in its place a new Madison Square Garden with a sagging roof, the epitome of architectural *kitsch* and probably best described as "modernistic," which is a fine, invidious word. They included, too, a slab of a hotel (twenty-eight stories) and a slab of an office building (thirty-four). The entrances to the Manhattan Bridge, particularly that on the Manhattan side, were close to absurd – the Bernini colonnade of St. Peter's Square tacked onto the Porte St. Denis, plus statuary, and the whole surmounted by a granite frieze (no one could see it in transit and certainly could not get near it in any other way) depicting Indians chasing buffalo – but they were familiar, endearing, and, for New York objects, reasonably old. The entrances were ripped down to make way for another of Moses' stultifying projects – an elevated cross-Manhattan expressway, which, if ever undertaken, would have made of a wide area of lower Manhattan, from the Holland Tunnel on the west to the Williamsburg and Manhattan bridges on the east, the same kind of gutted corpse that freeways made of downtown Los Angeles. Somehow, in one of those miraculous reversals of form, it was killed. As lagniappe to the letter writers, the city proposed to dump the station's eighty-four Doric columns into some kind of quaint classical arrangement in Flushing Meadow – a sort of Parc Monceau afflicted with a frightening elephantiasis – and to deposit some of the bridge's statuary and its frieze in the Brooklyn Museum. There are those who believe the future to be hopeless and some who profess to like what has happened and an overwhelming majority simply preoccupied with operating the mechanisms of living in the most complex city in the world. For the time being enough is left of the city so that one *knows* it is New York City, and not just any confection of glass and concrete in the Temperate Zone.

The very air trembles with prescience: the expiring shriek of a subway train rounding the last curve into Times Square, the sound floating upward through the sidewalk grates on hot, dusty, brazen puffs of air; the slosh of high-pressure hoses washing down Fulton Fish Market; the contesting voices of produce salesmen in Washington Market; the solemn mumbling of the day's first passenger planes floating down to Idlewild and LaGuardia; a Bach oratorio heard faintly through the closed doors of a church on lower Fifth Avenue; the nasty scream of a police-car siren somewhere on the West Side; the click of the clockwork in a signal-control box at an intersection. Also, the high-pitched cries and hoarse grunts of baseball players in Central Park and the squeak of a window cleaner's squeegee (over the clank of his safety belt) eighty floors up; the hum, thump, and clack of an escalator in a department store; the bright noise of jazz spilling into Duffy Square; the disputes of starlings and the colloquies of pigeons; the roar from the Yankee Stadium and the rumble of a long freight over the Hell Gate Bridge; the ceaseless belling of telephones; the buzz of neon signs; the stomach-shaking voice of a huge ship departing and the fussy, hortatory piping of the tugs pushing her out of her berth; the creak of sets being moved out of the back of the Metropolitan Opera House after midnight; the waves of applause heard as the doors of a theater are opened on Forty-fifth Street after the final curtain; the bang and hiss of trucks, taxicabs, and automobiles. Great events are foretold in all the mutterings and shoutings. No city has such a voice; it is a voice with perfect pitch.

Of the day in 1524, when his ship became the first known to enter the Port of New York, the Florentine sailor, Da Verrazano, said, "We found a pleasant place below steep little hills, and from these hills, a mighty deep-mouthed river ran into the sea." To another sailor, Henry Hudson, eighty-five years later, the mighty river was no more than his possible passage to Cathay and its significance was lost to him: he *had* reached Cathay. The Port of New York is utterly unique. There is no cargo it cannot and has not handled. It is 423 square miles of water area and the biggest ship need not stand off it. Six hundred and fifty miles of water frontage will berth better than 400 deepwater vessels. Twenty-five thousand ships of more than 160 lines call at the port; 10 major railroads (nearly all of them in financial trouble), 500 trucking companies, and 39 United States and international airlines distribute their cargoes, which come to 36,000,000 tons a year. It is not necessary to come to New York to get to the rest of the country or the world, but the journey loses savor if one does not. For those who stay, the taste of the city is exotic in the extreme; it makes the tongue smart and years of rolling it on the tongue do not diminish the delicious pungency.

No matter where he comes from, what language he speaks, or what happens to a human being in New York, once he has heard the city's voice he will be haunted by it for the rest of his life, whether he settles here or 15,000 miles away; whether it woos or rejects him, lulls him, makes him fearful, or distracts him to the point of ecstasy or despair. So will its face affect him. The illuminated catenary curve of the George Washington Bridge at night strikes at the heart like the Twenty-third Psalm. The sky line from the promenade on Brooklyn Heights is an army with banners. Not to be moved to pity *and* anger by the prodigious slums still remaining on the Lower East Side, in Spanish Harlem and Negro Harlem, is impossible; even the city's slums are matchless. Optimism is not faked in New York and boosterism is not the city's way, outside of official press-agentry. New York, it is said over and over, is not the United States. The cliché is a monstrous one; it is, of course, true. No New Yorker ever bothers to argue the point, or to point out that the United States is not New York. He is too busy shoving his way into a subway train, retailing his private agonies to a psychoanalyst, subduing the prickings of impulse in a supermarket, listening to his neighbors (man and wife) conduct a murderous quarrel in the apartment next door (or timing the heavings of the bed), sprawling on the grass in Central Park or Van Cortlandt or Prospect, rubbing the ears of a dog while taking him out for a late walk, watching the sun go down behind the Palisades, and, always, staving off the exhaustion of body and mind that is the price he pays for living in New York. He is the most provincial of human beings – with reason, since he feels that nowhere else on earth could he be so completely fulfilled or so irrevocably deprived as in the city. There is no sensation, from birth to death, his being tells him, that is not heightened for having been experienced in New York. He becomes neither elated nor elegiac at the realization. His capacity for the acceptance of the universe (as defined for him by New York) is probably greater than that of any human.

He comes to know these things in small ways. Thus, it is said by outlanders that the rudeness and indifference of New Yorkers toward each other is unequaled and inexpungeable. There is at least one New Yorker (he is typical), however, who knows better, much, much better. One Good Friday morning – that year, the day was the eve of Passover, as well – he got into a cab at Sixth Avenue and Ninth Street. At Eleventh he told the driver to hold up while he picked up his newspapers at a corner store. He ran out of the cab, grabbing for change in a pocket, and, in his hurry, brought up his keys. They fell through the steel grating of a sewer eight feet deep. The man began to sweat and curse; the keys were the only set he had. He had just moved into his apartment and he knew no one in the building. The superintendent was out of town for the weekend. He was already an hour late for work. A man to whom desperation comes easily and brings confusion with it, the passenger told the driver to take him to his office.

"Listen, Mac," said the driver on the way uptown. "I got an idea for you. Call the city. Those guys that work the sewers. I mean, you never can tell." The man grunted, said nothing, paid his fare, and went to his office. Ten minutes later, after scrabbling through the telephone book, he located SEWERS BUR OF MUNICIPL BLDG and telephoned. After a suitably long interval he got a deep male voice and told his story. "Boy," said the voice, "did *you* pick a day. You know what day this is? Good Friday. Passover, too. Practically everybody is off." He paused to let this sink in. "Ah, hell," he went on, relenting, "gimme your number and sit tight. I'll call you back." He did, fifteen minutes later. "Are you in luck," said the voice. "There's an emergency crew in the neighborhood. How fast can you get down there?" In no time, of course, said the owner of the keys. He got out of the cab just as a big red truck with five men in it pulled up at the sewer. "You the guy

Eighth Avenue and Fortieth Street; subway fisherman. The delusion (not unlike that of wealthier New Yorkers) is that riches lie at the end of a length of string and a piece of gum at the bottom of a subway grating.

about the keys?" asked one. He turned out to be a foreman. The man said he was. The foreman looked him over wearily, hands on hips, and then turned to his men. "Okay, boy," he said to one of them. "Go get 'em." The grating was removed. The crewman, rubber-gloved, hip-booted, and oilskinned, went down into the muck. He came up a few moments later with the keys, which he wiped off and handed to the foreman.

"These yours?" the latter asked. Weak with relief, the man said they were, took them carefully with one hand, reached into a pocket with the other, and pulled out $20, which he handed to the foreman. "That's all right," said the foreman. "Happens all the time." He took the money. "We'll split it," he added. He slid into the cab of the truck, next to the driver, looked back at the man with the keys, and waved easily at him. "Happy Easter," he said as the truck pulled away. "Gutt Yontiff."

A DISTRICT POLICE REPORTER

I was born and raised on the West Side, the outskirts of Hell's Kitchen. I've been a district man forty-five years and things have got to the point where I go out of the city and I'm ashamed to admit I come from New York City, for the simple reason they think everybody comes from the city's out to be a wise guy or you're out to get something for nothing. But that's only part of it. I'd say it's a worse city to live in than it used to be. In fact, it stinks. You're not safe on the streets, you're not safe in the subways, you're not even safe going into your own home. You want the real answer to conditions? We have too goddamn much liberalism. And you got to figure your politicians are all in that liberal line these days because of the votes they're looking for.

You had that vicious murder down here on the playground on Forth-sixth, where those boys were assaulted and killed and they locked up that so-called Umbrella Man and that Cape Man. One guy's getting life and the other's been sentenced to the chair. And all the politicians crying in their beer – "It's a shame that this poor boy should be electrocuted." That's the way it goes all along the line, where you go into court and the judges sort of favor these young hoodlums that are being brought in and they just pamper them too damned much. Sometimes it gets to look as though the arresting officer was the perpetrator of the crime, instead of the guy that's being charged. For that reason, many officers kind of hesitate to make an arrest, because they feel eventually it'll be thrown out of court and they're just wasting their time. Also, when a cop gets in trouble over one of these things, his superior runs away from them, and they don't get any support, and, as a result, the morale of the Police Department is very low.

Let a cop go out and use his night stick, because, let me tell you, years ago, as a boy – I'm well into my sixties now – many a time I got smacked on my fanny by a cop with his night stick for getting into some little mischief and if I went home and told my father what happened, he'd say to me, "What did you do? The officer wouldn't've hit you if you hadn't done something wrong," and my old man

Forty-sixth Street, between First and Second avenues. The police flush some kid crapshooters. Somehow, despite superbly co-ordinated raids of this kind, the dope problem gets worse and the policy banks get bigger.

would wind up belting me too. Today, if an incident like that takes place, the parents come rushing into the station house making a complaint against the cop who slapped their darling son who they claim is always a good boy and never did anything wrong and they want the cop charged with police brutality.

Also, you have your Puerto Ricans, who come into the city and make life miserable for everybody, worse than Negroes ever were. They don't hesitate to push you right off the sidewalk. You go into some of your restaurants and they have nobody but these particular people as help and they sort of have the attitude they're doing you a favor letting you come in and eat. They insult the customers and if you have any complaint they just walk away. Instead of sitting down and enjoying a meal, you're aggravated by your contact with these particular individuals.

You run into another condition today – more goddamn degenerates running around the streets than ever before. Male prostitutes. You can't even go into a toilet in the subway or some of the bars or grills without being followed in by a fag or being annoyed. They say the reason there's been such a heavy influx of them is mostly show business. Show business and TV, and whether these particular individuals *are* the same as in show business, I don't know, because I never contact them. Most of our murders recently have been of so-called fags who have gone out and got acquainted with men. The usual practice is to pick up a soldier or sailor, invite them to his apartment for a drink, and, of course, it all depends on how the individual takes the proposition, whether he accepts it or rejects it, whether he just wants to rob the guy or gets mad and kills him.

Years ago, a woman could walk around even in the toughest sections of the city without being molested. Now she can't even walk on Broadway after dark. We have lots of cases where women are not even safe when they go into the apartment houses where they have these self-service elevators. You've read about certain areas where the churches aren't even able to hold services at night because the women are afraid to go out. I say, take the handcuffs off the cops and allow them to go out and do the job properly. They'd need backing up from the district attorneys and the grand juries, don't forget that. But you put their night sticks back in their hands and you'd correct conditions in a hurry.

MRS. RUTH LINDEN
Telephone operator for the Jewish Guild for the Blind

It must have been 1933 when my eyes became infected and I was operated on. Complications set in and I lost my sight. I never even had partial vision. I went from perfect sight to total blindness. I was a very observant individual when I had my sight and I still am. But the city's changing so rapidly now, I almost can't tell what's what. Of course, I've grown with it, and if you grow with something, you really don't see the changes. Someone will say to me, "There's a new building going up here," or I can feel there's a sidewalk where there used to be grass, and right now I feel New York is a very glamorous place, a wonderful city. I don't travel by myself, you see; I like to have a guide with me. But those who do travel alone find people are wonderful. They chat with them and they get a feeling of warmth they might not somewhere else. Naturally, it's easier where there are a lot of people.

And then, we have an agency like the Guild here, that does a great deal for people like us. There is nothing like it in small cities. What's more, we're nonsectarian. Why, the girl I'm training right now is a Baptist. I'd say sixty per cent of our people are not of the Jewish faith. This city gives them jobs more readily than other places, too. We have contract shops in which the blind work side by side with the sighted. We no longer have places for the blind to work exclusively —we try to have them help themselves as normal human beings. It's still a fairly prevalent feeling in many cities that blind people should have make-work and that's alien to the thinking of most professional agencies in New York.

The only thing I have to complain about is that the doors aren't opened for capable blind persons to work as switchboard operators. We can't seem to break through that barrier. There should be a good many Braille switchboards in New York, but the only ones are here at the Guild and one in Queens and in the Bronx. "Why should we take in a blind girl when we can get a sighted one?" is what they say. They have opened up outside of New York—a factory in Buffalo, a hospital in Utica.

Beyond the loss of my sight, nothing has changed for me, nothing at all. I don't feel the city's more difficult to live in. I still like the sensation of getting into the crowded subway—I live in the Bronx—even though my wallet was snatched once. And I doubt I would have left New York even if I were not blind. It has so much to offer; it has all the opportunities for those who will see them, and if you have the ability, you can find your niche. I came to the Guild twenty-six years ago. I heard typewriters going. I said, "I'd love to work here." They didn't have a switchboard at the time and no openings for typists. They put me to folding outgoing mail. The first day, I earned a dollar and I said to my husband, "Now I can make money, even though I'm blind. Let's frame the dollar." We didn't actually. Then the switchboard was installed, and, when I saw it, I said, "This is what I want to do," and I have been doing it ever since.

WITNESS

THEODORE WALTER (SONNY) ROLLINS
Tenor saxophonist

Jazz isn't just colored people's music, but music of the country and of the world, and that is one of the messages I really want to send. It's an important one. That's been proved more in New York than anywhere else. That's why jazz moved here. The social conditions made it possible. It's become easier in New York for whites and Negroes to play together than even in Chicago. In fact, in Chicago, they still have a white local and a colored local. Not here. Here, it's 802 and that's it, and there's a great deal of intermingling. It's what New York should be, and is, in the finest sense—a unity of people—and jazz exemplifies that more than anything.

In a material way, it's not as lucrative a city as some of the others. In other words, you can't make as much money as you can out of town, but that way you

One Hundredth Street between
First and Second avenues,
north side. When the rats occupy the houses, the people
live in the streets.

The Lower East Side; three stores. Three languages as well.

have to stay on the road all the time. I think it may be because the competition is so keen here. The guys come from all over to make it. The record companies are here and so on. So that means the best from every place are trying to make it here and you've got to test yourself against all of them. If you pass, you got it made anywhere in the world. It's essential to be here, even if you make less.

After being in Chicago and San Francisco and Paris and all those places, I realized that, as the song goes, once you leave New York, you're not going anywhere, and that's even though I was born in Harlem in a tenement house on 137th Street. I always had an image before I went, that Paris would be the place for the artist and people wouldn't be too concerned with the material aspects of life and would be striving for the aesthetic ones. It wasn't entirely true. I found there were many things in Parisian life that were more materialistic than they are in New York and then I realized that right here were the things I thought had existed in other places.

I live on the Lower East Side. That's what this country is all about – Chinese, Slavic peoples, Jewish, Irish, Italian, Negro, Puerto Rican, more or less living side by side, going to the same schools, very little or no racial friction at all. Everything is here.

It happened I stopped playing in August of '59. I was going too fast and I wanted to stop and think about what I was doing and where I was going. Sometime the next spring, I was sitting at home on a Sunday afternoon and all of a sudden the urge came to me to get out of the house – I'm somewhat of a mystic, by the way, but not in the weirdo sense – and walk. Maybe this bug was in my head, or had been for a long time, but I went in the direction of the Williamsburg Bridge and walked out over it.

It was just like going to heaven or something, to be on top of everything. It was beautiful. That bridge had been there all this while and I had never thought of doing what I did. Later, I started playing my horn on the bridge, at a particular spot. It is the most apropos of all places in the city for me, a beautiful thing. Not only can I be alone there, but it also gives me the complete grandeur of the city. I think there is a greater potential for a good society in this country – exemplified by this city – than anywhere else in the world. I have an optimistic outlook, rather than a pessimistic one, and I feel that if good things *are* going to happen, there's a better chance of them happening here than, say, in Idaho, or somewhere else.

MRS. JESSICA GUSHIN

A housewife and mother of a three-year-old daughter

In New York, your aspirations, if you suffer from a lack of confidence, become warped by the accomplishments of other people. Let's say that if I had the time and freedom to do something about them, it might be easier, but it's more difficult in New York being tied down with a child because of the expense of substitute help and the difficulty of getting to know how good that help is. There's no place for amateurs in New York; it's too easy to have dreams broken here. I always wanted to be a writer or an actress. Coming back from where I was and not being these things has made me very bitter. Maybe if I'd stayed in the Southwest, it might have been better. There's so much success flaunted in New York that it's an easy place to be bitter.

I was born in Linden, New Jersey, in 1934. I went to Douglas, the women's college at Rutgers, but I wanted to come to New York, because it was the center of everything and Douglas was very provincial, and I transferred to Barnard. I came to New York to live in 1954, got married in 1956, lived in the West Village, moved to Staten Island – Stapleton – which is a graveyard. (They do, as a matter of fact, have a great many graveyards on Staten Island, or so it seemed to me.) Then we moved to Arizona – my husband is a doctor and he worked among the Indians out there for a couple of years – and returned here about a year ago.

I used to like New York, the noise, streets, crowds, the coming and going at any hour and finding something to do. You could sort of blend into it and be nobody very comfortably. I found myself on that very vital, dynamic campus at Barnard

Central Park; a Sunday afternoon.
The miracle of the city is that, however briefly, innocence is to be found in it.

with people from all over the world. They like to collect them up there, you know, to give you that cosmopolitan feeling – one sari among the knee socks is supposed to do a lot for you. Anyway, I majored in sociology. God knows why, and He won't tell. I did a research project with some of the other students in the slum areas around Morningside Heights, and, although it told me a lot about the city – its filth, human beings that were non-human, decay and disintegration – it was divorced from the New York I loved then. I simply split off the real horror. The only thing any of us thought was, "Ugh, God, if they moved next to us, wouldn't it be terrible?"

There was nobody to interpret or explain. I had no child to ask me, "Why is that man lying in the gutter?" The Village was quaint; the Village was lovely; Bleecker Street was charming – I didn't have to walk down it with a stroller and brush flies off a child or a great big, filthy-dirty piece of newspaper blowing into her face. I also had the freedom to come and go as I pleased, which you do not have in New York with a baby. I love the theater, but we can't afford to go. I liked going to the stores a lot, but that's an almost impossible chore now; I liked the ethnic neighborhoods, but where are they now?

I think if you're disillusioned with a place it means you're disillusioned with yourself. I know that, but to me the contrast of the vitality of the Southwest with the death in New York is a real one. The buildings go up to the skies; there is no room on the ground for people; no place to walk at night where it's safe in this horror of human degradation. I realize this feeling set in only after I came back with the child. A quaint neighborhood isn't interesting to a child; the city's too cold in the winter and too hot in the summer and you just don't have the freedom, the money, or the time to get out and *use* New York.

New York is to be *used*. It's not to be enjoyed so much as *used* – to be *had*. I can't see any future here. They choke us with traffic. They wreck neighborhoods they should restore; they put up apartment houses and other buildings in a completely unpremeditated way as far as good city planning goes. It would be very nice if we were all birds in New York – all the space is up – but where we walked and children played has been ruined. There's plenty of space to curb dogs, but none for a child.

There is an overwhelming fright in New York and when you are frightened you don't want to be alone. This is such an easy place to be alone and it's very difficult to come to know people. I do have my husband and child, but my husband is gone eight hours a day or more and you don't know anyone in the building or anything about them or anyone who knows anything about them. I'd leave if I could, but I don't have too much of a choice because my husband will probably continue to work here. What will I do? I suppose I'll try and pick up the threads, is what I'll do. I'll try and unravel them, but I'd rather do it some place else. In New York, as far as I can see, nothing worth while is being built, either physically or spiritually.

When you live in the Southwest, sheer physical strength is important; you have to be able to dig your car out of the snow or mud; you have to know, if you're stuck in the desert, what to carry in your car. In New York, none of this matters. You don't need to depend on your own physical strength. If you can afford it, things are done for you. To bake bread in New York is no virtue.

JOSEPH WILLEN
Executive vice president, Federation of Jewish Philanthropies of New York

I've been puzzled all my life, as I look at New York, by two things. (I was sixty-six in June, 1963, and I came to this country in 1905 from a little Polish town called Kushnitza.) The two things are public indifference, on the one hand, and the great concern of individuals who make up that public, on the other. It exists here more than in any other place because here the public is such a mass. I've lived in three apartment houses in which I never knew a neighbor. That gives you one image of New York. Yet, if someone had called up and said, "There's someone on the nineteenth floor in trouble," I'd have done everything in my power to help. Here, one often feels that he is part of the mass, but he acts as an individual. As a community, New York rarely rises up to do anything.

But what extraordinary things are done in this town by small groups. Nowhere else in the world will you find so many involved in music, ballet, hospitals, theater, museums, universities, religious institutions, whatever. We have an anarchy of organization, yet a universality of taking care of neighbors. It is a kind of planned anarchy. This apparent chaos, which puzzles so many people, is the only way in which we can function effectively in this city. Because if we didn't operate that way we'd be destroyed by the bigness required to handle every problem centrally. Bigness would soon get in the way of really reaching out. The New Yorker, who is part of this bigness, escapes it by being part of something small. It sounds like a dualism, but, in large measure, it is the only way in which the individual saves himself from the inevitabilities of overwhelming size – big government, big business, big labor, big everything.

New York has five medical schools. No city in the United States can match that. New York has eighty-seven voluntary hospitals, yet it wasn't possible to get them together for a central building-fund drive. Their greatness is expressed by their individuality.

There is another thing about New York that, I think, is the beginning of an understanding of our whole American community: it's no longer white-Protestant-Anglo-Saxon. The trend is everywhere, but perhaps more so in New York. Do you like irony? The McCarran-Walter Act has had the strangest impact on this city and country. Its fundamental purpose was to keep America Anglo-Saxon-white-Protestant. What happened? It kept out Italians, Hungarians, Greeks, Poles, Jews. The Negro and the Puerto Rican poured into New York. If the politics of our city are different today than they used to be, the McCarran-Walter Act was a factor. By the way, no group voted harder for the act than Southern congressmen.

Here is yet another irony. One used to say that the forgotten x per cent would – when it became a large per cent – inevitably upset the political applecart. But that is not so. Today the well fed are a majority and the underprivileged no longer have the built-in political power to make themselves felt as they once could. They no longer have as many allies. Sometimes, this fact exposes us to the great danger that we forget there are many among us who are underfed and underprivileged.

East Harlem; junior high school playground at First Avenue and Ninety-ninth Street. Cyclone fence, iron playgrounds, and skyscraper housing are the ideal solution – except for human beings.

Central Park; bird watchers.
In the midst of chaos, their absorption is admirable.

When I was young, almost everyone had poor relations and poor friends, no matter how well off he himself might be. And, in effect, we lived together in a close community of interest. There wasn't a sharp division. Today it is different. If you are an executive, the chances are that you rarely meet people who aren't executives or employees of executives. Your association with those of a lower economic level are in terms of those who serve you—the elevator operator, the cab driver, etc. And while you are aware of those whose economic level is much lower, they are no longer your friend, your brother, your neighbor. They are somebody else. Where once you might have said, "There but for the grace of God go I," today, with so much opportunity available you may think that those who aren't in your class don't have the capacity or the ability or the cultural insight and thus, in effect, can't make it.

One of the prime consequences of this in New York is that the Puerto Rican and the Negro are the *clients* of our community and very rarely the *managers* of communal services. Unfortunately, to date, we are doing too little to change this situation. Many of our agencies say that they serve regardless of race, creed, or color. Yet the Negro and Puerto Rican are seldom on the boards of directors or on

One Hundredth Street between First and Second avenues. Among the games played on this neglected block are shooting, knifing, mainlining, policy running, and exploitation of the helpless; the banks deliberately deny loans, either building or private, and starve such streets.

the medical staffs. They are handling the service ends of the business; they are the porters and the elevator operators. Can there be any more non-democratic process than that which sees such a sharp division between the served and the server? "Regardless of race, creed, or color" must be truly that in all aspects of our institutions, or we are getting ready for some explosions.

The great number of people who are coming in from the South and from Puerto Rico have also affected our educational setup. More and more New York youngsters are being sent to private schools or are the excuse for the exodus to the suburbs because parents don't want them in inferior public schools. Many of our leaders of the community speak out vigorously and eloquently on behalf of good public schools – even though, let's face it, they may not send their own children to them. *Many* of those who are responsible for the educational programs of our

Sixty-second Street between Second and Third avenues. The price of sinking roots in nine-teenth-century New York comes very high.

city do not send their children to our public schools. The result is that in many areas our schools are not representative of the community and inevitably this must downgrade our educational standards and community life.

Finally, let me say a word about the aged in our city. I've spent a lifetime working for the social services of our community and still I do not know the answers to this problem. Ours is a city in which to be old is hard. Perhaps nowhere in the world are the aged so alone as in New York City. You see them on the benches along Broadway, in the parks, on the subways. Millions of people surrounding them and yet they are alone. It's a point I made earlier: we are a city of no neighbors. It is the agony of being so big. Close to a million of our people are over sixty-five, and our efforts to reach out and touch the hand of an old person and say "We know your pain, your sorrow, your loneliness," are pitifully small and inadequate. Well, this is how I see our city. This is New York.

GEORGE C. SCOTT
Actor

This is a conniving town, see, a screwing town, a deceitful town, a depressing town, a retrogressive town to live in and beget children in. I've tried to think of an image or a symbol that stands in my mind for New York and it's not easy, but the clearest picture I get is one of bitterness; it's the strongest image I've always had – bitter professionally, bitter personally, for a good many years. But in my profession, I had to come here. Unfortunately, this is where the theater exists and so I am kept here. I wish it were everywhere, not just in New York, because, frankly, I don't think New York deserves it. It's been taken over by people who use it like a dead whore or a dead horse. Somehow, it doesn't matter how many thousands of marvelous little-theater groups there are around the country, and people who read good plays and are devoted to the theater – they're not Broadway.

Maybe Broadway *has* something essential to the American theater, but, by the same token, it's that same Broadway that's responsible for the death of the theater. I've used the word before about it – cancer. The theater is being eaten away from the inside and New York is responsible for that – oh, very definitely. I think the theater can flourish and grow healthy and big-time elsewhere eventually. What the hell, there're only a few basic elements in it, like any other great formula – talent, dedication, audience, money, and guts. That's what sent me into the wilderness to produce plays in Michigan.

A-a-a-g-h, but you can't get away from the power, the immense power – I keep coming back to that word. It's a disturbing thing. The whole damned city is a disturbing place to be. That's why I don't go out much any more. When I was broke, I was not one of those people, I'm sorry to say, who could find comradeship and beauty in New York. I know people who can. Many of my friends, not so fortunate as I've been, can keep on with that hideous charade of a bottle of chianti and a couple of stuffed pillows and a cold-water flat – and the cockroaches – and tell themselves it's not always going to be like that, and, by the very virtue of that belief, faith, and innocence, create their own beauty around them. I can't do that.

I look around me and all I see and feel is great pain and confusion and tremendous power; forces that smash and crash against each other; people narcoticized to go through their lives as nearly unconscious as they can get. Something like this is true in any urban place, but in New York whole legions of people appear to be operating on one cylinder, because to operate at really full capacity would drive them insane. Perhaps now I'm getting a better image of New York – a beast, a mindless beast, a great, blind Samson. Samson, at least, had a mind when he pulled the temple down, but this is aimless, brutal, and pointless.

New York is a city without color to me. A great deal of electricity, but no color. It is a gray city, full of gray people; a morass, a quagmire, a swamp. Someday I might do a film about New York, a city in which you can go from the highest plateau of wealth and intelligence and compassion and experience to the Dark Ages in five seconds. You can do it on any street, not just the East Side or Hell's Kitchen or the West Side, but on Fifth Avenue, too. I'd like to show some of that. But what would be the motive for doing such a movie? Unless you just wanted to show man what a monster he is and that seems to be pointless as the city itself. If you could take a camera and see the things I've seen in this city – I'd like to show the faces of people as they walk by; a drunk with his face bashed in where he's hit the concrete – they always have some old wound, a cast on one arm that dates from the clinic a week before; a well-dressed woman curbing her damned poodle.

There's no spirit of pride in New York at all – I mean in the civic way of the best of the old Greek cities – on any level. I get the feeling that everybody hates it, this city of smells, horrible smells. The streets stink; the rivers around it stink; the air stinks; the effluvium hanging over it stinks. I know there is real beauty here and it's always shocking and marvelous and surprising when I see it – a cat and a kid, a junkman's horse, a cop's horse; young people, perhaps; a smile; two hands holding each other; now and then, old people concentrating on some object; innocent things unlike New York.

I hate to be prone to seeing so much ugliness, but, by God, I can't help it. What's registered on the retina is there. I suppose it's the hangover of those early years I thought I'd never get over. I'd like to be able to say that I've been able to rise above all that, but it's not true. There's no way of removing yourself from this place, except to leave it entirely and never come back. Strangely enough, though, I always do get excited when I come back to it. There's that *power* again, that feeling of, goddamn it, something's going on here, something's happening, good, bad, or indifferent. I'm happy in New York now, but why is that? It's because of the people and not the damned city. My wife, friends, acquaintances, children. I'm happy because I see goals in front of me that have nothing to do with New York, and you can be happy in hell if you have goals; you can be happy in jail thinking about how you're going to get out.

The George Washington Bridge, east to Manhattan. The bridge supports only anarchy on wheels.

ANARCHY ON WHEELS CHAPTER 3

Twice a day, every business day, some 2,000,000 people intent on getting into or out of the nine square miles of Manhattan south of Sixty-first Street, an area in which, for anything they may tell themselves to the contrary, their Domesday Book is kept, descend into the maelstrom of the subways with the haunted resignation of lemmings, there to die the small death of the rush hour. Their resurrection is recurrent, rapid, and rumpled. The subway rider issues forth from a car door like breakfast food shot from guns, with the important difference that he is shrunken rather than puffed. Entombment in the subways bears some resemblance, anthropologically, to that of Ben Jonson, who was buried standing up in Westminster Abbey – although with considerable ceremony and no shoving. In New York, the ritual of subway burial is casual, involving only the dropping of a fifteen-cent token into a turnstile. (The bodies may wait a long time in line to be interred; attrition among changemakers is almost a matter of policy with the Transit Authority.) Rarely is the loved one accompanied to the entrance and once on the platform he is on his own.

In the cars, he stands on roughly 1.4 square feet of floor space or on somebody else's feet. There, he may stare glumly at the disingenuous posters pasted up by the Authority, adjuring him to use the "Three Magic Words," "PLEASE," "SORRY," and "THANK YOU." (Occasionally, from the quagmire of a copywriter's subconscious, a slimy stump of this kind will surface: "COURTESY IS CONTAGIOUS – LET'S START AN EPIDEMIC.") He is asked, more firmly, not to push or block, and warned (under penalty of the law) not to smoke, litter, spit, or deface, all of which he does, if only inadvertently, at one time or another. At Christmastime, he is urged, with bright meretriciousness, to buy packages of tokens as gifts for the person who has everything. The subway rider is a sullen example of the incredible compressibility of the human frame. There are seats in all cars, but it is the fixed belief of most travelers that these are occupied by paid agents who do nothing but ride perpetually over the system's 237 miles.

In common with the dead, the subway rider is beyond frustration. Year in and year out, winter and summer, he is bullied and beaten by his fellows seeking the same Nirvana, a skyscraper in the morning, an apartment in Brooklyn, the Bronx, or Queens at night. To this end, he suffers the grisly folksiness of the Authority's publicity (legitimate, paid advertising on car cards has declined steadily for years), his hat to be mashed, his glasses to be knocked off, his unread newspaper to be shredded, and his nose to be assailed by smells more pungent than those in a North African casbah. He endures dank tunnels and windswept platforms in winter, choking dust and stifling heat in summer, and the muscular importunities of station guards in all seasons. He once voted for a $500,000,000 bond issue for the construction of a Second Avenue subway and seemed not the least surprised to find out, years later, that all the money had been spent on wages and patches for the old ones. (The system even sold its power plants, despite a lot of puerile grumbling, to another monolithic outfit, the Consolidated Edison Company, the archness of whose public posture is fully the equal of that of the Transit Authority: "Dig We Must, For Growing New York.") So passive is he rendered by "The Safest Railroad in the World" (every time there is a breakdown, the figures are whipped out to prove it. They make no mention of reliability), that on his crowded, thunderous wanderings he manages to lose or forget or have stolen from him such items as outboard motors, artificial arms, hearing aids, television antennae, fishing rods, false teeth, and the crutches that bore him into the trains in the first place.

No sociometric ruler has as yet been found to measure the traumatic effect (a vogue concept of the Sixties, like cholesterol) of the daily getting into and out of southern Manhattan's nine square miles. There are, however, abounding statistics – those compiled by the Regional Plan Association are irreproachable – to show that the number of people performing the feat (it is nothing less) was actually about half a million smaller in 1960 (about 3,350,000) than in 1948. (It started to go up again in 1961 and 1962.) Fewer people were riding the subways. (The Transit Authority thoughtfully omitted any mention of the abominable off-hours stretchout that saves it money: shorter trains, longer waits, and every car filled with the swirling kitchen midden tossed away by New Yorkers whose amorality in civic affairs comes to them directly from their betters, the city administration.) Fewer passengers were riding the dreadful commuter trains. (These were bankrupt, or close to, both financially and as a source of folk humor. Their bone dryness as a wellspring of laughs is easily gauged: both the New Haven and the Long Island began to make bad jokes about themselves years ago. At no time, of course, did they forbear to disgorge volumes of statistics designed to show that their on-time records were 101 per cent or better.)

The number of interurban bus passengers remained reasonably constant over a four-year period up to 1960. Buses in the city, privately or publicly owned, were carrying fewer people. (For a halcyon three weeks early in 1962, there were no privately owned buses on the streets at all. What happened was that a transit sharpshooter named Harry Weinberg, having made good in Dallas and Honolulu in the rude, nineteenth-century mode of Commodore Vanderbilt bought up the Fifth Avenue Coach Company's lines and thought he could get away with it in New York. He was the victim of a cultural lag. He wanted to raise fares a nickel and cut down on service. He tried to fight City Hall *and* the Transport Workers Union, between whom there are thousands of blood ties, all Democratic. Weinberg fired a few men for openers, as they say in poker; the union struck him cleanly and beautifully; the city virtuously grabbed his equity and ran the lines, keeping the fare at fifteen cents with the same sort of quasi-concealed subsidy granted the subways.)

The really significant figure compiled by the Regional Plan, which is supported by 1500 businesses, governments, and individuals and takes as its province the twenty-two counties in New York, New Jersey, and Connecticut (with their blindly

Eighth Avenue, Thirty-ninth to Fortieth streets;
the Port Authority bus terminal on a weekday morning.
Their Domesday Book is kept in Manhattan's
nine square miles south of Sixty-first Street.

Times Square; the subway at the evening rush
hour. The rider is a sullen example of the incredible compressibility of the human frame.

and aggressively independent government bodies), within a fifty-mile radius of Times Square, was that the number of automobiles, trucks, and taxicabs piling into Manhattan's hub every day had gone up from 200,000 in 1924 to almost 600,000 in 1960. This was the result, at least in part, of what the Plan people, with mortifying accuracy and a hint of pride, termed, in their Bulletin Number 99/ December 1961, a "pioneering development" fostered by them since 1929; the bulletin added that "the network of radial and circumferential expressways of the Region" and "the substantial growth of effective municipal and county planning" had "now been achieved in most of its fundamentals." This is a shining instance of how Americans, not simply the Regional Plan, live bewitched by the *juju* of statistics. They are historically incapable of accepting the evidence of their senses. Like its supporters, the Plan is, naturally and without any sinister intent, willy-nilly committed to the internal-combustion engine on wheels. It has always hugged to itself the theory, convenient but as yet not susceptible of proof, that the way to reduce congestion and speed traffic in the city was to build more and bigger roads, bridges, tunnels, accesses, egresses, cloverleafs, crossovers, under passes, by-passes, and so on around it. For some peculiar reason, the theory has not worked. Where the city once had a traffic problem, it now has a way of life – anarchy.

Unless one is willing to get stuffy and adopt the broadest philosophical outlook (also known by the odious expression, THE BIG PICTURE) – a species of Marxian-cum-Spenglerian analysis that the whole world is going to hell in a high-powered handbasket driven by capitalist hot-rodders – it is impossible to assign any respon-

The Staten Island ferry on a weekday morning. Their dance is the lockstep.

sibility anywhere and nobody is to blame for anything. The phenomenon is not unique to New York, only more readily observable because of its pre-eminent position. It displays some of the qualities of foam rubber: it can be poked but not dented. It is the height of fatuity to suppose that the rascals can be turned out, since the rascals are of both parties and immutable. They may feign anger and righteousness publicly, denounce each other ringingly, pledge themselves to institute this and wipe out that, but contrapuntal to the noise may be detected a strain of the purest *politesse,* a touching solicitude, the throaty gurgle of mutual accommodation. Nobody gores anybody's ox. A butcher is broken on the wheel of justice for putting a thumb on a scale or too much fat in hamburger; a landlord in whose lousy tenement a Puerto Rican child is bitten to death by rats (his parents pay $25 a week to house themselves, three other children, and the rats in one room with a foul toilet in the hall) is fined $250 when the city can bestir itself to catch him. To return to the particularity of transportation, however, a cop puts a $15 parking ticket on the mayor's car; the mayor sends his chauffeur to court to pay it, and the anarchic traffic gets worse hour by hour.

The behavior of New Yorkers under a pressure so remorseless is indicative of their wonderful, misapplied flexibility. When, for example, alternate-side-of-the-street parking (a regulatory measure of notable complexity) was instituted (as much to permit the streets to be cleaned as to speed traffic), drivers exerted all their cunning to move their cars from curb to curb at the last possible moment (one entrepreneur went so far as to publish – and sell for a dollar – a 40-page listing of free parking spaces and the hours at which they were available); many ignored the regulations and regarded summonses as what they called "paying dues." If the police mean in earnest to clear a street (they find it inadvisable to try too many at a time) for, say, a parade, they tie on all street furniture paper signs that say, "No Parking Today," especially over metal signs which, since time out of mind, have exhorted, "No Parking at Any Time."

For a short while, late in 1960, the ordinances were enforced with sweaty integrity. The occasion for this convulsive adherence to duty was cosmic in its irrelevance. Commissioner Stephen P. Kennedy got it into his head to forbid the police to hold outside jobs. The cops' lodge, the Patrolmen's Benevolent Association, took bitter exception to the edict. Downing night sticks, of course, was unthinkable, not to say illegal. On October 26, the cops struck back by, as it were, going limp, ticketing twenty-three per cent fewer cars than they had on the same day the previous year. Traffic violations bring in a lot of money to the city and few people, not excluding the guiltless, do anything but pay up, behaving in Traffic Court like a race of lumpen proletariat. Kennedy threatened his men with severe disciplinary action. The response of the force was memorable: between October 27 and November 28, it issued, give or take a few points, a hundred per cent more summonses a day, or better, than was usual. "If summonses is what they want," said Patrolman John J. Cassese, president of the P.B.A., "summonses is what they'll get. It's a bad situation all around." He added that it was "too bad the public is caught in the squeeze"; he was "certainly sorry" about that. The delicious struggle ended with the departure for private life of the commissioner and the utterance of a mealymouthed pronunciamento that, in effect, permitted the cops to go right on moonlighting.

Possibly more instructive was the workmanlike dismantling of Traffic Commissioner Henry A. Barnes. Shortly after Mayor Robert F. Wagner, Jr., was re-elected in November, 1961 (he was, mystifyingly, cast as a crusading reformer and wore the look of a man patiently going along with a gag), he fired the incumbent traffic man, T. T. Wiley. Wiley was a quiet, highly competent engineer who had been allowed to putter around harmlessly for years. Barnes was brought in from Baltimore (at $5000 a year more than Wiley) on a favoring gale of publicity, much of it self-generated and brash, but amusing; years before he got to New York, he was writing articles on how things ought to be done there. An angular, upstate New York boy in his early fifties, he played the drawling apple-knocker engagingly and wore a tie clasp with the letters YCDBSOYA on it. He explained with bucolic slyness that it meant, "You Can't Do Business Sitting On Your Ass." With the customary pious snigger, the newspapers put a dash in place of the unmistakable word. Barnes got reporters and photographers up to his hotel at eight o'clock mornings to accompany him on whirlwind tours of his new demesne. He viewed with misgiving and predicted freely and was visibly warmed by the reception he got on the editorial pages. He let it be known the mayor had told him he was his own man.

On January 12, 1962, three days before he went to work officially, Barnes received – through the newspapers – a glimpse of the foreseeable future. Wagner said his new commissioner would be given "all the tools we possibly can," appending, "I'm still the mayor and I make the decisions and will continue to do so." Whether this cast a tinge of liver on Barnes's eupepsia is conjectural. On his way to the office the first day, his car was blocked for eight minutes, within a hundred feet of Traffic's headquarters just south of the Brooklyn Bridge, by a huge wrecking crane and iron ball. (The crane was in the neighborhood for the purpose, among others, of knocking down a landmark, the handsome Greek Revival Lorillard Building of 1837, a cultural annoyance standing in the way of still another new Brooklyn Bridge approach.) Barnes merely wondered why the crane couldn't be used nights and said he thought his job was "going to be a lot of fun." The briefest accounting of Barnes's first three months or so is a veritable necrology. On January 16, he inveighed loudly against double parking by physicians, saying he was glad "New York has a wealthy privileged class," and disclosing, too, that he planned to revoke the immunity enjoyed by lower-ranking employees of foreign consulates. His statement of the day, couched in his firmly rural vernacular, was, "Congestion here sure is a dilly." On subsequent days, the following signs and portents and manifestations were recorded:

January 17. – The president of the New York County Medical Society observes tartly that doctors' incomes have nothing to do with parking or traffic problems and that "a doctor's car and where he can park it is almost as essential to his practice as a stethoscope." A telegram is dispatched to Barnes suggesting he look for a national solution to traffic troubles before "passing out pronouncements to the press." January 21. – Barnes reiterates his stand on minor-league diplomats; Police Commissioner Michael J. Murphy informs him they enjoy no such immunity to begin with. On a television program, Barnes says stubbornly, "I'm not retracting what I said about doctors. I'm not picking on them, either, but if you give special privileges to one group you will be pressed to give it to a lot of others. The big idea is to move traffic." January 25. – The "scramble," or so-called "Barnes Dance," is instituted at Forty-second Street and Vanderbilt Avenue; all traffic is stopped for twenty-three seconds so that pedestrians may cross any way they please. It costs nothing and disturbs nothing. January 27. – Barnes reports a taxicab driver, unprovoked, has pumped his hand in gratitude for "going after the doctors." The hackie tells Barnes, "You know, I work in this cab ten hours, and if I jump out a minute to go to the bathroom, when I come out I've got a ticket." "I never realized," Barnes tells newspapermen, his tie-clasp humor to the fore again, "that getting ticketed for going to the bathroom was one of the hazards of cab driving." January 31. – Following Barnes's complaint, the United States Post Office orders its drivers to obey the law. "I believe," he comments, "we'll have excellent relations." The same day he lets reporters know things are getting done: he has fixed the door check on a toilet in the men's room at Traffic Headquarters and it now closes.

February 4. – Barnes estimates it would cost $100,000,000 and take five to eight years to solve the city's "amazing traffic mess." Of the articles he had written, earlier and at a safe distance, he concedes, "It was pretty easy to write what I thought should be done in New York when I wasn't there." (At about the same time, police accident figures for January, 1962, revealed that traffic deaths were double what they had been for the same month in 1961. The poor showing was attributed in part to unfortunately fine weather – it had brought out cars and people untimely.) February 6. – Barnes repairs a jammed parking meter with a penknife. February 7. – At a conference with representatives of the Medical Society, he points out that 35,000 of the 50,000 summonses issued to physicians in eight years had been disposed of with painless suspended sentences. He thinks doctors' wives are doing a lot of the illegal parking. Told that there are more than a thousand woman physicians in the city, he answers, "I'm sure they all wear high heels and park on Thirty-fourth Street near Macy's while on calls." February 15. – He announces that within thirty days he will wreak a "major change in Manhattan that will be quite startling and have a tremendous effect on traffic." He has been told, he goes on, "that there is really nothing I can do about it. I don't think so at all." February 19. – At a dinner of the City Club, he suggests that buses be used to transport commuters on city parkways. "I'll hear from Robert Moses on that one," he predicts with poignant accuracy. February 27. – He plans a dramatic revision of the traffic pattern from Canal Street to the Battery.

March 4. – Having had what the New York *Times* mercifully called his "first heart-to-heart talk" with Mayor Wagner, the commissioner, as the *Times* put it, "put up a 'go-slow' sign yesterday – for himself." These included the conversion to one-way traffic of Fifth and Madison avenues ("Little need to rush into that," Barnes said of something that had been promised regularly by the mayor as early as 1957), the building of more municipal garages, expansion of departmental operations, and so on and so on and so on. He dropped his February 15 plan to make a "startling" announcement and said the newspapers had "inflated" it, anyway; how much it had been blown up was a secret he clutched grimly to his breast. March 12. – He comments innocently that he has taken no position on the Fifth-Madison Avenue conversion and tells the Broadway Association, rather wistfully, that it is "almost impossible" to enforce parking restrictions against people who think they are entitled to park where they live. "I had," he says, "the odd idea that streets are made for moving traffic and not for parking lots." March 13. – The Barnes Dance is instituted at Wall Street and Broadway. March 15. – With evident asperity, he tells a luncheon meeting of the Civic Executives Conference that "never in my twenty-five years" in the business "have I run into such red tape and interference from every city agency that you can think of." He had waited ten days to get three holes drilled in a floor and had even asked for a drill so that he could do the work himself; on the eleventh day, though, three men showed up. (An aide to the mayor clucked sympathetically. "We don't," he said, unsmiling, "like red tape any better than he does and we do our utmost to keep it at a minimum.") Barnes declares he will not "take the blame for any foul-ups in alternate-side-of-the-street parking." (These are the indubitable privileges of the Police and Sanitation Departments.) He concludes, a little shrilly, some feel, "I may be disgusted, but I am too damn mean to leave and I am going to stay in spite of it."

March 21. – To the New York Board of Trade, the commissioner confesses that he is "fed up with trying to iron out jurisdictional problems," that he is "getting resigned to delays, politics, and frustrations" and that he wouldn't dream of being "foolish enough" to try any changes in the garment district. (Two days later, at Church and Fulton streets, a pedestrian who had twice before been given tickets for jaywalking, pulled a gun on a cop determined to give him a third. The man was disarmed and charged with felonious assault and violation of the Sullivan Law.)

April 1. – He is told his budget for the forthcoming year, while $1,000,000 higher than his predecessor's last, would, nevertheless, be $840,000 less than what he had requested and that half of the increase would be whittled away by mandatory salary increases and the rising cost of materials. April 18. – His prediction that he would hear from Robert Moses on the proposal to use buses on city parkways comes true. "Mr. Barnes," says this tablet sent down from Moses' Sinai, "of course, has not been here long enough to develop any pride in our accomplishments or to be sensitive about baseless criticism." Moses speaks of Barnes's "100 per cent" ignorance of the illegality of his proposal and flicks the commissioner off his lapel with the observation that if he "insists on making lurid announcements and random unsupported wisecracks at the expense of those who have duties to perform, he will find New York a tough town." April 21. – The commissioner presses a button changing a red light to green to open officially the International Automobile Show at the Coliseum on Columbus Circle.

WITNESS

JOSEPH DICKMAN
A liquor salesman

As far as drinking is concerned, people here are much more sophisticated about liquor and drinking habits in general. No one looks cockeyed at men hanging around bars in the afternoon. Out of town, these same guys would be considered the town bums. The only way you can tell rich from poor these days is what

Seventh Street east of Third Avenue; McSorley's Ale House.
It has endured, unbelievably and without women, since 1854.

they'll buy in the liquor stores. Where people are well to do, it's the high-priced scotches and bourbons. If they're *really* rich, however, they don't get fooled by labels. They buy the house brands. They know their friends know they don't have to think about prices and they don't have to put on a show with labels. In the poorer areas, it's the blends – what they call rye, only you don't see a bottle of real rye around any more.

Somehow, I still love New York in spite of many stupid things I see happening around. I miss the old saloons with the family entrance and every saloon like a public meeting place, where neighborhood issues and problems were pretty much thrashed out. I hate to see those things go by the wayside for luxury apartments, which are bringing back people into New York who never really understood New York and what it is, except they can live in a fourteenth-floor apartment and look out the window and say, "What a beautiful view." Who are they kidding? I like the beatniks in the Village – they remind me of the early Thirties, they're non-

Third Avenue saloon; P. J. Clarke's. First the interior decorators took over the street, then the Madison Avenue boys, then the homosexuals; finally, the real estate developers pushed them all out.

conformists fighting back against those steel structures that go up with no heart in them.

I lived in a brownstone fifteen years and I knew who my neighbor was and this was great, this was New York. Now, I live in an apartment house – they tore down my brownstone – and there's a door right opposite mine and a dozen doors down the hall and I don't know who lives in them. When I lived in the brownstone, I used to sit in my window – I was on the ground floor – with a highball in my hand on a Sunday afternoon, looking out at all the people walking up and down Twelfth Street and my friends would come by and yell, "There's that Mexican whore in the window again." It was a great compliment to me. It gave me a feeling of great warmth. They knew me, I knew them. And they'd come in and we'd drink the afternoon away. Who can see me sitting in a window on the fourteenth floor?

This used to be a city of people. Now, it's a city of marionettes. They run, they disappear into buildings, they have no identity. Once they get inside, they're gone, you don't see them any more. Today, it's a city of big buildings and slums. I'm "lucky" enough – put that in quotes – to be living in a big building, but I'd rather be back in the brownstone where the floors, instead of being nailed down, were put in with wooden pegs. The streets have changed. If they put up a tree, it's a sickly thing for big-building dogs, not humans. For humans, no one has any consideration. The neighborhood stores are gone, too. I used to like the old butcher and grocer. He knew you. Oh, he might put a finger on the scale, but you allowed him the extra dime. Today, everything's streamlined. You buy a corned beef, say, and you get it in a supermarket and you get it already wrapped in one of those damned shiny, transparent packages *with* the instructions right in there how to cook it. Christ, that was something the butcher told you personally. The few neighborhood saloons left, you can't get into because the tourists jam 'em. By tourists, I mean the rubbernecks from the big buildings – their necks get stretched out of the fourteenth floor – who come running down into the nice, dirty saloons we knew. It's reached the point, too, where an old-time bartender doesn't remain long in one place, because if he *does* get to know the customers the boss'll fire him. He has to be completely impersonal.

It's odd I should still love the town, but I do. I stay, I guess, because I was born here – I was born in Chinatown, believe it or not – and my roots are here. It's home and no one ever feels hurt in their own home. I always felt safe in New York, like being in my mother's womb. Out of town, it always felt hostile to me. I'll tell you something else about the New Yorker. Out of town, he's the biggest chump you ever saw. He acts just like an out-of-towner does in New York. He goes to the bellhop in his hotel and asks where can he get a broad or where is there a bustout joint. The New Yorker is actually an appleknocker, you know that? That's all he is. I love him for *that*.

I even love the crap the politicians put down Primary Week and Election Day and forget about a week after. We all know about that and we all go on voting the way we do because New York is what it is and we all go on yelling, "You'll never have another LaGuardia." I hate the subway, but I wouldn't do without it. I despise the bus drivers, the crude, arrogant bastards, but still I love the city. I hate the rumbling of the garbage trucks just about when you're falling asleep at two in the morning, and by the time you get downstairs to go to work, the streets are crummy again, but still I love the city. I must be nuts. I know that.

MRS. GERTRUDE DICKMAN
A teacher in the public elementary schools

My teaching career is in two big chunks. It started with ten years in Harlem, many more than I needed to stay there, because I had the right to ask for a transfer after three, but I stayed because I felt that, with the experience I had, I had something to contribute; I felt I understood these people more, perhaps, than the new person sent to replace me would and that I had built something in terms of a relationship. Before you can become accepted in an area like that, you must prove yourself; the burden of the proof is so heavy on you. Frequently, you were the first white person these children had ever seen. Their mothers would return from an eight- or ten-hour day working for that white lady up in the Bronx and she would tell her tale of woe to her kids, built up out of whatever resentments she was harboring – usually more real than not – and these would, naturally, be transferred to you.

In the course of a day, you might be called a white Jew bastard as well as not if you were to reprimand somebody for his behavior in class. It took long years of having the older brothers and the sisters and the cousins of these children in your class to teach the kids that followed that you weren't a white Jew bastard. Then, you might get off the subway and walk down 144th Street toward the school and somebody from a fourth-floor window would call out, "Hi, Mrs. Dickman," and you knew you had it made because you had proved you were their friend and not just somebody who saw the kids five hours a day. I learned that these children had the most magnificent ability to survive, an ability that our coddled, middle-class children could never achieve. I learned that these latchkey kids would have to get up and cook their own breakfast and iron their white shirts to be ready for assembly and look as spick and span as anyone could hope to have them look. They couldn't have tried any harder to get on with the job of learning in spite of all the hardships.

The conditions they had to cope with were the conditions of no father in the family and a string of "uncles" passing through; the mothers working from eight in the morning until eight at night; the housing problems that are so well known – no beds of their own, rat-infested buildings, outrageous rents for what they got, and all the rest of it. The ones who didn't make it, the ones who needed help most – well, for instance, you'd get a child in a class of thirty who was present when his father shot his mother. The psychological results of this, of course, would be self-evident in later years – he'd end up in the psychiatric ward at Bellevue or worse. This child tried to commit suicide. Two weeks later he was back in class. What do you do with a child like that? I harbored him, I gave him the usual T.L.C. – Tender Loving Care – which is about the only panacea for all emotional disturbances of children. What happened to him after he left my class I don't know. Who knows what further horrors befell him?

I've stood at the threshold of my classroom waiting for the bell to ring for lunch and a block of wood came sailing down the hall – not intended for me – but catching me on the bridge of the nose with enough force to make me black out. You could multiply this a thousand times. Yes, I guess what kept me up there ten years was the fact that I could still understand why these things were happening, that it wasn't the kid who was doing this to me. He was doing it out of his need to free himself of his hostility toward the environment in which he was living. I could at least attempt to change it, or make it a little better, the five hours a day he spent in my care, and I got the feeling that maybe I was doing a little good.

I left Harlem in 1952. Frankly, I felt that if I didn't, I wouldn't have had any other kind of experience in the school system and I would get too set in my ways to make a change. Besides, my personal life and physical condition were such I felt I had to ease things for myself. Yet here I am in another depressed area – the Lower East Side – which is the nearest thing to a United Nations situation I can think of. We've got complete integration here. Where else in the world could you find a child of Chinese parentage, for example, who went to Trinidad for a few years and came into your classroom with a beautiful British accent and by her very manners raised the standards – immediately – of everyone around her?

I think New York should be kicked solidly for not doing something more. I would say the school system *is* really trying harder now, but it's got a long, long way to go. This city, with all of the money at its command, could have given those kids in Harlem a better chance – probably still can. Smaller classes, for one thing; many more special services. When I was there, we were fortunate to have one full-time psychiatric social worker, but that lady would have needed three heads really to function and handle the full load.

I have never lived anywhere else in my life, although I have been to Europe

*Hunter Elementary School for Bright Children.
Gifted children play just as hard as any others.*

*Central Park; the climbers. The adaptability
of urban children is matched only by that of
the city's tired trees.*

several times and all over this country and Canada, and I don't think I *could* live anywhere else. This city satisfies me every way, except, of course, when I get the need occasionally to look at a mountain, let us say, and even then I can find one by taking a boat ride up the Hudson. Ironically, I lack the will to go out and get all the things one can find in New York. They're there and I don't take nearly enough advantage of them. I know that and I know that whatever is lacking is not the fault of New York. It's within myself.

WITNESS

RIKURO TAKAHASHI
New York agent of the Fuji Bank, Ltd., Tokyo

I have been here twice before, once for six months, once for two weeks, and – it is not a matter of like or dislike, just an impression – the buildings are so tall, the streets so dark, there is no sunshine. Perhaps it lends some kind of dignity. I have the feeling now that New York has become more quiet than Tokyo and seems less crowded. Tokyo is becoming more and more similar to New York, though, in many ways; the buildings, naturally, are not so high – ten stories is the limit – and the roads are straighter in this city. In Tokyo they are crooked. Also, they are as dirty there as they are here. And our traffic is much heavier and worse. We call Tokyo taxicab drivers *kamikaze* – suicide pilots. New York drivers are next to *kamikaze*.

I find Tokyo a livelier city than New York. Compared with others, of course, New York *is* a very active city, but there are, in Tokyo, many more – what shall I say? – bars, places to drink, and more night clubs and cabarets, and more people walking around at all hours. The night life is quite different. Those places are served by girls. They do close, it is true, earlier than they do here. And then, too, there are the geisha houses. Whether such establishments are more stimulating or not than New York's depends on the person. Here, many couples dine in restaurants. In Japan, such places are only for men. Of course, I am a man, and so I find Tokyo more stimulating.

Here is a paradox. In this country, we all understand, there are no pure Americans, most of them being of foreign origin, so that most of the American people are, more or less, indifferent to country of origin. In Japan, all Japanese are Japanese and we are always cognizant of the foreigner. Now, Japanese, generally speaking, are very *kind* to foreigners, but in Tokyo to be a *friend* of a Japanese is very difficult. In New York, I can say that since all of us are foreigners, there is a possibility of being a *friend* of someone, but New York is not especially *kind* to foreigners. Japanese are *kinder* to foreigners; here, people are *friendlier* to them.

As to banking, this is an international monetary market, but if you compare New York with London, I think London is still far advanced in terms of international finance, even though the United Kingdom has been losing its economic strength. Nevertheless, it is now absolutely indispensable for any bank of the first rank to have an agency in New York and I can foresee that eventually the city will be on a par with London. I must say also that Japanese banks are trying very hard to institute many of the methods of New York banks. Before the war, our banking methods followed the European, the Continental systems; since, we have been trying to adopt American methods. For example, small deposits and consumer loans; the Taylor System – rationalization – the use of many machines, although no machine can ever replace the abacus. For a long string of figures, an adding machine, but for just two or three or a short column, the abacus, in the hands of a trained man, cannot be equaled.

For a business life, this is a good place, an efficient city, but for a private life, it is not. Here, I live in New Rochelle. In Toyko, also, I live in the suburbs. It is my ambition to live in the country.

Orchard Street, south from Stanton, on Sunday. Law or no law, one man's Sunday is another's Monday.

HYMIE POMPER
Owner of a fruit and vegetable store at 146 Avenue C

It's a dog's life, the worst business you could think of to get into. I have two married daughters and a boy going to City College. The boy's going to be a clinical psychologist, at least that's what he's studying. But I wouldn't let him *smell* this business; I don't even let him come in the store and help me. I want him to have a better life than I had. I came here from Poland in 1925 and worked for somebody else on a pushcart on Rivington Street. I graduated from Public School 91. After a while I went out floating. Floating is you take a pushcart from corner to corner until you get chased by the cops. For me, it was mostly on Avenue C. When you were floating, in order to stay on a corner, you'd all chip in and give the cop a couple of bucks. Then I got a permit to have a steady place – one of those places LaGuardia didn't get rid of the pushcarts.

I went in the army in 1944 – I had three children before Pearl Harbor – so I didn't volunteer – they drafted me – and I got out in December 1945. I was wounded in the left hand in the Battle of the Bulge. I'm here in this store since 1948. No more pushcarts for me. They should be off the streets. In this time and age, there's no call for them to be staying in the streets in the snow and rain and all kinds of weather. This place cost me a few hundred dollars in painting and so on, but that's about all. It never was a fancy neighborhood, but now I'd like to move out. Who knows, maybe this *is* my last year here. I won't regret leaving; nobody's here any more I know. The housing projects hurt me; the rules drove out the people who dealt with me because their incomes got too high. The supermarkets did me damage, too. Understand me, what I am saying has nothing to do with race or color. I am a Jew. But, when I went into business for myself, this neighborhood was Poles, Jews, Russians, Ukrainians, Italians. They bought from me. Then they started to tear the neighborhood down and build these projects and people moved out. The Puerto Ricans moved in. Nobody else wants to live here today. For me, it has nothing to do with their being Puerto Ricans. It's that they buy from their own stores that speak their own language. Maybe the landlords are better off with Puerto Ricans, but not businessmen.

You get my point? The neighborhood shouldn't be so one-sided. On the other hand, one thing is a little better now. You only go five times to the market a week. It used to be six. You have an extra day to catch up on a little sleep. Otherwise, there was no night, no day, you couldn't go any place. You don't feel like going somewhere after sixteen, seventeen hours a day. The routine is always the same: get to the market – Washington Market – two, three, four in the morning with the station wagon. I live on Eighth Street. I go down Avenue C to Houston Street, turn right to Essex, left on Essex at Broadway, right on East Broadway to Worth, up Worth to Broadway, left on Broadway to Chambers, right on Chambers into the Market and park at Chambers and Washington. Then I make my rounds. Maybe a dozen places. Coming back, it's Franklin Street all the way to Broadway, left on Broadway to Houston, right on Houston to Avenue C, left on Avenue C to the store.

I open at seven in the morning and close at seven at night, but I'm in the store before, packing out. Packing out is putting fruits and vegetables on display. In the summertime I put a stand outside and have a boy to help me. It's too hard to pack outside in the heat for me. Maybe what it'll take to get me out of here is they're moving the market up to the Bronx eventually. The only reason I stayed here was I didn't have far to travel. I'll probably get a job – I'm still only forty-five – but I wouldn't go back to this business if I gave it up. I won't blame what I am, either, on New York. New York is my home; home is where you make it, what you make it. Maybe I just didn't have the thing to get up and go. I was content with what I was doing – in spite of myself. I should, maybe, have had a little more gumption to get out and try and better myself.

A Harlem street. The richest city in the world generously permits them to survive.

MARTIN BREGMAN
Associate general agent for a life-insurance company

New York is a jungle and a lie in a lot of ways, but if, say, you take sand and sift it, work on it, take your time – and if you like sand – you'll be able to separate the dirty from the white and so I have to come out crazy about New York. Oh, sure, I've found sand elsewhere that's white and filthy, but it doesn't have the *consistency,* the *grade* we have here, dirty or clean. As a kid, born in Harlem, raised in the Allerton Avenue section of the Bronx during the depression, New York was cold, impersonal, ugly, colorless, and drab. In my neighborhood, celebrities were the guys who broke out by getting a scholarship to an out-of-state college. Well, my family managed to *send* me to Indiana University. I screwed up; one year. You want to know why? The transition was no transition; it was Allerton Avenue all over again.

I came back to New York and did a year at a chiropractic school, which I hated, but I had to do something. I didn't finish that either. Now, I'm not knocking chiropractic; I never found out what it was because I quit and opened an office. It was probably illegal, but nobody stopped me. Interesting, eh? After three months, I decided what I was doing was phony. I realized I was treating people not knowing my ass from my elbow – or theirs, either. My office was at 1650 Broadway, the same building Irving Berlin is in. All music and show business. One of my patients was an agent. We opened a theatrical agency and set out to conquer the world. *That* lasted three months.

Right after that time, I was approached to go into the illegal liquor business. Some guys were starting up a moonshine still out in Jersey. I didn't go in. I was too damn scared. I'll never forget the night I met the local bigwig that ran the liquor concession on the Upper East Side – around East 100th Street. This man was of medium height, kind of heavy set, black coat, gray felt hat with a broad brim, and he walked with four other guys right behind him. Gangster movies. First thing he said to me was – I swear it's true – "I like you, kid." He was really

The Eighties, off Park Avenue; street photographer at work. He, his pony, and his camera are almost as archaic as the hurdy gurdy.

playing the role. "I heard a lot about you," he said. "You're the kind of guy we're looking for. We're thinking of opening up a new operation and we need a bright guy to run it."

All the time we're talking, deliveries are being made to the back of the candy store where we're standing and from there to the local bars. Ever see those five-gallon syrup tins? That's what they use. Right out in the open. It seemed like two days I was standing on that corner before I said I'd like to think it over. Think it over! Hah! Like I was applying for a job at B.B.D. & O. But that gave me a new insight. I learned I had a choice. I could walk away from this man. I wasn't involved. I was so *not* involved, all I knew was this guy's name was Joe and I didn't know if it was his first or last name. I walked away because I was scared and I'd never done anything really wrong. My Jewish stock came out, I guess. I realized how close I was to screwing up my life and I thought if somebody has the opportunity to screw up their lives as easily as this, then going in the other direction couldn't be any more difficult. It would just be another direction, wouldn't it?

I tried going back into show business but I found out in order to be a success I had to do something I didn't enjoy. I had to lie—keep one lie constantly in the air in order to maintain I don't know how many others. My whole business was built on one lie after another (when you're at the bottom, it can't be helped)—lies about talent, lies about pay, so many lies it was like the bootlegging operation. I got married and went into the insurance business at the same time. It was just going to be a temporary arrangement until we'd carpeted the living-room floor. Then I discovered something quite by accident—that what I told people about my product was true and the insurance I sold would do exactly the things it was supposed to do, perform just as written, as specified. I've sold about $15,000,000 in the last nine years. Now, also, I sometimes get the feeling that it's only because of insurance that millions of people are fulfilling a very important need for their families. There's a great satisfaction when somebody depends on you, and you're in a position to come through for them. It sounds corny, but it's true.

AN AUTOMOBILE BODY-AND-FENDER MAN

In this town, anything goes. In a small town, which is where I came from, you pull a stunt once or twice in my kind of business, everybody knows it and it's dangerous. In a big city, particularly in this one, you steal and you're respected. Why is it everything runs by rackets, by money? What have you got that's honest? *You* tell *me*. The rate here is fifty bucks a hole for plugging bullet holes in a car. During the war, we used to get twenty dollars a number for changing serial numbers on a motor block. There's a way of doing it. If you just grind and cut a new figure in, acid'll bring up the old number. The thing to do is grind a little deeper, throw a weld over it, regrind, and then put your numbers on. But that doesn't pay any more. Now, you steal a car and what you do is this. You go to a junkie—a junkyard man, not a hophead—who's got a wreck, let's say it's a '60 Caddie. You buy the registration from him. Then you go out and steal one just like it. Get it? Where's a cop going to look? At the engine number? He doesn't even know where it is and he hasn't got the time, anyway. Color? Repaint, that's all. License plates? That's a joke. Then, there's twenty-five General Motors keys'll open practically any GM car. Fifteen Ford keys'll trip any Ford-make lock open.

Then, there's disappearing cars – cars that *have got* to be lost. For the insurance. There's a nice dollar in that. The car's garbaged up – cut up – immediately in the shop. The engine is busted up and sold for scrap. It isn't worth rebuilding and changing the numbers these days. A lot of the other parts can be sold, too. Mechanics won't touch tire stealing any more. It isn't worth it the way it was during the war shortage. But there're more dishonest guys in the body-and-fender line now than there ever were. Wherever there's insurance money involved, you'll find that. If an adjuster can't make a buck on you, he'll make sure you never get another job. Some shops get blackballed by insurance companies. All an adjuster has to do is turn a guy in and a car'll be pulled out of your shop if it's found there. Adjusters work on ten per cent of the repair estimate. I'd say that was a pretty fair shake. All right, now, suppose you want to work with a chaser – that's a guy with a tow car, not a lawyer, the way most people think. You can always buy a job from him. The average is around fifteen per cent off the top. Let's say the job is a $500 one. So, there's fifty bucks for the adjuster and seventy-five for the chaser. I didn't mention the cops who work with the chaser. They'll take around forty. What's that leave? Who needs it?

Did you know this? Most mechanics hate doctors. The doctors themselves make a buck on the side – splitting fees – and they're always damned sure a mechanic's doing the same thing and they can't do anything about it. What does a doctor know about the inside of a car any more than one of his patients about his own insides? There's the mechanic beating the doctor at his own game. I'm fed up with it. I'll say this much for New York, though. If you can't make a dollar in New York, you can't make it any place. I started in business with nothing. Now, I've got some property free and clear that pays me rent. There's no mortgage on my home. What I want to do is work out of the town where I live. It's in another state. First, I want to become an insurance adjuster there – I got a pretty good name with the insurance companies, believe it or not – and then I want to do adjusting in my own shop out there.

WITNESS

DAVID SCHWARTZ
President of Jonathan Logan, Inc., ladies' garment manufacturers

We did business with Lepke Buchalter. Who didn't in the garment business? We *had* to pay the racketeers in order to operate freely. The reason that came about was the union was weak and these men worked for the union *and* the businessmen and we paid them to avoid trouble. I knew Lepke very well and Gurrah Schapiro, too. Lepke was a brilliant man, brilliant. There wasn't anything he couldn't have done if he'd wanted to. I know that at the end Lepke tried to go straight, but they wouldn't let him and he wound up in the electric chair. So then, Tom Dewey took our books away and investigated. It was a terrible thing.

80

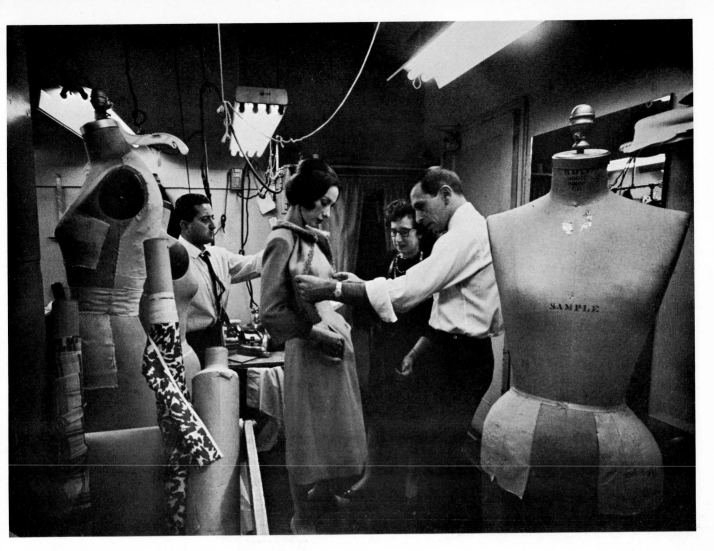

The garment center; a Seventh Avenue fashion house.
Paris proposes but New York disposes.

They tried to get us to talk. We were afraid to tell the truth. Every day somebody was getting killed. Whoever went down to the district attorney's office to tell the truth got killed. We tried to lie our way out of it and we wound up being fined, oh, around $20,000 for some state-tax violation we weren't even guilty of.

The thing that saved this industry was the new laws Roosevelt passed, because as soon as the union got legal power they got rid of the racketeers. Dewey did a wonderful job of police work, but I don't think that had anything to do with the stopping of the racketeers. The union got rid of them themselves. Since then, others have appeared, like the ones who tried in 1949, because I was non-union, to collect $200 a month to move my goods. So, to avoid getting mixed up with the underworld again, I joined the union. I called David Dubinsky. I met him at the Harvard Club with my lawyers. For four and a half years we never made a contract, just shook hands, and we have been with the union ever since.

I was born in Harlem and started to work at a very young age. When I was nineteen I went into business with a patternmaker and I have been very successful. There is no problem getting the price for merchandise if your styling is

The garment center. The figures show that fewer dresses get made in New York, but the head knows where the styles are thought up.

The garment center. What used to be said of the Jews and Italians holds good for the Negroes and the Puerto Ricans: they were born with a needle in their hands.

right and fashionwise and you move right away. There is a market for everybody. Along about 1945, I was making money in seven figures before taxes. I had two young children then; my daughter was nine and my son was six. I thought I wanted to retire and I locked myself in my office and thought about it. I decided I couldn't do that to my kids because they would have nothing to look forward to. I decided to stay in business and make it a very high-class one.

About three years ago, we made our merger with Butte Copper, at which time we received $3,000,000, which I put into making knit goods. We had had a tremendous amount of trouble in the Fifties, because we were overcapitalized and, being a family-owned business and not giving out any dividends, we were being overtaxed heavily. We made poor investments. We decided to merge with a public company or go public ourselves. I met the heads of Butte Copper and we sat down in my office. The one thing worried them was they said the garment business is a one-man business. They had never even seen a garment manufactured. I told them I could prove that General Motors was a one-man business. One man, I said, the president of General Motors, caused the last recession – they overproduced, the stock was split three for one, the country produced entirely too much merchandise. They said, "Dave, you're right and I recommend we sell out to you." I believe we were the first people in the dress business ever applied for listing on the Stock Exchange and got it without any bankers involved, just by passing the requirements.

Without the Puerto Ricans and the colored people, we would have no garment business in New York today. These people are born with needles in their hands. And still, it's impossible for us to get enough help to operate a plant in the city. That's why we manufacture elsewhere. Will New York ever lose its place as the center of fashion? Never. There is manufacturing done in Los Angeles and Texas. I have a factory in Venezuela and in South Carolina and in Jersey. But it is here that everything has to be created.

People say the garment business is a jungle. Not for me. I *enjoy* my business. I feel I have accomplished something. I have met some of the finest people. It has done a lot for me. I have donated to the Albert Einstein College of Medicine over $1,000,000, about $500,000 to Brandeis, $100,000 to Georgetown University, N.Y.U., $25,000. This year, also, $25,000 to the Federation of Jewish Philanthropies and I have pledged $100,000 to the Federation's building fund. The garment business has been very, very good to me. My wife didn't want my son to go into the business. When he left college I gave him a gift of a trip to Europe. When he returned he said he wanted to go into the business. He took over our knitwear division and made millions for us. This twenty-three-year-old boy runs it himself; goes to Europe for styles; takes care of selling. He is a king in his own right.

Wall Street; the Stock Exchange. Behind the classical façade, everything is quite, quite up to date.

WITNESS

WALTER K. GUTMAN
A partner in Stearns & Co., stockbrokers

New York is such a part of me and I'm such a speck in it. I have so many different sets of memories of it – love ones and sad ones and crazy ones and business ones. It's unlikely that I'll live anywhere else, certainly not in the United States. I think of what would have happened to me if my father had not moved to New York in 1914 when I was a kid. I'm a rather passive person, you see – you can be active and passive as well – so that New York really made me. In any other city, I wouldn't have found the combination to suit me. I wrote for art magazines for a good long while – almost up until the Depression – and then I went into the stock market where I am now. I had a certain amount of beginner's luck, which is very exciting, and I thought, "This is great, better than art magazines," and that's where I've been ever since. It suited me exactly, what with my analytical temperament and my liking for spectacle, my abstractness and my artistic temperament.

The financial district; the Chase Manhattan Bank.
The lines of power are clearly drawn.

I wouldn't be what I am now had I not lived here. I wouldn't have had the artists *or* Wall Street. I integrate with all these business people and all these artists. The only people I guess I don't mix with are gangsters, although I have known a few. Very specifically, New York has Negroes and without Negroes I wouldn't be me, because my education in sex and love came, in many ways, from Negroes. I wouldn't want to live without the life I have had with them.

They understood and liked me and I liked them. My understanding came late, about 1949, when I finally *met* them, as it were. It was terrific, fabulous; it still is. You know the Manet painting, the *Olympia?* Well, my first experience with Negroes was when I went to a hotel room with a woman they called "The Princess." It was one of those crummy little places. I opened the door and I saw her lying on the bed. What a sight! She was hustling, all right – for fifty bucks – but she was very proud, too, and there was that beautiful body lying there on that soiled white sheet in that crummy room, all the shades down, maybe one light from a naked bulb. I thought then it was just like the Manet painting, except that it was a black woman lying on the white sheet. The contrast in the colors was incredible to me.

America is where these two races meet and live together and New York is where they do it with the most sophistication and the least barrier to communication, particularly in the arts – you're almost never going to meet Negroes in business. New York is the center of the arts, high and low, and in the arts you're pretty much on your own. Also, I've met people who are hooked on drugs, hung up, smoke pot – and I like them. If the element of shame were detached from it, if you had hundreds of thousands frankly hooked, it wouldn't be so bad.

There was one other thing – psychoanalysis. I had a total of ten years under two very good men. When I started, New York was one of the few, if not the only, places in America, and one of the few in the world, where there was a large group of analysts. Such decisive moments as my discovery of Negroes came after analysis. Maybe that's not quite true, but it's pretty damned true. Perhaps if I had lived in another city and been analyzed there, I would have come to New York, but I probably would not have been analyzed in another city. Not only because the technique might not have been available at that time, but the anonymity which I needed would not have been available, either. It was through analysis that I finally grew up and developed and if there is one final thing that New York means to me, it is that it is not only the place where I have lived most of my life, but the place in which I grew up. Perhaps that's a little too lyrical, but you have to grow up somewhere.

A BOOKMAKER

The heat always comes in cycles, like when you hear of a plane crash, you know you're going to get one or two more, and then it slacks off. Making book is always easy as long as you know the right people. Who are the right people? Use your imagination. You start with whoever bothers you first – the cops. It could be a cop on the street or a detective on the Vice Squad. That's who you go to first and try to buy your way out. How much you pay depends on how big you are, how much they got on you, and how much it means to the individual himself, his sense of dignity. You take that Vice Squad. They are the worst criminals. The prostitute, the narcotics men, they live off them. From the cops it goes to the lawyers, the bail bondsmen, the politicians, the judges, everybody. The whole thing is a farce.

Don't kid yourself. No matter where you go in New York City, there's got to be someone somewhere picking up the horse action, the policy action, football, baseball, you name it. There's no such thing as you can't get a bet down. A book that operates regularly in the same spot is always paying off. And if you keep paying off, you're still not left alone. Maybe some cops you're taking care of get transferred. They pass the word along to someone else and the new guys'll come around to get on the payroll. I'm not a big operator. Let's say I gross in bets $300 a day. At the end of a six-day week, that's $1800. My payoff runs from

The Aqueduct Race Track; mutuel windows. The hole is just as bottomless as it is in the Stock Market.

thirty to fifty bucks a week and I clear three to four hundred. I'm like an ordinary businessman – calm, a good family man, a guy sees to it his children are well kept and brought up.

I like to go out like any other businessman – to a restaurant, or dance, or go to a wedding. I'm no freak. I lead a normal life. The only time it's nervous is when you're being watched and you can't conduct business properly. A bookmaker has more scruples than most big businessmen. They believe in paying off their debts, not welching, and that, in my opinion, makes them a man. Let the cops and the politicians concentrate on more central things – I mean like dope, mugging, murder, and rape – and relieve them of this by legalizing bookmaking. Put the book under bond. They'd gladly pay it out in taxes instead of graft. They're not criminals. In England they're gentlemen.

I work off the street. There's less expense not having your own place. Also, when you work out of a place, you've got to be afraid they could close it down on you. The best they can do when you're in the street is tell you to get off if they got nothing on you. It's usually the players who get the book pinched. A player, *his* mind is always in the clear. It's only what *he* wants to do that counts – play the horses, get his bet down. He doesn't look for cops watching and he walks right up to you with a scratch sheet in his hand. The silly bastard. When you work in the street, you try to do most of your business in the lunch hour – fast – and duck the slips wherever it's convenient. You're dead, of course, if the cops find them on you. Sometimes you're dead even if they don't. You got to watch out for a frame. They know you're making book and they'll push you in a hallway and frisk you. They'll take their hands out of your pocket and what do you know, they got a couple of slips in them, saying it's yours. All the while those slips have been in their hands. There's many a book got a conviction and a fine for frames like that. There's a lot of guys take all their action late at night to avoid trouble. Players know where to find them.

All this talk about hoods and violence. All that about violence is a lot of bull. The hoods, the mob, syndicate – you call it anything you want – they don't bother with small handbooks. If they're a big operation, they try to get all the small books to turn their hedges into them. A hedge is when a book thinks he might have taken too much action on a certain horse and he turns it over to a bigger one. A small book operating by himself is not dangerous, but if he gets to be really big, someone'll approach him – not in a mean way, but just to say, "Now look, you're in this territory, how about giving us your hedges?" That's all, and they let you operate. It figures. If they take over, they got to take over the payoffs and all the other headaches. All they want from you is the hedges. They regulate, too. Let's say a small book is operating in a factory, maybe two hundred men, and hedging his big bets off properly and another guy comes in and he knows there's already a book there. You automatically get in touch with certain people and he's told in a nice way he can't operate. Oh, he'll lay off. Believe me. He's in the wrong and he knows it. If he goes to see anyone else, they'll say, "You're in the wrong," and that's the end of it. Nobody threatens. They don't have to. It's a very clean-cut business.

A patrolman checks in at the precinct.
He can check his head off,
but that won't stop the action.

The Solomon R. Guggenheim Museum.
Frank Lloyd Wright's ambiguous legacy to New York
is patronized like a carnival in redneck country.

THE BUSINESS OF ART CHAPTER 4

Toward the end of his life, the sculptor Constantin Brancusi arrived at an agreement with the city of Paris to leave his entire collection to the National Museum of Modern Art provided the authorities would desist from knocking down his decayed shanty of a studio-home in Montparnasse – it was on the proposed site of a hospital – and leave him to die there in peace, which he did at the age of eighty-one. The government later acceded to a clause in his will stipulating that the museum house the collection in the veritable shack. Shard by shard of peeled plaster, pane by pane of flyspecked window, tired walls and all, it was removed from the Impasse Ronsin and set up in the museum with as much fidelity as that accorded any château shipped to America by William Randolph Hearst. The idea of an artist finding a corresponding trace of *tendresse* in the breast of a real-estate developer in New York City borders on the grotesque and

The Solomon R. Guggenheim Museum.
No giant milkshakes are served at this drive-in.

his chance of being canonized by the city administration is much less than minuscule. Nonetheless, New York is beyond question the creative center of the art world today (as well as its principal market), a fact which may be regarded as one of the tenuous triumphs of mind over money.

This was indelibly illustrated by the surrealist scuffle between the city and its unexpectedly obdurate community of serious, non-commercial artists, the largest and most important there is. More than 30,000 painters and sculptors, roughly eighty-five per cent of this country's artists, all in a boil of creation, live and work in the metropolitan area. Shortly before the Second World War the focus of art began to shift to New York from Paris, partly because of the immigration, permanent or temporary, of such European masters as Mondrian, Hofmann, Matta, Chagall, and Ernst, and the return of such expatriate Medicis as Peggy Guggenheim. A New York School characterized by, among other things, the enormous splatterings of Abstract Expressionism, succeeded the School of Paris, not unself-consciously and a little to its own amazement. Museums aside, there are above 300 art galleries in the city, a threefold increase in the two decades since 1940. About 200 are in Manhattan alone, from Fulton Fish Market to 125th Street. The most important, a fragrance of *fraises des bois* in clotted cream, are located in the Fifties, Sixties, and Seventies, with Madison Avenue as their axis; formerly the axis was Fifty-seventh Street, from Sixth Avenue to Lexington; an entire street of substantial avant-garde galleries also grew up brightly in the otherwise unpromising soil of Tenth Street east of Fourth Avenue, a tangle of officially blighted blocks, blocks to bring an itch to the palms of urban renewers.

Greenwich Village.
The Real Thing.

The Museum of Modern Art; sculpture garden. Had the Modern not come into being, the Met might not own a Jackson Pollock.

In any case, a short while before Christmas of 1961, the city and the artists ended almost a year of guerrilla warfare in a seasonally pink glow (Alizaran Rose and Geranium Lake, with a winsome touch of Municipal Whitewash) of good-fellowship. In essence, the city agreed to let live and the artists to go on living and working in the rundown ateliers out of which the law had been trying to run them. These are the upper floors, or lofts (the artists came to be known as the Loft Generation), of hundreds of old downtown business and manufacturing buildings – century-old, cast-iron buildings with rows of delicately fluted columns and intricately ornamented lintels; heavy masonry structures of the Eighties and Nineties, proliferating with fake loggias, balustrades, entablatures, imbrications, rinceaux, swags, bezants, rosettes, and all the other endearing truck of the Beaux Arts; buildings comically Frenchified with oversized mansard roofs; beautiful, dilapidated, doomed, red-brick homes a hundred and thirty years old, with ruined, eyeless Greek doorways; and disgraced brownstones. They are scattered all over lower Broadway, the streets around Fulton and Washington Markets; Canal, Chambers, Grand, and Fulton streets; Fourth Avenue and Lafayette Street; whatever remains of Chelsea that has not yet been torn down for superblocks of antiseptic housing; almost anywhere south of Thirtieth Street to the tip of Manhattan.

Exactly how many painters and sculptors are in these lofts nobody really knows, not even the city, but a competent consensus in art circles is that they number in excess of 7000. They include artists of every aesthetic belief, from such abstractionists as De Kooning and Sidney Geist, to such representational painters as Raphael Soyer, Edwin Dickinson, and Jack Levine. Primarily, of course, artists levitated to the lofts for economic reasons – the rents were low, although not so low as they had been before the war – and, secondarily, for aesthetic ones. There seems to be some sort of mystic interaction between the size of a loft and the square footage of the work painters and sculptors turn out these days. They work big and the phenomenon is one that has provoked a good deal of metaphysical argument, like the disputed priority between chicken and egg. As one sculptor, who works with huge masses of scrap steel and an oxyacetylene torch, put it, "Who was it said, 'First, we shape the building and then the building shapes us'? My loft has turned out the best sculpture I've ever done. It's *demanded* more of me."

Until the city intruded on them, nobody, with the exception of artists, collectors, critics, and gallery owners, gave any more thought to how artists lived or where or on what than they did to the *moeurs* of machine operators extruding plastic doilies in the same loft buildings. What happened was that inspectors of the Buildings and Fire departments undertook an unexpectedly conscientious enforcement of fire and safety laws in factory buildings. The principal victims were artists, who have always been notorious for never having met a payroll, anyone's payroll. In addition to being philosophical anarchists and refusing to get up at seven-thirty in the morning, they actually were violating the law, but with rather less guile than the payroll-meeters, and getting hauled off to court. Thereupon, they formed an Artist Tenants Association and threatened a strike. The A.T.A.'s marvelous fancy was to withhold the work of its members from galleries and museums unless the city laid off. It was a staggering conceit. Mayor

Wagner, yielding to no man in his keen appreciation of art, concluded a bargain with the A.T.A. (this was prior to the election of 1961), which had to be re-affirmed later when the artists somehow got suspicious that they were only a trifle less enforced against than before. (For two off-election years, between 1959 and 1961, the mayor sturdily kept in check his appetite for art. In budgets of over two billion dollars each, he found himself unable to scrape together $63,000 a year to pay the salaries of twenty guards for the Metropolitan Museum of Art and forced that institution to close on Mondays for the first time in seventy years. Later, he raised his own salary and those of some of his janizaries by an amount far exceeding the needs of the Metropolitan.)

One winter afternoon following the famous victory, James Gahagan, Jr., a painter and former chairman of the A.T.A., a thin, black-haired, clean-shaven, and, by any standard – bourgeois or bohemian – unexceptionable-looking man in his mid-thirites, observed to a well-swaddled conformist caller, "You don't *get* this kind of life – you *earn* it." The statement was made with an absence of bathos that might very well have plunged Henry Murger into gloom or caused

The Metropolitan Museum of Art. Theirs is the proper awe owed to $2,300,000 worth of painting; they are looking at Rembrandt's Aristotle Contemplating the Bust of Homer.

Puccini to make Mimi a lady wrestler. "It becomes a sort of contest of values," Gahagan said. "Do we give up our personal freedom and artistic goals and a way of life for job security, a developmental higher salary, Blue Cross, and a new car? And is it a fair trade? We've decided it isn't. In the end, we feel we have more, not less. Most of us earn under a thousand a year from our painting and sculpture, but we wouldn't change the situation." Probably no more than thirty to fifty artists make enough from their vocation to live on it; the rest must work at almost anything, preferably part time, for sustenance enough to hare after their elusive grail. One artist sweeps floors at the Museum of Modern Art; others are qualified art teachers in the public schools or give private lessons; they have been clerks, house painters, plumbers, and electricians; manual-training instructors, occupational therapists, playground supervisors, ushers, dishwashers, art critics, telephone operators, jazz musicians, and ditch diggers.

In a way, living in a loft, apart from the presumptive spiritual toughening, is a kind of pioneering in the most built-up city on earth. There is, to begin with, a frontier, one that works in peculiar reverse and is constantly shifting. That is, the Indians, or artists, get to invade the wilderness only *after* the lofts have been sacked and abandoned by the white settlers – the paper-box manufacturers and fabricators of brassière hooks – and they occupy them in the full, melancholy knowledge of imminent redevelopment, a synonym for real-estate speculation, luxury housing, and glass office buildings. Unless he inherits his loft from another Indian, which is getting to be more and more usual as lofts get to be fewer and fewer, the artist puts in a good deal of scouting on foot to find one. He will pay his landlord anywhere from $35 a month (for what one sculptor called "wall-to-wall flooring") up to $300. Landlords have lost whatever naïveté they might have had concerning artists. They know that a few uptown galleries will foot the rent bill for a $300 layout if their man is having a vogue. They are well aware, too, that in an artist they are getting a built-in night watchman and fire warden. With or without justification, the painter or sculptor cherishes his work as the most precious possession he has on earth. He is not only on the premises after business hours, when the moneygrubbers have left, but he is apt to be much more scrupulous in sniffing out fire; the costume-jewelry people below are not only not there but take an abiding comfort in insurance.

Furthermore, it is difficult for an artist to do anything but improve the place. What he gets, barring inheritance from a colleague, is a bare, filthy shell, cold, dank, dusty, dark, unpainted, and generally strewn at least ankle deep with the exhausted leavings of the departed manufacturer tenant. The customary procedure in opening up a loft is not, as might be expected, for the sensitive creator to throw open his windows to the world and dilate his nostrils in an access of feeling too great for anything but deep breathing, but to close the windows and replace broken panes. He installs a sink and toilet, if they are lacking, has the place wired (or does it himself), hooks up a stove, plasters the walls and whitewashes them (no inconsiderable task; some lofts are seventy-five feet long and forty wide and their ceilings may be fifteen high), and repairs or covers the floors, which may be splintered or uneven. (Sculptors, who need a true surface, are particular sufferers from wavy floors.) He constructs the tall racks for stacking his paintings and only then does he move in his Spartan pallet, his few,

The Metropolitan Museum of Art. Always a good show.

humble sticks of furniture, and the blessed tools of his art. By comparison with, say, some advertising and television people, the artists lead lives in their lofts of disappointing respectability. A fairly high percentage are not only married but have children. One burning painter is known to have overcome his fiancée's misgivings over the starkness of his loft by building her a three-room house in it; it was fitted out with windows, doors, and a peaked roof with eaves.

However, any inference that artists are anchorites is a libel on their calling. The chances are that for sheer size (the dimensions of lofts abet this) and noise (nobody is going to knock up in a deserted business building) parties thrown by them are without equal. They generally start late any night of the week, continue until four or five in the morning, and attract as many as five hundred guests. The host may prime the pump with a case of liquor, if he can afford to, and ask his guests to bring their own bottles. Inevitably, a good many uninvited outsiders are attracted to these affairs and not much trouble is taken to keep them out. At one party, a drunk wandered in off the street. He kept asking for a drink and was casually directed on and on – the loft was a long one. Finally, he walked out a tall window fronting on an alley, fell two floors, got up, shook himself, and walked off. Outsiders go to loft parties in a fever of anticipation, brought on by bad novels, of Lord only knows what unspeakable goings-on. For some reason, artists have a passion for dancing in public, and, young or old, the stamina to keep it up all night. Slumming laymen tend to puzzle over this and then be chagrined and it is easy to identify them: they leave first and rarely after midnight. Beyond an occasional fist fight and the nuzzling of someone's wife by someone else's husband – lofts are too open spaces for much else – a loft party presents all the orgiastic aspects of a rush-hour dash for a commuter train.

The luxuriation of art in New York has nurtured another growth, an identifiable form of entertainment – the opening. As is sometimes observable in symbiotic relationships, the parasite looks to be doing better than the host. An art-show opening is a highly developed and gratifying form of riding to the hounds of culture (up the hills of status, down the dales of acceptance; in full cry, baying at the heels of the Philistines), and its original function, the exhibition of art for sale, is, like the vermiform appendix, vestigial. From mid-September to mid-June, forty shows or so a week open – weeks of a hundred openings are not unheard of – in a disorderly clatter. Often as not, depending less on his reputation than on his credit (neither has much to do with the other), the artist will pay part of the expenses. (What drives the iron firmly into the souls of those who have yet to arrive financially is that those who *have* would sooner imitate Maxfield Parrish than pay anything.) The whole thing is as stylized as an old-fashioned fairgrounds clambake, although a good deal less muscular; clambake protocol used to require the participants to gorge themselves on steamed clams, corn, and chicken, sped down in a roil of beer, and then to throw shells, cobs, bones, and bottles at each other until the cops came. For those who attend them, openings satisfy, by ritual incantation and writhing, the need to belong to a higher community of the mind by simple proximity rather than talent.

The art lover, journeyman or apprentice, is in a peculiarly fortunate position of intellectual impregnability, safe behind the crenellations of ignorance, since the same things are said and done, whether in the presence of Abstract Expressionism, Magic Realism, *Neue Sachlichkeit* or "New Thinginess," Synchronism, Constructivism, Social Realism, or Neo-Plasticism. A quick triangulation is made upon entering a gallery. The visitor first locates the bar and then the artist, postponing a visit to the first in passing deference to the second. The former is always set up between two large, glowering chunks of pre-Columbian artifact, Henry Moore sculpture, or blowtorch bronze. These have holes in them and are used for ashtrays, thus unexpectedly demonstrating the late Louis Sullivan's dictum that form follows function. (A minimum of half a dozen drinks will be dropped, three women drenched, and two glasses broken.)

When the artist has been sighted, the well-wisher shoulders his way through the noisy press – a disciple swimming up the Ganges in flood to get to Gandhi, impatiently brushing off crocodiles as he thrashes ahead – seizes his hand and murmers, with egregious candor, "This is your best." The artist replies, "Thank you. I'm glad you could come" – Gandhi handing the disciple a spinning wheel. He is fully cognizant, and the other knows he is, that the likelihood of the paintings having been seen, much less appraised, is remote because (a) they have been blocked off by the other art lovers rooted in the classic pose of openings – elbow in one hand, glass in the other, back to the canvases – and (b) besides, the artist somehow spotted the man charging into the gallery no earlier than twenty-two seconds before. In the event a guest has a cocktail-party critical position to maintain and is unwilling to commit himself prior to being told where he stands (this may take a few days; professional critics rarely go to openings), a large supply of conversational gambits is at hand suitable for these routs.

"Interesting," "lively," and "mysterious, very mysterious," are fine, but *"épatant," "formidable,"* and *"fantastisch"* summon up the image of the traveler, tanned and graying at the temples, who got to the opening from Spoleto by way of Brussels via Air France. It may be said of the show that "It's a marvelous hanging," and a good way to run an artist down is to call his work "charming," "seductive," and "energetic." Paintings and sculpture "move," are "felt," "experienced," and "realized"; they "work" or "come off," while artists "mature," become "freer," "looser," and "stronger"; enter a "new phase" or display an "inner quality" not immediately analyzable. The inner quality can vaguely be demonstrated: "He has a certain . . . ," says the demonstrator and raises his hands as though he were kneading a lump of putty in mid-air. He then drops them helplessly.

Part of the *mise en scène* – as requisite as a brass goboon on a Western-saloon set – is a contingent of graceful young men with 35-millimeter cameras slung about their necks and another so stylish that the cuffs of their pants have been transferred to the sleeves of their jackets; they have the eyes of does. It is almost impossible to learn their last names or what they do, but in an unobtrusive way they are death on hors d'oeuvres and Scotch, and the bartenders who work the galleries regularly know when to cut them off. Balancing them is a group of girls who are either spectacularly beautiful or so unprepossessing that they are fascinating. (A woman judges the success of an opening by whether she is invited to dinner afterward; failing that, she goes forth to chew the burned hamburger and drink the bitter aloes of loneliness, ultimately shuffling home to bed with book and bellyache.) Lastly, there are *prospective* collectors – not *collectors* – people with money who, to coin a phrase, don't know art, but know what they are told to like and might be induced to spend some of the first for some of the second. They are inordinately flattered at being invited to so special a *fête*.

Aside from the torrent of productivity, the War of the Lofts (a pathetic one, not too different from Blenheim, since eventually neither laws nor cops but bulldozers will pry loose the artists), and the foolish striving at the periphery, the ascendancy of New York can be symbolized by two events half a century apart. In 1913, the International Exhibit of Modern Art opened in the Seventy-first Regiment Armory on Park Avenue at Thirty-fourth Street to a foofaraw of outrage, critical and general. Theodore Roosevelt, teeth bared nakeder than usual, denounced the "modernists" as lunatics. The genius Caruso was dragooned into coming down to the Armory, where he drew caricatures of Cubist art (among them Marcel Duchamp's *Nude Descending a Staircase*) and scattered them to the howling know-nothings.

In April, 1962, nine influential galleries staged – the word is exact – something unique in art history. They simultaneously celebrated Picasso's eightieth birthday with a loan show of 309 of his paintings, drawings, and sculptures drawn from public and private American collections, dividing them up among themselves in periods to make a noble progression. "It's unheard of," Picasso commented, but he had no conception of the justness of his observation. The exhibition opened on a mild, clear night and the display of chic along Madison Avenue from Fifty-seventh Street to Seventy-eighth was choking, more dazzling than the *son et lumière* at Versailles during the tourist season; a turnout to make the Master a convenience or an irrelevance. The chivalry wore dinner jackets; the beauty was in evening dress, coifed within a foot of its scalp, drenched in all the perfumes of Araby and tottering daintily in jeweled heels. Heads inclined graciously upon meeting; the shriek and twitter of colliding celebrities could be heard on the night air. The liveried chauffeur in the rented Rolls-Royce was sedulously attendant. The peasants gawked. There was champagne at every gallery stop.

(For whatever the irony is worth, the nineteen-day extravaganza, which took months of genuinely selfless effort and noteworthy co-operation among competing galleries to get together, was a benefit – admission was charged – for the Public Education Association, an organization devoted to improving the city's public schools. A month previously, the city's schoolteachers struck for a day in troubled desperation, trying to force the city and state to come through with pay raises that had been promised and promised and promised.)

The *respectability* of art of every kind is assured. The sharp rise in museum attendance is a vulgar measurement. The Guggenheim, Frank Lloyd Wright's appalling frozen-custard stand on Fifth Avenue (cannibalized sardonically from what were yellowed plans for a parking garage with the same spiral ramp), gets built and is patronized by people with the hot-eyed avidity of Georgia rednecks lining up to see a girlie revue in a carnival tent. Several blocks south, the Metropolitan Museum of Art, the finest all-around museum in the Western Hemisphere (if, architecturally, the relict of William Morris Hunt's pastry-chef classicism), spends more money for a painting than has ever been spent – $2,300,000 – outbidding the Cleveland Museum of Art, the Carnegie Institute, and the Baron Heinrich H. von Thyssen-Bornemisz of Lugano, Switzerland, for Rembrandt's *Aristotle Contemplating the Bust of Homer*. Whether Rembrandt killed the people or the contemplation of the price glazed their eyes, Homer and Aristotle were socko at the Met. (It is noteworthy that part of the south wall of the American Wing at the Metropolitan is the scavenged marble façade of the United States Branch Bank, the old Government Assay Office, on Wall Street, built in 1824 and torn down in 1915.) As John Canaday, the New York *Times* art critic, wrote of the Metropolitan, in another context, "If ever things get so tough that the Metropolitan Museum has to go into business instead of keeping its doors open to the public, it could take over the slogan, 'Always a good show.'" Canaday's observation was made before the Metropolitan borrowed the Mona Lisa from the Louvre in 1963. It was not seen; it was filed past. The French, for all anyone knows, may have enjoyed the awful breach of taste.

If any institution in this country can be termed the most potent influence over contemporary art, it is the Museum of Modern Art, founded as recently as 1929. The politics of art are as convoluted, subterranean, and nasty as those of government, and the museum's executives get jumpy and distressed when the implication of their power is dilated upon. It is, beyond any doubt, the peerless

Greenwich Village; Outdoor Art Show.

popularizer of contemporary art, the arbiter of taste, the Dow-Jones Index of collectors, very nearly the last court of appeal, if not the determinant, of the direction art takes, and, through its international traveling exhibitions, a mighty influence abroad. The role is one the museum insists it finds uncomfortable, one it says was thrust upon it, that accrued to it by default. For what it thinks of as an ardent and honorable search for the best, it has been as hissingly denigrated as loudly praised. Such sinister machinations have been attributed to it as the buying up of certain works of art and the ignoring of others for the purpose of protecting the investments of its patrons. Aline B. Saarinen, a critic sympathetic to the museum, on the whole, still felt impelled, on its twenty-fifth anniversary, to write: "Officialdom and near-monopoly of power are corroding in any field, both to the institution and to the 'product' involved. The vitality and health of modern art depend not only on the continued excellence and effectiveness of the Museum of Modern Art but on the increased strength and independence of the rest of the modern art world."

To the uninstructed, however, some conclusions seem inescapable: without the museum, nine galleries might very well not have banded together to do homage to Picasso and Rosa Bonheur's huge *Horse Fair* at the Metropolitan might be taken seriously (the Metropolitan might not own a Jackson Pollock, either); the artists (many of whom are bitter about the Modern) might not deem it worth while to fight City Hall for their lofts; the Guggenheim might still be the tiny, *recherché* Museum of Non-Objective Art hidden away in an office building; and the commonalty who go to look at art might be (a) fewer in number and (b) alarmingly larger in proportions of Neanderthals to merely harmless middlebrows obediently stuffing themselves on the museum's extremely digestible and varied diet – from comely spoons and well-designed bobsleds to stained-glass windows by Marc Chagall to the pulped-up chassis of an old automobile.

A MANHATTAN SECRETARY

I was born in Palermo and I came to this country when I was four; my father, who'd come here first, brought us over. We lived in the country until the hurricane of 1938 demolished my father's farm and he opened a butcher store in the city. He's retired now. New York has done something for me that the country never did and that no other city might and I would have been a different type of person not living here. It has given me an understanding of humanity and changed me a great deal. Quite often, we Italians are very clannish and I know that my early years were very narrow. I had no childhood whatsoever; I was kept very, very strict. There was a time I wouldn't read a book not sanctioned by the Church. Now I've learned I'm old enough to know what's right or wrong. A book isn't going to make me immoral. From everything you read, you learn something.

The first time I was allowed to go out with a fellow, I was nineteen and a half. I had to be home at ten o'clock, and, believe me, until I married my husband – he was only the fifth fellow I ever went with – it was ten o'clock. Until him, I

Revlon Beauty Salon. The coiffeur prepares another kind of dove for flight.

hated all men, because my father was a tyrant and I pictured all men to be the same. Now, I have been married for twelve years to the most wonderful man in the world. Once, I couldn't understand if a girl went out with two men. I didn't approve of divorce, either. I do now. I had to. I married a divorced man. At one time, I wouldn't have. Here's something very much the same: when I came over on the boat from Italy, I had never seen any colored people. The first time I did, I said to my mother, "Look at those funny people."

I'm not prejudiced. They're humans, the same as you and I are; they have a right to live. The only thing I don't approve of – for now, anyway – is inter-marriage, not because such people can't love each other, but because of the children; they have no place, the majority won't accept them. Perhaps that will change. It should. Let me tell you something else. We're not as enlightened in this city as you might expect. We have just as much prejudice here as they have down South, maybe more so, but in the South they're more sincere in their prejudice; we're inclined to be hypocrites up here. Where colored people, for example, moved into a neighborhood with whites, the minute they move in, the whites move out. If we'd sort of live together, this sort of thing wouldn't happen. And we'll have to. That's what New York has taught me if it hasn't the others. It's a thing we'll have to accept and I personally think it would make life much more pleasant.

EDWARD HONG
A Chinese lawyer

I was the second Chinese lawyer to practice in the city of New York and the first in Illinois. I was born in Toishan, China. My father, a United States citizen born here, brought me up in Danville, Illinois. Most of my practice is among Chinese, not just because I speak their language but because they take up all the time I have; I have no time left, it seems, except for the Chinese. Ah, there's no city like New York for speaking your own tongue. New York has been very good to the Chinese, at least by comparison with the other big center for us in this country, San Francisco. San Francisco's no damned good, as far as the Chinese are concerned, but that's always been common in the coast states. Perhaps it will change. New York, at least, has let the Chinese alone and we, in turn, have left New York alone. I don't have to tell you we have the lowest crime rate of any minority group in this city. Industriousness, respect for the family, thrift, abiding by law are still characteristic of the Chinese.

We are not confined to our ghetto here as they are in San Francisco. We are distributed all over the city and those of us who stay in Chinatown do so out of choice. Now, as to Chinatown. Unless Chinatown itself gets together and proposes a *modern* Chinatown with a good, a real Chinese atmosphere, instead of just those run-down tenements, I think it will be wiped out. The only reason our people want it as it is now is they're sure of what they *have* and they're not sure of what they'll *get* if there is rebuilding. The only thing important to them is to receive no less than what they have. Keep this in mind, too. There is a new generation of Chinese who don't want to be waiters, cooks, dishwashers, and laundrymen. These are the younger ones and they don't much care what happens to Chinatown. The younger ones have been educated and they buy homes all over New York. We have younger ones, in large numbers, I should add, for the first time in our history in this country. Prior to World War II, how many Chinese children did you see? Very few. The Exclusion Act prevented wives and children from being brought over.

Since the act was repealed and the end of the war, I'll bet 10,000 Chinese women have come over and they have given us this new generation. Would the Chinese be better off if they were dispersed? Yes and no. In New York, where the size and cohesion of a minority affects it politically, it would be good for the Chinese to stay in one section in order to carry enough weight to get political

Chinatown; Mott Street.
Its families are a
model of family life.

advantage. Dispersed, they would be nothing. On the other hand, it would be good for them to separate, because then they would assimilate into the community and their political interests would be on a different basis. As far as business is concerned, there are those who say that if you clean up Chinatown, rebuild it, it will bring in more business and then there are those who say that, if you do, its business will be scattered and destroyed and the atmosphere lost.

But what do you have there now? Chinatown should be a show place. It would be advantageous for us and good for our pride to show people exactly what the Chinese are, rather than what people think they are from reading Sax Rohmer. The way Chinatown is still represented – still, believe me – is as one big den of ill repute: opium dens, people getting lost in underground dungeons, white slavery, and the whole nonsense. Tourists still ask a cop, "Is it safe to walk through here?" They're looking for a mysteriousness that isn't there and maybe never was and they're disappointed. Very well, then. Why not give them a Chinatown where the real Chinese culture is on display, where the shops sell typical Chinese goods, not plastic backscratchers made in Japan? All a tourist gets now is dirty streets, gift shops where he buys the same stuff he can get at the Statue of Liberty (and, as I say, most of it made in Japan), and some restaurants. Nothing is contributed to his knowledge. Chinatown could be made into an exemplary community for visitors. Good housing and, yes, a pagoda, a Chinese museum, some genuine Chinese art pieces. And so on. How many thousands of years of Chinese culture are there? I think it would be a service to both the Chinese and the people who come to see Chinatown. And nothing Chinese need be lost. Broken-down tenements and Japanese souvenirs aren't Chinese.

WITNESS

THE REVEREND JAMES A. GUSWELLER
Rector of St. Matthew's and St. Timothy's Protestant Episcopal Church

You might say this is two cities – a city of light and of darkness; of heroism and deprivation and degeneration. It contains our greatest centers of culture; on its side streets are the stench of garbage, rats, and the darkness of the slums. Which of the two cities will extirpate the other is the big question. I had a nice New Jersey parish when I accepted a call to New York in 1955. I was thrilled at the thought of coming here. I used to say to my wife, "This is the heart of civilization, a place we look to for hope, just as millions of deprived people in the world looked at the Statue of Liberty as their symbol of hope when they came to this country." And yet, we don't really fulfill that hope.

What has happened is that the Church in the city has lost touch with the mass of the people as well as with the business and political community. It often acquires endowment support so that, carrying on its functions with that kind of money, it neglects the masses of people in the heart of the city. It tries to draw parishioners from outside. Many of the wealthy churches spend fabulous amounts of money on music budgets and luncheon clubs to keep commuters who once lived here, but are now outside the city and the parish. I know of one that has a music budget alone of almost $100,000 a year. We get along on about $45,000 for everything.

When I was first invited to come here, I spent a few days walking around and seeing what the neighborhood was like. On Eighty-fourth Street, I saw Negro and Puerto Rican children. I talked to old residents and they told me this had once been a quiet neighborhood; brownstones had housed one family; railroad flats a family a floor. Now you find twelve families in a brownstone and in the railroad flats a family per room. I was struck also by the fact that there were no trees on the block, nothing but stone. In the back yard of my church there is a tree, an ailanthus–what is called the Tree of Heaven–the tree that grows almost without light and water and the things trees must have.

It seemed to symbolize the neighborhood to me. The ailanthus is a slum tree. Nobody likes it; it causes an itch if one comes in contact with it in the fall and spring; and yet it is beautiful. In a sense, it is very much like the Negro and Puerto Rican children. They, too, grow up without sunlight, the proper food, a family life. And yet, they, too, are beautiful. People don't like them, because they itch the conscience and there are too many of them. When I came here, this church had nothing to say to these people. Its remaining members lived outside the neighborhood; its doors were shut. I have the firm conviction that a parish church must be a cell of the Body of Christ in this world. It must *minister,* just as He would. I have learned compassion for these people. Recall Jesus and the Pharisees. "Why do you sit down and eat with these sinners?" they asked him. He answered, "I came not to call the righteous, but sinners to repentance."

I found utter depravity in this parish. The children grew up without homes, literally without families–like the ailanthus. Half the narcotics in the United States are sold in New York. What I'm upset about is that the authorities aren't truly aware of the correlation between narcotics and all the petty crimes, the apartment rifling, the purse-snatching, the mugging. You can't treat the addict as a criminal. He *must* steal to satisfy his urge for drugs; he's forced into being a criminal. What I'd like to see is a method of treating him realistically–cheap prescriptions for drugs at clinics, and, if he says he wants to get off, they can withdraw him gradually. A quarter for a prescription instead of five dollars for a fix and he won't have to be a criminal. It's been done in Europe; it would work here.

The *impossibility* of life here, especially for the teen-age kids. They grow up in a ghetto; they know nothing but the menial job opportunity will ever come their way. They have no incentive in school. What difference does it make to the Negro kid or the Puerto Rican one, anyway? The success stories are very few. These kids even lose the will to desire. When a kid gets to be fourteen or fifteen in this neighborhood, he doesn't even have the desire to go to camp in the summer when the opportunity is given him. He'd rather just sit and look at the asphalt streets. What's the use? That's the attitude. Many of the Puerto Rican kids are caught between two languages so that they end up knowing neither. They apply for military service, but the army won't take them–they can't pass tests. What's left? Nothing. Nothing but a path of crime.

The city is so big that corruption is visible in almost every department; you just can't live here and fail to see that. It's under every stone and it's worse than anything I ever knew. But everything is relative. We're going to get somewhere here, eventually. I think certain changes have already been effected on the West Side. The city finally realized it had to do something. There is a certain amount of concern now. But I'd very much like to see the Department of Welfare, for example, do more case work, instead of just sending money to clients.

I haven't been offered another parish, but I wouldn't accept one if I were. I've got a lot of work here. I've got to build my community center and then I want to get into the realm of housing. I want to influence wealthy people, if I can, to rehabilitate some of this slum housing. I feel if we could fix up some of these

The Cathedral of St. John the Divine. It has been building since 1892; the date of its finish is still conjectural.

brownstones and make them livable it would help considerably. Public housing is no answer to all problems, and, besides, there just isn't enough money for that much of it.

I get a lot of encouragement from my new parishioners. They have a fresh approach to the Christian religion. It's a rather unsophisticated one, but it has helped me. They'll say such things to me as, "I'se in the drinking world; you'se in the theology world." I've found out they're not so very far apart, if there is compassion. And the Church has got to have it if it is to mean anything to people.

WITNESS   RABBI EDWARD E. KLEIN
                 Of the Stephen S. Wise Free Synagogue

Religion in New York, like religion almost anywhere else in the United States, has witnessed a revival, but I'm not sure it is a significant one. I'm afraid that much of it stems from a desire to conform; some of it is a desire to escape; while a

Harlem; Puerto Rican children. Rats and slum landlords are their familiars; they are bitten by both.

small but significant part comes from genuine commitment. I do think this: if religion remains aloof from the problems of big-city living; if our churches and synagogues are simply little islands of peace in a chaotic community, then religion will become stagnant. Religion belongs in the market place, on the street corner. Every church and synagogue should be a community center, where young and old can come for creative activity, for example; as the Latins put it, nothing human is alien to religion.

I suppose we have the worst slums in the world in New York and some of the most difficult behavior problems, although statistically we're no worse than other American cities; it's the bigness that constitutes the problem. These slums have to be cleaned up, but not by a bulldozer that's going to ride roughshod over a lot of people who have nowhere else to go. What is called for are sensitive programs of urban renewal and a decent regard for the least of the dispossessed. To me, this is a religious challenge. Too many religious groups have looked on this as secondary. If religion is to be pure theology, then it'll be pie in the sky when you die. If religion is to be pure social action, then it's a matter of expediency only. The role of religion is to join ethical imperatives with day-to-

Temple Emanu-El. It is appropriate to its congregation.

day social action, which means no compromise and dedication to duty and all the dynamism that can derive from religious inspiration.

If the prophets of Israel were living today, Amos would be preaching on West Eighty-fourth Street. I am thinking of Father Gusweller, whose church is on that terrible block and whom I know well. The exposure of some of the horrible slum conditions there have come from tough, fighting clergymen like him. Thirteen years ago, I helped to found the League of West Side Organizations, headed by a priest, a minister, and a rabbi. It has been addressing itself to this particular problem – not to save our parishes, but to save the city and its human resources, which are the greatest in the world. One very effective thing the religious groups of this city did accomplish was the passage of its Fair Housing Practices law. It was the Protestant, Catholic, and Jewish clergy who came out for the bill and strengthened the mayor's hand. I feel, too, that we've done a good job in educating people in an understanding of the law and how to use it.

People are not leaving our neighborhoods now in numbers as large as in previous years. The new projects being planned are creating a new confidence in the area. Also, I think, religious leaders have made it clear that they don't want any such renewed area to be an economic or racial ghetto. We want the complexion of the community to remain the same. People will join those synagogues and those churches that answer their felt needs, give them a sense of purpose, evoke from them a commitment to ideals. They don't want any spiritual Miltown, but rather faith that things can be better if man makes them better.

I am an incurable optimist. I recall that the Seabury Investigation was precipitated by two religious leaders – Stephen S. Wise, the founder of our Free Synagogue, and Dr. John Haynes Holmes. I'm hopeful for the future of this city and hopeful for religion. The function of religion is to apply an ethical measurement to day-to-day problems. The prophet Amos used the figure of a plumb line. Religion is a sort of plumb line. Where society doesn't measure up to what we know to be God's law, the fact has got to be shouted from the housetops by religious leaders.

A CATHOLIC PRIEST   WITNESS

I would say that the Catholic clergy in New York is more conservative than elsewhere in this country, less ready to accept change than, say, the priest in the Midwest would be; certainly than the priest in Europe. I'm thinking here mostly of reforms within the structure of the Church, liturgy and so on. On the other hand, we in New York are more sophisticated in the use of social organizations outside the church – psychiatry, social work – mainly because such things are so much more available here. I *could* say the conservative element is fully in power in New York, but it wouldn't be quite true; there are many young priests who are taking new tacks in their approach to different problems. It's not true, by the way, that the Church regards New York as more difficult. It's simply difficult in a different way.

The way I see it, the problems facing the Roman Catholic Church in New York are these (they are not unique, mind you, but perhaps more pressing because of the nature of the city): materialism, for one thing; the emphasis must be on the importance of spiritual values, family life and social conscience, the vocation of work and the like. Then there's integration. I'm thinking of the Puerto Rican in particular. He has come into an already established Catholic Church in this city, one which had, outside of the upper classes, two main elements – the Irish and the Italian. The Irish were predominant by virtue of numbers and the fact that they came earlier than the Italians and they spoke English. And, just as there was resentment on the part of the Irish at the advent of the Italians, so is there on the part of both toward the Puerto Ricans. *In* religious matters, you see, as well as outside of them. I'm afraid the Catholic as well as the human idea of charity is not as prevalent as it should be.

The intellectuals and the bourgeoisie are a third problem. In the past, the Church in our country has not had to deal with intellectuals. The vast majority of the population, Catholic or not, had all they could do just to keep alive, let alone have a chance at education. So that, today, the old conception of the Church having all the answers satisfactorily in every area is no longer the case. And most particularly in New York, because of the high number of university graduates. The Church is no longer in a position where it can merely restate its teachings. It must now rephrase and re-explain them in a language that is understandable and acceptable to new currents of thought.

Now, as to divorce and the laws of New York State. We know the only ground for divorce is adultery; we know of perjured testimony. And the accusations made against the Church – that *it* is responsible for the situation. Well, the basic foundation of our country is one of majority rule. Possibly I should say democratic process. Until such time as the majority of the people of New York State wish to change the law, it won't be changed. On the one hand, the Church feels that this is actually divine law, something not even open to discussion; on the other, of course, there are all those who are not Catholics. I'm sure the Church never feels it is thwarting the rule of the majority. The Church is accused of maintaining a lobby at Albany that has prevented even a discussion of the problem. What I can't understand is this: if it is Catholic lobbying that has thwarted changes in the divorce laws of the state, why aren't opposing views presented equally strongly? In any change, let me add, you would have to include what the Church regards as its right to defend what it considers to be divine and natural law.

WITNESS

AL RYLANDER

Vice President for promotional services, National Broadcasting Company

I don't care where the factory is, the television industry emanates from New York. I don't care where a man makes it, creates it, or how he does it. If he doesn't have a New York outlet, he's small time. And I'm content to stay in New York; I have no desire to travel. To be a television executive here is to be part of every-

St. Patrick's Cathedral. When the Lord is risen, traffic stops.

Park Avenue; boater above, scooter below. Chic comes in small packages.

thing that happens all over the world. In the course of a given day I can be part of Africa, the United Nations, Shakespeare on the Avon, California, South America, Asia. I get drama, literature, religion, escapism, thrills. Everything that's possible in human experience. A television network executive's New York has only two boundaries – the hands on the clock. Nothing else matters and you're constantly fighting those hands. This is the only business I know of in which, when you make a mistake, there's no post-mortem on why. You cannot be a second-guesser, you have got to be a first-guesser. Sure, you could be wrong, but you must make a decision and make it fast. Once the hand on that clock goes from five to six, there's nothing can be done about it. You've got to be worrying about it going from six to seven and what has to be done then, not what should have been done when it hit five.

I think the fortunate TV executive is the man who, in falling in love with a girl, by the grace of God gets a wife who understands the business he's in, who shares his excitement and the minute-by-minute action. Offhand, I'd say for a man to be a success in TV he must have a home compatible that way. Otherwise, he must fall by the wayside, because an incompatible home must create diversion in his thinking. This industry, I admit, has the greatest mortality rate of any. The pressures are twofold—trying to do your job and trying to keep your sanity. And it is the individual who, through training, or maybe just chemistry, has the make-up to really live what the doctor tells him—leave your problems in the office. Me, I go to sleep on a dime. I can wake up in the middle of the night, think of a stunt, an idea, a program suggestion, jot it down, and go right back to sleep again. From years of knowing, from my past track record, the chances are sixty to forty I'll be able to do the job and so there's no use worrying about it. Besides, the people I report to are human. They don't expect you to be right a hundred per cent.

I say the good we do by far outweighs the evil. We carry the opera and the public-affairs shows and so on; we work awfully hard on them and they lose money. TV is no different than anything else in living. You've got to know the difference between right and wrong here, too. Why did NBC lower their sights in some ways? Because ABC was making the money. NBC had to buy the action stuff to meet the competition. It was ABC that pioneered in the Western, in the private-eye shows. They pioneered in the volume and the violence.

I used to be a movie press agent. In the movie business, it was simply a matter of opening a picture and the customers came in. If a guy working for you in the ad agency wasn't compatible, you got a new account executive. No problem. You were the boss. You had a field man you didn't like? You got a new field man. All down the line you dealt with people mostly who were in show business—the exhibitors. Here, you're dealing with people in a big industry and one wrong move can discredit the image of a corporation that took years and years to build.

In the movies, my job was to get the customers into the theater. Here my job is to get the viewer to the set. But the big difference is that there I could do anything as long as it created an effect. Here, it must be done with dignity, taste, and decorum, because this is something that goes into the home. I've got to make it conducive for people to stay home—that castle, that private fortress. Nobody gets in but me and that TV set and, if their sensitivities are rubbed the wrong way, I've lost a customer. He's going to go to the movies—maybe—or more likely tune in another network. What I do now has made a big difference in my life. From a *somewhat* in the entertainment business, let me tell you, I've become a *somebody* in industry.

TWO PRESS AGENTS

EDDIE JAFFE

In other cities, you can dream; in New York you can do something about it. I came here out of an orphans' home in Ohio right after the '29 crash. It exhilarates me when I think of the challenges this city offers; it depresses me when I think of how little I've done to accept them. I have lived the way it was safest for me, which is to say I *created* a world in which I was comfortable, one like the world of my fantasies, populated only by exciting people almost all of whom had cut themselves off from their own families and societies. Some may have been defeated, but they never gave in and they found in others like them the affection and acceptance they couldn't get anywhere else, whether they were actors, thieves, writers, lawyers, doctors, dreamers, soldiers, scholars, whores, drug addicts – the works. It's no coincidence that I became a Broadway press agent. It kept me near such people.

For a good many years, I lived in a hotel that was, except for me and another roomer, a hotel for call girls. It was more moral than any apartment building I ever lived in. Why, the management wouldn't let *us* have company in the room. It wasn't until the Seabury Investigation that I found out what kind of place it was and that the bellhop who used to thank me so profusely for a dime tip had an income of $3500 a week from the girls who rented rooms to take their johns to. Today – and this is what saddens me, because it's symbolic, in a way, of what's happened to my business – the hotel's charging relief families forty-five bucks a week for a room and making more money than it ever did.

BILL DOLL

Odd McIntyre outlined it for me before I got here from Grafton, West Virginia, a long time ago. His New York did exist, although they used to say he made it up, and it still does. I don't believe he falsified too much. They say the city's changed, that it's a whole lot more sophisticated than it used to be, that you can't get away with the kind of stunts you used to. That's a lot of nonsense. You can still get a show girl into a New York paper walking under a ladder on Friday the thirteenth. What about the Madison Square Garden party Mike Todd threw for *Around the World in Eighty Days?* I was with him then. People talked about that long after Mike was laid away. You can always find a character to work for here. Lately, I've been lucky to dig up Joe Levine. He fascinates me. He's an individualist, really, not a character. I don't know how it happens, but they seem to gyrate toward me, whether it was Brock Pemberton, Jed Harris, Frank McCoy, Mike Myerberg or Monte Proser, or John Ringling North or George Hamid. I've fought every son of a bitch in town on one thing. Everybody's trying to get me to be classy and do the Madison Avenue bit and call myself a public relations counselor. I'm a press agent. Hardly anybody else calls himself that any more. We call ourselves press agents on our letterhead and my high-class Southern clients say it's dreadful. It does give us a little renegade taint, but I've stuck with it and it's paid off.

The Victoria Theater on Broadway. There is unquestionably a neurosis, if not a broken heart, for every light on Broadway.

The entrance to Twenty-one, 21 West Fifty-second Street. Given enough years and the right kind of management, even a speakeasy can become the epitome of fashion.

Above: Washington Market. Here is the huge maw through which New York ingests its fruit and vegetables, its butter, eggs, and cheese.
Below: Mulberry Street; De Lucca's Cheese Store. Nowhere in the world can an Italian eat so well as in New York.

THE MARKETS

For whatever the coincidence is worth as a symbol of the metropolis' endemic, greedy *arrivisme* (a principal source of its power and pre-eminence), by the time the newest New York World's Fair opens in 1964, two of the landmarks by which the city best identified itself, Washington Market and the Fulton Fish Market, may have been pulled down and set up somewhere else, mostly in the Bronx and the remainder in New Jersey. They are, so to say, warty anachronisms on the otherwise fair face of what New York calls progress. Thomas F. Devoe, a cultivated butcher, member of the New-York Historical Society and author of a history of various public markets published in 1862, wrote of Washington Market (with as much annoyance as others have of Fulton, too, early as 1772 and late as yesterday), "This market is without doubt the greatest depot for the sale of all manner of edibles in the United States [but] the small passageways are so obstructed, that to pass through is almost impossible; and if the attempt be made, the person must be prepared to receive a greasy, dirty or torn coat or dress, besides being crowded or pushed, or the danger of having his pocket or basket relieved of anything valuable." Mayor O'Dwyer begged members of the International Apple Association in 1948, "Mr. Visitor, please don't go down to the market." At least one chairman of the House Committee on Agriculture, Harold Cooley of North Carolina, once looked it over and declared, "A disgrace to the city and nation." Said the Commissioner of Markets: "It just doesn't belong."

The truth is that the old markets are among the most expensive working antiques the city has. Every year it costs more and takes longer to bring in and get out fewer things for which there is increasingly less space in the fine, desecrated buildings and narrow streets. But even in their decline, their very real, sad economic decline, they are beautiful. They lack the lacy glass and iron and formal expanse of Les Halles or the Palladian grace notes of the Boston Public Market, but they have their own richnesses. Almost nowhere else do places exist where New York's historical continuity is so movingly apparent – prints and plaques and prettied-up sites are static and remote – and where the city's diurnal rhythms can be felt so strongly. Also, the establishments in them are among the remaining few whose owners and laborers work side by side and are practically indistinguishable in appearance, from overalls, sweaters, watch caps and heavy boots, to baling hooks and hatchets (which are called tomahawks), the principal market tools. Brotherhood has nothing to do with it. "I'm out of here two days and I lose the feel," a wealthy produce man said. "Absentee ownership is unknown down here. With perishables, things happen too fast. If I *have* to go on a trip, I'm in touch by phone once, twice a day." Prices are still quoted in terms of the ancient English shilling, twelve and a half cents; a sale is a private treaty. The markets are unself-consciously Breughelian in aspect, peacefully brawling, good to look at, to be in and smell. They are the largest primary markets in the world and in them occurs the great daily gulp by which the city ingests most of its fresh fruits and vegetables, a good part of its butter, eggs, and cheese, and all of its fresh fruit.

Into Washington Market every working day comes an average of 310 carlots of produce (a carlot – not a carload in the market – is defined arbitrarily at fifteen tons): 125 different kinds of fruits and vegetables from everywhere in the United States and twenty-odd foreign countries. In addition, the market also disposes of about 670,000 pounds of butter a day (Wisconsin, Iowa, and Minnesota); 20,-000 pounds of cheese (Wisconsin, Ohio, the Netherlands, Switzerland, Denmark, and Italy); and 18,640 cases of eggs (New York, New Jersey, Iowa, Minnesota, Georgia, Alabama, the Carolinas, and Virginia). The produce part of the market is long and narrow. It begins at Barclay Street, runs twelve blocks north to Hubert, and extends west from Greenwich to West, with only Washington Street, its spine, between, for less than 150 yards – some forty-nine acres altogether. It includes, too, three Pennsylvania and Erie Railroad piers – 27, 28, and 29 – north of Hubert to Desbrosses. Roughly a third of the fruits and vegetables headed for the market are sold at auction on these piers and only a minute percentage moves through the streets. The butter-and-egg-and-cheese stores – any wholesale business in the market is called a store – are mostly east of Greenwich to Hudson, in the side streets between Chambers and Harrison, luckily out of the way of the produce houses; a collision with the produce business would have forced both out a long time ago.

Of the produce entering the New York area, a fraction less than sixty per cent (including what is sold at auction on the North River piers) is Washington Market's share and that share has been going down at the rate of one per cent a year. Another twenty-two is taken by the chain stores, which set up their own receiving warehouses to cut the cost and trouble of getting things out of lower Manhattan; the remainder is channeled into borough and metropolitan-area markets. Nearly half of what does get downtown these days arrives by truck; roughly forty-seven per cent by rail (which, in any case, has to be transshipped by truck to get to market, since the nearest railhead is a good two miles away); and only five per cent by boat. The phenomenon of frozen and processed foods diverted a lot of fresh produce. But the villain of the piece is the twentieth-century truck stalled in eighteenth-century streets lined with nineteenth-century buildings.

Fulton Fish Market is straight across town on the East River. From Fulton and South streets, it extends north through Beekman, Peck Slip, and Dover; and back from the river front through Front to Water. (The names are evocative of anything a man could want to evoke of the city; what is to be conjured up out of a street in the Bronx Terminal Market known as "Exterior Street"?) On Piers 17 and 18 are the eighteen stands of the Fulton Market Fishmongers' Association; on Pier 19, the sixteen of the younger New York Wholesale Fish Dealers' Association. (At one o'clock in the morning of Tuesday, August 11, 1936, the massive

Fulton Fish Market. It is a marvelous excitement of movement, clutter, and smells.

steel and concrete structure put up by the Wholesale Fish Dealers' Association in 1908 collapsed with a rumble and a shriek and slid tiredly into the East River. The only people in it, a truck driver and a watchman, were rescued. Five hours later, 500 marketmen would have started a day's work in it. A new building was opened by Mayor LaGuardia three years later.)

Across South Street are the independents and the so-called specialists, the fillet and shellfish dealers, some located anyhow in blackened houses with steeply pitched roofs dating to well before the Civil War, some in a reasonably recent block-square, one-story brick building. The fresh-water fish sellers line both sides of Peck Slip to Front Street. From 181,000,000 pounds in 1949, annual receipts at Fulton have dropped to 164,000,000 or so a year. But it is still possible to choose from 135 varieties of salt-water fish, 35 of fresh-water, and 20 kinds of shellfish. However, no more than seven per cent of what Fulton receives comes in by trawler or dragger. Eighty-five per cent rolls in on the ubiquitous over-the-road truck and the remainder gets there by local truck from railheads and airports.

The sight of the buildings in Washington Market can cause an aching pleasure for a past the looker cannot have known. Scarcely one is less than a century old; some have the French roofs of the mode of 1860, some the earlier gambrel, some the peaked, some the flat. They were comfortable homes in the days when the market's work was done on the North River piers. There is a dark gray, four-story warehouse of historic importance at the northwest corner of Washington and Murray streets. Put up in 1848 to the design of a distinguished in-

The Fulton Fish Market, Peck Slip at Front Street. These, among the most beautiful buildings in New York, will soon be gone; beauty is a gamy irrelevance to a real estate developer.

ventor, James Bogardus, it was the first iron building ever completed and the precursor of the skyscraper. (The chances are that the cast-iron buildings of Bogardus and Daniel Badger permitted the use of as much glass in their façades as any of those monstrous triumphs of architecture *soi-disant* along Park and Third avenues.) Almost all the others are of masonry, their red bricks painted over and over in greens, browns, whites, and yellows, and, ultimately, not painted at all; soiled and faded and darkened where they have not been rendered uniformly dun by the weather. Here and there, a wholesale house advertises itself by painting its name in black letters on a white band high up across the face of a building. The letters stand out bravely between rows of blind windows. The windows are blind because most of the old structures are dead above the second floor. The street level is used for receiving and selling, the second floor usually for offices, and, possibly, makeshift locker rooms. One rich wholesaler,

Longshoremen in a saloon on the West Side. What is the song of the shape-up, the Skylock, and the broken sling?

an elderly man, keeps such long hours that he has fitted out an uncommonly luxurious bedroom above his store for recuperative naps. Another, whose grandfather would have hooted him out of the business for the effeteness of the idea, rigged up a golf driving range on the second floor of *his* store and had a professional down three mornings a week to give him lessons. But, for the most part, everything above the street is boarded up and walled off; rats squeak and scrabble in the dark and raise clouds of dust that cannot be seen and skitter downstairs during the off-hours to gormandize on garbage.

The life of the market is in the streets, surging, loud, and assertive, redolent and splashed with raw primary color. That anything at all gets done is astonishing and the working day has been strung out to twenty-four hours. (It once began at about midnight and ended at 7 A.M. or so.) There are days when less than three quarters of what comes in goes out and the additional cost of doing business because of delay and subsequent spoilage, has been estimated conservatively at about $11,000,000 a year. The produce people add $1,000,000 in thievery, the job of inventory control in quarters so badly squeezed being comparable to that of a quartermaster trying to count an army's toothbrushes in battle.

The office staffs of the big receivers, wholesalers, jobbers, and repackers, who occupy some 200 "stores," show up for work when other white-collar people do, but theirs is a muted arrival. The market's day really begins, its theme is stated boldly, around noon, when the big trailer trucks start to bang and snort and clatter into West Street under the elevated highway, the end of their thousand-mile and longer trips announced with an exasperated sigh of air brakes. Their length, thirty-three feet or more, keeps them out of Washington and Greenwich streets; their cargoes are transferred to smaller trucks which park three abreast, so close together that a man cannot get through. The average north-south Manhattan Street has a seventy-foot roadway paved in asphalt; its cement sidewalks are fifteen feet wide. These streets do not handle traffic very well. But Washington and Greenwich streets, which must accommodate something like 4000 trucks every day, are just thirty-two feet wide and paved (Greenwich last in 1913, Washington in 1932) with what the city calls its Standard Granite Block, a spring-breaker eight inches long, four wide, and five deep. It is impossible to estimate how many outside rear-view truck mirrors get broken every day in the contest to get by each other in the market's streets. No truck is without its dents and deep horizontal scratches from cab to tailboard. The congestion is such that a good many vehicles of approved length never get into the district at all. They have to be parked five and six blocks away and their consignments moved in dozens of agonizingly slow (and maddeningly expensive) hand-truck trips from store to truck.

Offhand, no one can recall when a new piece of sidewalk was laid down, and, anyway, not much sidewalk can be seen; fruits and vegetables cover them most of the time. By late afternoon, stores and sidewalks are choked with thousands and thousands of odorous crates stacked high as the naked electric bulbs under the sheds that hang on cables from the second floors of buildings. A walk-way just wide enough to let hand trucks get through is all that is kept and that is apt to be broken, cracked and sunken from steel hand-truck wheels or packages set down hard. (Any container of whatever weight is a "package" in the market.) There are anise, asparagus, and artichokes from California; beet tops from New Jersey; cabbages from Texas, cantaloupes from Mexico and *cipollino* – a small onion – from Morocco; Belgian endive and South Carolina mustard; Israeli lemons, Chilean melons, and Florida oranges; potatoes from Long Island and Idaho; apples from New York, New England, and the Northwest. Trade argot for the marvelous array is surprisingly meager; all brands are known as "marks"; cantaloupes are "lopes"; pineapples are "pines" and asparagus "grass"; the vegetable, broccoli rab, "rape"; and a citrus fruit from the British West Indies, *ugli,* is called "ugly fruit."

A marked acceleration of movement can be felt and a rising, indistinct tide of sound can be heard by six P.M. The daily passage at arms between sellers and buyers has begun. Between then and midnight, the streets are a clutter of purveyors for hotels and restaurant chains, secondary wholesalers and brokers working for out-of-town customers and retailers, pinching fruits, shaking ice out of lettuce and celery samples in open packages, bargaining, threatening, cajoling, pleading, turning away from salesmen in elaborate disgust and back in reluctant assent; shouting, conspiring in stage whispers, wandering from store to store (eyes sharp and hands behind backs) to get the turn of price, somehow avoiding the bruising thrust of hand trucks clattering over the walkways and ultimately departing. The sellers call sharp customers "undertakers" or "gravediggers," and the saying goes that when an undertaker buys cheap he has killed another shipper.

It is miraculous in the awful congestion that people manage not to get in each other's way, but they do manage. They move with extreme slowness, in a kind of disorderly ballet that, if watched long enough, is seen to contain a style and logic all its own. Out of all this milling around, the wholesaler develops his feel for the immediate market. He gets daily reports from the Department of Agriculture and is on the telephone day and night with growers everywhere but he is given to making his last-minute decisions on the basis of the night's movements in the streets. "If you got a lot of little retailers still running around frantic at six or seven in the morning," one wholesaler has noted, "looking that hard that late, you know you're in a hot market and it'll probably be stronger the next day. There's another barometer, too. If we get guys we sell to once in a blue moon, we know we've either got the best stuff, or, more likely, the market's short."

Seventy-five per cent of the market's business is over by midnight. Between then and seven A.M., the field is left to parties of stragglers – the small neighborhood re-

The Bowery, north of Canal Street. A man will bargain his pants off here to buy a drink.

tailers and the last-ditch bargainers. On cold nights, street fires are lighted in bent, rusted oil and paint drums called fire cans. They don't give much warmth outside a radius of three feet. (For some reason, all fire cans in Washington Market burn coke; in Fulton, they are fueled with broken fish boxes.) Men stand as close as they can to them, with their backs turned, slapping their sides with gloved hands for a few minutes, and then move off regretfully to work once more. (More than one homeless alcoholic or wino hustling in the market for enough money for a pint or two and a flop – the unions try to see to it that they are not employed, but they do get hired irregularly – has been found dead, a dirty bundle of rags, next to a cold fire can on a winter morning.) When the sun rises, it rises on a battlefield strewn with the debris of defeated produce. It gets swept up carefully. The salesmen pull in their delivery benches, high podium-like stands at which sales are written up, and get ready to go home. They invariably say, "Good night."

The one market activity that is conducted practically in private is the auction. Two companies (one of which, Brown & Seccomb, was founded in 1798) auction off tomatoes (at midnight) and fruits (at eight-thirty in the morning) on the railroad piers. The produce, lightered across the Hudson, is lined up in the huge, echoing pier sheds for inspection and auctioned off in harshly lit, dingy auditorium-like rooms upstairs. The auctioneers work in a hard nasal chant understandable only to themselves and buyers, bidding up prices a nickel at a time. The bidders respond with winks, twitches, flicks of the catalogues that are printed up daily, and almost imperceptible nods.

The day in Fulton Fish Market starts around one or two o'clock in the morning, although selling doesn't begin officially until six on Mondays and Fridays and seven on Tuesdays, Wednesdays, and Thursdays. Fulton is the successor to the seventeenth-century Fly Market (Fly was a corruption of the Dutch word for valley; the Fly was located at Pearl Street and Maiden Lane. Of its lady vendors it was sung, "At dawn of day, from short repose,/At hours that might all townsmen shame,/To catch our money, round or square/She from the groves of Flatbush came. . . .") At one o'clock in the morning South Street is in deep shadow under the Franklin D. Roosevelt Drive. The street lamps are helped out a little by the modest pools of light from the windows of Cappy's Bar off South on Fulton; from the Paris Restaurant in Meyer's Hotel at South and Peck Slip; and from Carmine's bar at Front and Beekman. Meyer's was built in 1873 and its forty rooms are occupied only by a few crusty, retired marketmen and by the transient truck drivers and fishermen forced to lay over in New York for a night or two. Kroos and Bose's Restaurant doesn't open until three A.M., nor does the Fair, one flight up on Peck Slip. Sweet's, on Fulton, which is a century and a quarter old, used to feed clipper captains steak at four in the morning, but the place keeps daytime hours now and so does Sloppy Louie's around the corner. Even P. Sobel's, a kind of tiny general store next door to Sloppy Louie's, which sells insulated boots and boning knives, work pants and caps and rubber gloves to the market people and fishermen and retailers from uptown, doesn't open until four A.M.

Over-the-road rigs park under the elevated highway from one in the morning on. Then the unloaders – they are known as taximen – start to show up to get the fish boxes out of them and set them up before the closed gates at the piers and the locked doors across the street. Anything fish comes in is called a box. There are Southern boxes, shrimp, smelt, flat, Long Island, and Jersey boxes; New Bedford and Boston, West Coast, salmon, and Candadian boxes; and 500-pounders, which have no special name. The nomenclature has to do with weight, point of origin, and custom. From three o'clock on, the journeymen, who move boxes from stands into customers' trucks, come to work with the lumpers, who unload fishing boats when there are any in port. Owners come on the job by then and with them come the salesmen, the bookkeepers and cashiers.

The trawlers and draggers from New England work out of Fulton Market only between October and Easter because there is no money there for them the rest of the year, when they sail from and put in at their home ports where their catches are processed and canned or frozen and shipped by truck. The fishermen, most of whom are of Portuguese birth or descent, are among the last individuals in one of the remaining few individualistic enterprises in this country. Even unionization has not affected their historic practice: they are still paid in shares. Sixty per cent of the proceeds of a catch are divided evenly among the crew – save for a small bonus to engineers and cooks (after expenses have been deducted for groceries, oil, twenty tons of ice a trip for preserving fish, fresh water, and wharfage); the captain gets a tenth of the owner's forty per cent in addition.

On a midweek morning late in the winter of 1962, the *Golden Eagle,* a typical East Coast fisherman, nosed into Pier 19, alongside the Joseph H. Carter Company, with 60,000 pounds of porgy, butterfish, sea bass, fluke, whiting, and squid. She had been out four days, fishing for two, on the grounds eighty-seven miles southeast of Ambrose Light. She had come back because reports – carried over her ship-to-shore telephone – indicated prices weren't high enough to warrant staying out any longer. The *Golden Eagle* is a Gloucesterman, wooden-hulled, a hundred feet long, diesel-powered, and equipped with just about everything there is to take the guesswork out of fishing – radar, loran, and an electronic fish-finder that "sees" schools of fish as deep as four hundred fathoms. She was built in Thomaston, Maryland, in 1942 and carries eight men. At that – as her men complained – she is neither as big, fast, and modern nor as well-equipped as the Russian and Japanese boats she has to compete with.

Over breakfast, the vessel's captain, a Portuguese in his early thirties named Eduardo Militeo Fragata, said the voyage had been uneventful, except for a day of heavy snow and high winds. "We still fished," said Fragata, a black-haired, round-faced man with good white teeth. "Three drags." The length of a drag is about an hour and a half to two hours. "Shall I tell you the facts?" he went on. "Fish is too cheap. But you got to look for it whether the price is there or not. Fishing has its ups and downs. I say it's in the blood. I never did anything else, nor my family. I came to this country from a fishing village twenty-five miles from Lisbon. I was fishing on my eighteenth birthday. My father was lost at sea three years ago off a Texas shrimper; two years before, an uncle out of New Bedford. I lost my right eye in 1948, cutting cable at sea; an end hit me in the face. In 1952, off Cape Sable, on the Fourth of July, my ship foundered. A wonderful day, though. We got off in a dory. Another vessel picked us up. For all that, I say it's in the system. I am my own boss. The life is good. I am glad to

Sunday shoppers on Orchard Street. Here, the meshpocheh *and* la familia *are one in the eyes of the storekeeper.*

get away and glad to get back, but I don't like staying ashore more than a day or two. We're not used to this city life."

A penetrating, exciting smell of fish filled the air as the *Golden Eagle's* cargo was swung overside and packed into boxes. The business day had begun in the market. (Between the leaping flames from wood-burning fire cans and the irregular but glaring illumination over the doors of the fish houses, the market becomes almost as light as day hours before work begins officially.) Retailers' trucks pulled in as the trailer rigs moved out. The hoarse shouting of selling echoed under the pier sheds and highway as buyers and sellers crowded each other in the stands and on the streets. Fish are still sold on old-fashioned hanging scales. For a hundred years and more, each house has had its own selling code – a sentence ten letters long, often unprintable. The first letter, of course, stands for the number 1, the tenth for 10. Price is called out by the salesman to the book-keeper in letters. No bookkeeper ever confuses a shout from a salesman in his own company with that of a man from another, although they may be no more than ten feet apart. The codes, in fact, are obsolete, since everybody pretty much knows everybody else's, but the practice of long years dies hard.

For all practical purposes, selling is over with by ten o'clock in the morning, but it goes on desultorily until two or three in the afternoon when the concrete floors and the cobbled streets are rigorously hosed down of scales and skins, the merchants close up, and the watchmen come on duty. Something gray has crept into Fulton Market, like a drab fog off the East River, for alll the movement and noise. It is the miasma of dissolution and disappearance, the presence of impermanence. Nobody dances barefoot in a box of live crabs any more out of sheer exuberance. Nobody gets liquored up and tries swimming to Brooklyn. Of the last two men who did – decades ago – one drowned and the other collected a five-dollar bet. The market boys no longer play baseball in South Street while waiting for the Fall River steamers. There aren't any steamers and the trucks take up all the space.

"There's not much sentiment for the place down here," one man remarked over a cup of coffee in Kroos and Bose's. "Where there's labor of this kind, there's no sentiment. That's for tourists – *they* don't have to work here. Funny thing is we don't even get too many of *them*. I'll show you how few fishing boats come in, too. Couple of weeks ago, an advertising agency tried lining up a trawler to pose a model on – one of those Miss Rheingold things. They had to give up and they faked something with another vessel at another pier not even in the fish market. But, somehow, there *is* a magnet attached to the place. Men go away a year, two years, and – boom – they're back. They come home to roost. Don't ask me why. Ever notice how many *old* men you can find working here?" He swallowed some coffee and signaled at the counterman for another cup. "The old free-and-easy is gone," he went on. "Not a proprietor doesn't know what it costs to open his gates every day; they make a chemical analysis of every motion. Sure, it was inevitable we'd be out of here. What logical reason is there for us to *be* here?" Without waiting for an answer, he finished his coffee, bounced two dimes on the counter, and walked off across the street, pulling on his gloves as he did so.

A SENIOR VICE PRESIDENT IN AN ADVERTISING AGENCY

A large part of advertising is a big goddamn suburb. The guys look alike and talk alike and it gets a little boring. One way for me to stay fresh is to stay away from them. There are more guys in advertising like me than you might think. I was away seven and a half years in the suburbs – we moved back here three years ago – and I didn't know what was bothering me. I started going to an analyst in the suburbs. It's possible if I hadn't gone to live there I'd never have known an analyst. I could spend days criticizing advertising for all the reasons anyone's ever given. I could also spend twice as much time defending it. If I've gained any insight in recent years, it's that I find this is the kind of work for which I'm best suited. I thrive on crises; I love emergencies and challenges. I guess I even like the idea of being up and down – up one day because someone liked an ad I did and down the next because a commercial I was involved in got a low Schwerin – a kind of rating they have for commercials. I like what I have to do in my job – selling new ideas to people.

I spend a lot of money to live here – on my home, on cabs, on restaurants, on night clubs, on air conditioning – but I'm incomparably comfortable. I admit it takes far too much money, but I'm willing to spend it. One year since we came to New York, I made over a hundred thousand. I'm broke. That's *very* New York.

Fifth Avenue at Fifty-first Street. Hot chestnuts are only a step from Cartier's.

I think the only time New York bugs me – and I'm a native, don't forget that – is when I start playing the sick game of comparing myself. I'm told I've gone very far, but for me it isn't far enough. I've got a beautiful apartment, but I want a beautiful town house. A friend of mine spent a quarter of a million for a town house, so I've got to spend a quarter of a million for one. It's a terrible confession to make when I see how well I live – almost anyone would say I'm ridiculously rich – but then when I see how others make the scene (You ever hear an advertising man use that expression? I mean, as a usual thing?) I get dissatisfied. I want to drive even harder.

I've seen a hell of a lot of that in Hollywood and Detroit or wherever, but it reaches its most exquisite pointlessness here. Nobody lives it up the way New Yorkers do. They do it with very nearly less show than anywhere in the world, yet somehow they're more flamboyant than anywhere else in the world. I watch New Yorkers come on – in a room, a restaurant, a theater. You suddenly realize they've got more and do it better than any royal couple you ever saw, or any movie star. That goes for advertising. In the hinterland, advertising is always second place. This is the old Palace of advertising and all the cats want to play here. This is the place you got to make it; otherwise, forget it. I've had tremendous offers to go out of town and turned them down. I might die way out there. Forgive the corn, but it'd be like leaving the big leagues to play Triple A ball.

The only thing I'd change for, I guess, would be to be a writer or painter. I'd give a great deal, for example, if I could see just one poem of mine published in a magazine that counted. Or a painting bought because someone thought it was good.

As a movie man, who respects and loves his business, I don't think the heart of the industry ever really was in Hollywood. If I am wrong about this, and certainly the point could be argued, I feel even more certain that its mind and other necessary equipment were never in Hollywood. People forget that the only reason why motion pictures went to Hollywood was because in those days there was a lot of sun out there. It sounds funny, but it's true. You have to remember how slow films and lenses were in those days, and that you needed a great deal of sun, and that pictures, for the most part, had to be shot outdoors. For me, Hollywood was mainly a manufacturing center for the film industry. It wasn't the heart, or the guts, or the mind, or the nervous system of the industry. All of these things, in my opinion, were in New York, but we New Yorkers somehow let the myth be perpetrated that the motion picture industry and Hollywood were synonymous. The president of almost every company was always located in New York. The top executives and the board of directors were also located in New York.

The guy in Hollywood, even though he was theoretically in charge of the factory, had little or no say-so, in many cases, about what he was manufacturing. I always felt that one of the worst things that ever happened to the American motion picture industry was the separation of the manufacturing from the rest of the business. New York is the number-one city in America in terms of creative talent, and a geographical separation from the Broadway stage, book publishing, and magazines makes it impossible to keep up with all of the new talents, whether they be actors, actresses, writers, directors, etc. The movie business is very dependent on all of these things and on the people who make their headquarters in New York. We are, in a very real sense, a derivative business. When I had occasion to live in Hollywood, I would find that there was a terrible break in my knowledge of what was really going on in the creative arts and talents. I would find myself more and more dependent on what I heard, rather than on what I knew from direct observation.

You can't ever forget that basically the economics of the motion picture business are determined in New York. With the exception of a few banks like the Bank of America, almost all of the fundamental underwriting of motion picture companies is done here. Without the support of Wall Street, I don't think a single motion picture company could have stayed in existence over the last twenty-five years. The head executive and sales offices, domestic and international, of all companies are still located in New York, and I think that is a good thing. New York City has had a great opportunity in recent years to become the center of the entire motion picture industry, but our city administration has done nothing to encourage it, and has done a great deal to hinder it. The situation is nothing short of stupid. We are the international city of the world, and movies are an international business.

There is a great deal of conversation about the motion picture industry coming back to New York, but I would rate the difference between shooting a picture in

The financial district. As they say in the movie business, the light may be fine in Hollywood or Rome, but the generator is down in Wall Street.

New York, as compared with Los Angeles, as ten to one in favor of Los Angeles. Out there, motion picture companies get immediate co-operation from the city government. Here they get little or nothing but talk. It's that sort of plain stupidity that's driving a lot of other industries out of New York. In spite of all of the talk about a motion picture industry in New York, I don't think you will find an average of more than two to three top pictures a year turned out here. It is not only the fault of the city administration, it is also the fault of the heads of the movie companies who lack foresight. They are stuck with that expensive studio operation in California, and in spite of the fact that studios have become one of the great drawbacks economically, they still insist on operating as if they were in the dinosaur age. Or they did until practically this morning.

I think New York *has* to become, if not the head center, at least as important as Hollywood in the next five to ten years. There is nothing in Hollywood, in terms of technique, that you can't get equally well in New York. The only advantage of Hollywood is that they have better studios, and these are physical things that can be built in and around New York, along the lines of the dream Zeckendorf had.

Our business, because of the separation between Hollywood and New York, became, to a large extent, a business with an artificial kind of talent, which was really a personality-dominated talent. I believe that if the industry was in New York to a greater extent there would be a more effective balance between real talent and personality, and the business would benefit from this.

The critics don't mean too much. Certainly they can't kill you the way they can in the legitimate theater. It is true, however, that the only critics who are important are the New York critics. They can't kill you, but, if you have an art-house picture and you get rave reviews, the whole job of selling is made much, much easier. While I feel that the New York critics are the only important motion picture critics in the country, I don't mean to imply that they are the best. I would say, for the most part, they are hopelessly untrained for their jobs and are barely competent, if that. Most of them have no respect or liking for the medium they are criticizing. They are picked in a hit-or-miss way. I would think that the editors and publishers of the New York papers would be a mite more careful in selecting critics who would have respect and a liking for the medium, and who would take the trouble to learn the first fundamentals about it.

As far as New York City itself is concerned, I was born in it forty-eight years ago, went to school in it, and for most of my life made my living in it. But at the moment, I would say my affection for it is at the lowest ebb. I live here mostly because of the relationship I have with the people I grew up with and so on. Certainly the city itself has little or no appeal to me physically. The architecture is being changed in a way that would drive me out of New York. It all looks like what I call bathroom architecture – cold, hard, and so inefficient that it doesn't work. New York City today, in my opinion, is dirty, doesn't afford the proper police protection, has terrible schools and a bad hospital and medical problem. Its traffic is an abomination. The town has become, in a very real sense, a menace to its citizens and their children. For the first time I am contemplating moving to the suburbs permanently and for selfish reasons. There is still enough in New York so that I would want the benefits of living near it, but

I don't want to live in it. I don't want my children brought up in the kind of New York we have now. I am very much opposed to having to send them to private schools because I am opposed to what I call economic parochialism. Yet I am forced to do exactly that. There simply is not a decent public school to send them to in the city of New York, and I feel that public schools are the absolute cornerstones of a working democracy. I don't like parochialism whether it be on a religious basis or on an economic basis.

The political cynicism that runs New York today almost compels you to arrive at the conclusion that if you have to make a living here – okay – but I don't want to live in New York, and don't want my kids to be brought up in New York.

WITNESS

MITCH MILLER
Television and recording personality

I think when Hemingway really wanted to renew himself, he always came back to New York. Whether it was Tim Costello's bar or the Plaza, he was here reviving himself, in a way. If he had been in New York at the end, he might not have felt so bloody alone. I don't want to play God and say he wouldn't have killed himself, but who knows what he *might* have done? Whether it's a thick-skinned agent or a sensitive artist thinking about his future, both are motivated by this mysterious chemistry of New York, its ability to renew creative talent. New York has widened me and broadened me and given me every chance to exercise every tangent of talent I thought I had and some I hadn't suspected, and it may give me the chance to exercise some of whose existence I'm not aware now. A city is like someone you love. You don't demand things of it. You get from it what you can give – you get back, absolutely in proportion, and with interest besides. Somewhere else, they would say, "This is your mold, your place," put the blinders on you, and shove you down the street. The most bitter and sardonic people in New York are those who have never given it anything and so they got nothing back.

New York likes to root a champion up the ladder like no other city I know of and when he gets there coddles and lionizes him. But only for a while. Then it wants a new champion or a new achievement. Anyone who thinks, "I've made it and I can lounge around from now on," is a fool, whether he's Mitch Miller or Mickey Mantle. But always there is this strange boosting and promoting of talent on the way up and a complete evaluation of it in ways that cannot be had in the tightest or the smallest or the coziest little city in America. I came here from Rochester in 1933, at the bottom of the Depression. I don't know whether it was because I was a musician, an oboist, but I found that as soon as people recognized I had a purpose, New York became the most open-armed, multi-opportunitied, multi-faceted place in the world.

My purpose enabled me to make a living. That gave me the independence not to have to clutch at the first thing that came my way if I didn't think it was right for me. If there hadn't been so many opportunities, I wouldn't have had the patience. After all, how long do you live? As a working musician, I played in thousands of recording sessions and I learned that end of the business. I

Central Park; Shakespeare in rehearsal. The Prince of Morocco and the Duke of Venice take a break on the Rialto.

began to see how to achieve the extra ten per cent that meant the difference between good and excellent in recording. When the chance came to get into the record business, I had subconsciously prepared myself for it. Where else could that have happened? I was, successively, musician, conductor, and arranger. Then came the step of working with popular artists as an A. and R. man – artists and repertoire – helping them pick songs, trying to show them what was best for them. Out of all that evolved the children's records and the Sing Along records and the Sing Along show on television. The Sing Along records and the television program are definitely not New York, but they couldn't have happened without New York.

Now I'm criticized for "forsaking my true vocation," for doing popular things. That's typical of New York, too, that kind of cultural cultism. You're good only as long as you're narrowly appreciated, as long as you get the hipsters and the coteries. I rejected that one right off the bat. Let's take Errol Garner, for example. When he was playing piano in cellars and dives, he was appreciated by only a few "jazz aficionados" – I have to put that in quotes, because I don't mean it as

The North River and skyline. The serenity is deceptive.

a term of affection – and the so-called critics adored him. This is a town of self-anointed, self-appointed critics. But when his records start to sell by the hundreds of thousands and he goes to Carnegie Hall and plays better than he ever played, with 3600 people loving it all at once, these same critics suddenly find he's lost his appeal for them. Maybe it's because they don't have a job any longer of translating him to those who don't read him. They've lost that feeling of superiority that comes from being the cryptographers to the lower classes.

Sure, the city's dirty, the traffic drives you out of your mind, the tradespeople are getting touchier and more acid, and you have to watch out or the television repair man'll steal you deaf, dumb, and blind. But you're put on warning there; that's part of the game. If you can drink the true nectar of New York, though, you've got a magic potion that'll make you unafraid to fail with a new idea. That nectar is the immediate reward and it's not financial alone, believe me. You get it when you can walk past a construction job and have guys yelling down, "Hey, Mitch, that was a pretty good show," or parents coming up, wagging a finger in your face and saying, "I have a bone to pick with you. Why do you put your program on at ten o'clock at night so my children can't watch?" The immediate reward I'm talking about is they take you to their hearts.

New York is even more demonstrative and warm for me than it used to be. Life is less private now, I'll be honest, but it's also much less difficult. The less private part is automatic. You can't go anywhere without being recognized. That's no complaint. When an artist beefs that people won't let him alone, it's a lot of crap. It's the greatest compliment they can pay him. When I really want to get away, I can still go to that Italian restaurant I know, or the house in the country, and have my fun with my family and a few friends. I lived in Rockland County for years. One of the reasons I moved here was driving home and falling asleep at the wheel. I live on Central Park West. I walk to work every chance I get. If I have ten or fifteen minutes in the morning, I enter Central Park at Seventy-second Street and take that winding path. Nobody has to tell me how dangerous the park is at night, but any guy who wants to feel like an oriental potentate with thousands of acres at his disposal, for his personal pleasure, has only to walk through Central Park on a sunny morning at a quarter to eight.

OSCAR GOODSTEIN
Owner of Birdland, a jazz club

Two thousand miles we're out to sea on the *Independence* and the guy who shines shoes calls me on the phone, he'd heard Oscar Goodstein was on the boat. He calls to tell me that if I turn the radio on I can hear Symphony Sid from New York doing the Birdland show, and, sure enough, I heard it. I heard it and I enjoyed it. On top of that, out of the crew of six hundred and eight, there were close to a seventh of them that came over to tell me how much they thought of Birdland. I even met a waiter on board who used to work here in Birdland. That's what New York means to me. Two thousand miles out to sea. Think of it!

When my assistant manager was killed – Irving Levy – that was a January 26.

He was buried on the twenty-seventh and on the twenty-eighth was his fourteenth wedding anniversary. He left a wife and four children and but for the grace of God there would lay I or anyone else who happened to be near this demented person at that time. There was no motive, no intent. I was in Vegas the night he got shot and they called me and I flew back at once. Now this will tell you what New York is like. I got innumerable anonymous calls, people kept calling me all day and night, giving me the names of witnesses and subsequently – that's how they got him – the name of the murderer, which I turned over to the police. I had never seen the man in my life. And when I asked some of the people why they were calling, the answer I got is, "You got the finest club in the world and we don't want to see any harm come to it." I don't know who called me. Literally.

People say to me, "What kind of a life do you live? You have no social life; you never get a chance to go out. How can you be so absorbed in what you're doing, regardless of how much you love the music?" It's a simple answer. We live a cleaner life and one that's a lot more enjoyable than the person who works from nine to six. Even though the club doesn't open until eight at night, at five every day we're here – my wife and me, she works with me, she's got arthritis and the doctor told her she should do anything, get out of the house, keep active – getting everything ready. We're through at four in the morning. By the time I check the business out, it's five. So what do we do? We go up to the Riker's at Fifty-seventh and Sixth and who do you think gathers there at that time of the morning? Everybody in the business. People who just got finished work. They come there, sit and talk, eat and relax. Then we drive home to Brooklyn, where we live. You never cease to marvel at that sort of thing in the city.

WITNESS

ELMER RICE
Playwright

I'd say that the changes that have taken place in this city between the turn of the century and now could not possibly be matched by any change in a comparable period in the future, except, of course, in the event of a nuclear war. I was born in 1892. I grew up at 106th Street and Madison Avenue. One of my first recollections is the horsecars on Madison Avenue with their potbellied wood stoves. In the winter, the horses might slip on the icy tracks and fall. There'd be great difficulty getting them to their feet and out of harness. If one broke a leg, a cop would come and shoot it. Sometimes the horse would lie there three or four days, frozen stiff, before it was carted away. Around the corner from me, there was a little farm with a wooden farmhouse and a kitchen garden. I think there was not a building on Fifth Avenue between Ninety-sixth and 110th streets then. It was all vacant lots; they made wonderful playgrounds. Some had hills and bushes and shrubs; others were flat and good for baseball. It's hard to conceive of any of that in New York now.

There's one thing you can't explain to anybody who grew up after the First World War and that is the sense of security people felt then. When I was young, every thoughtful person believed that with the progress of science and the advance of education there would be a gradual amelioration of the ills of the world, and so there was a kind of ease and relaxation. Two World Wars and the Depression have removed that. The whole tempo of the city has changed. All I sense now is tension, hurry, overcrowding, anxiety, noise, and stench. Mark you, it's a great city, but I wouldn't live here if you gave it to me. I moved to Connecticut in 1942. A few years ago I was forced to move back. I had a very big, spacious apartment on the West Side, very quiet and light, very comfortable. I lived here for another three years. Fortunately, I held onto the place in the country. I was unhappy the whole time I was here; I didn't have one comfortable day. I was conscious all the time of being hemmed in by the pressure of all these thick lives around me. I decided the hell with it and moved back to the country.

It's axiomatic that the professional theater, like everything else, is in a very bad way. A lot of its woes can be traced to the mechanization of society. Movies, radio, and television had their effect on the theater, and, of course, mechanization is responsible for most of our atomic war problems. I wrote *The Adding Machine* in 1923 and the curious thing about it is that the play is being done more now than it was in its first production, not because it was particularly outstanding, but because it does deal with this problem of mechanization.

I realize you have to take into account that when you get older you don't have the same fine, free, careless rapture you had in your youth. You're more sophisticated about things and disillusioned about some. Let me put it this way: if I were

The theater district, Forty-fifth Street, looking west from Broadway. It is a curious confusion of art and honky tonk, but the best this country has to offer.

*Forty-second Street, north side, between Broadway
and Eighth Avenue. It suppurates, like an untended sore.*

twenty-one now and starting out, I would certainly not find the theater as satisfactory as I did. That does away with the age differential. There's so much more at stake now, in terms of money, backers, of the need for instantaneous success, everybody demanding enormous sums of money.

The theater used to be simpler. You didn't have to deal with high-powered agents, for one thing. And what is a producer now? He's a man who has to go around, hat in hand, trying to raise money. In my time, nearly all producers financed their own plays; many of them had their own theaters. Let me give you a couple of examples. As recently as 1931; by which time I had been in the theater nearly twenty years, I put on two plays of my own. *The Left Bank* cost $8000 to produce and *Counselor-at-Law* $11,000. I did them with my own money. Today, obviously, *The Left Bank* would cost $75,000 and *Counselor-at-Law* at least $125,000. *The Left Bank* would never be produced or it would close in a week. Even then, I couldn't find anyone else to do it but myself with my money. And what happened? It ran for 250 performances and I sold the motion picture rights.

It's all very well to talk about off-Broadway, but when a play is done you want it done as well as is possible. The sad fact is that, as a rule, they don't do things very well off-Broadway. I would be hard put to it to think of an original play being done as well off-Broadway as in a good professional production on Broadway. If *The Adding Machine* were done off-Broadway today, I wouldn't have Dudley Digges, Margaret Wycherley, Edward G. Robinson, and Helen Westley to play it. I wouldn't have Lee Simonson to do the sets, Deems Taylor to write the music, and Philip Moeller to direct. Where could you get a setup like that off-Broadway? It isn't only the economics of it; you'd be willing to forget the royalties, but you couldn't get the people.

I know that if I were compelled to live in a city New York would be my first choice. It's the way you have an affection for a father, even though he beats you up occasionally. I can't honestly say New York beat me up; I have no sense of having been ill-treated by it. My professional career is here. So is a good part of my family and a great many of my friends. I have the advantage of living as I want to live and yet being able to avail myself of everything the city has to offer me. I have no personal grievance. I just think all modern cities are obsolete.

The Staten Island ferry on a Sunday. There is louder music inland.

SINGLE MOMENTS

Lower Broadway, an official reception.
New York is the endless celebration of everything.

White wing in the mist of Manhattan. Cold air vaporizes on the outside of live-steam mains below the street; the Mephistopheles with the broom materializes in it.

Fifth Avenue in the spring, south from Fifty-third Street.
The very air trembles with prescience.

Manhattan, looking northwest from the Pan Am Building.
From the left; Time-Life, Equitable Life, 30 Rockefeller Plaza, 666 Fifth, Seagram.

Trinity Church at the holiday season.
The money-changers may not be driven
out of the temple, but at least
they take time off on Christmas Day.

Forty-sixth Street between Ninth and Tenth avenues. Patrolman Gerald
J. Doherty's presence is after the fact a little; there was a double murder
on the street the day before.

Columbia University; steps of the Low Library. Few are aware of its full name: Columbia University in the City of New York.

The United Nations Secretariat shaft; the Security Council dome. The world's work, it is devoutly hoped, may someday be done here.

The United Nations; the General Assembly at its debates. Here one is almost persuaded of the possibility of peace.

Carnegie Hall; Artur Rubinstein playing. Had the artists not fought to save it, a red sky-scraper might occupy the site today.

Opposite page: The Metropolitan Opera House; a performance of the Kirov Ballet. When the proud Belmonts gave up the Academy of Music, the parvenu Vanderbilts graciously let them into the Met.

Fifth Avenue and Fifty-ninth Street; the Pulitzer Fountain. The lady, quite properly, is the Goddess of Abundance.

Fifth Avenue and Fifty-ninth Street; carriage, Pulitzer Fountain, and street Arabs. There are unpremeditated instants—no more than that—when the city will arrange itself in a loving tableau.

General Sherman marches through Central Park eternally, but the horse-drawn cab makes better time.

Bronx Park; the Zoo. The address is way uptown, but there is more space for the family.

Central Park at night.
The terrible and shaming truth is that it is not safe after dark.

Central Park; the Children's Zoo in winter. Noah's Ark will sail again and the whale will spout.

The Lower East Side; a pigeon loft on a tenement roof. The man fixes the pigeons in their orbit; the city fixes the man in his.

Coney Island. The Chamber of Commerce figure is always a million on Sundays.

Swimming pool on the roof of the Sheraton Motor Inn, Twelfth Avenue and Forty-second Street. The notion is utterly bizarre, but engaging.

The garment center. The rustle of heavy silk
in the House of Dior is enough to stop
traffic here.

Greenwich Village, Bleecker Street coffeehouse
exterior. There is more sin in Scarsdale.

Status symbol on the East Side.

WITNESS   VIRGIL THOMSON
                Composer and critic

When I was very young, I came from Kansas City to New York because artists always go from the provinces, if they were born there, to the metropolis. Later, New York was the jumping-off place from which I went to Europe. Paris, at that time, which was the early Twenties, was, artistically speaking, a rather grander metropolis than New York. Between 1920 and 1940, I came back from time to time for engagements and productions of works of mine. I *lived* in Paris. Going to New York from there was like going from New York now, say, to Boston, or Chicago, or somewhere else. I still have my little flat in Paris and I go back and forth, but no longer as one would from a provincial to a metropolitan situation, but rather as one living in a metropolitan situation would go back to his home town every so often for sentimental or nostalgic reasons.

New York is my place now. My publishers are here, my engagements come from here, mostly; I feel that I am in the center of the whole musical world as I used to feel I was in Paris and do not any more. With regard to New York, Paris is now, from an artistic point of view, at least a musical point of view, very much as, for example, Florence might be in regard to Paris – a nice, fine, handsome, cultivated city, but not really that active or central. There have been all kinds of New Yorks for me. Back in the Twenties, we used to produce our own works – Copland, Sessions, myself, others; we were always organizing concerts and doing things by ourselves and our contemporaries. In the Thirties, the young people wanted *us* to perform *their* works. They could muscle in on us or the Philharmonic.

And here, in the Sixties, there's off-Broadway theater – and music, too – and all organized by young people because they want to see and hear and play certain things and they realize the only way to change public taste is to go ahead and do it. The New York I inhabit now has the largest group of functioning poets in the world – far larger than in London or Paris – and it has broken the stranglehold of the conservatives. Tom Eliot had the veto power over publication of poetry in England and America for some twenty-five years. Now publishers don't have Eliots and there are 200 or more of these new little magazines and some of them are quite marvelous. Such things appear constantly, constantly, constantly. The city also has a large number of excellent composers, and, for ten years or more, the most active painting movement in the world. That particular movement, as such, may be drawing to a close, but the activity will remain.

You see, New York is no longer what it was forty years ago – a big-business city which consumed some art. It's a great metropolis; it creates art – painting, music, poetry, and literature – consumes it and distributes it. Metropolises always have mechanisms, but many have mechanisms that don't create – Buenos Aires doesn't create, only consumes. But if you have all the mechanisms, then you're capable of preserving and distributing the conservative work of older people and the successful work of the middle-aged, and there's plenty of money and mechanism and know-how around for young artists and their friends to produce and distribute their work without having to ask the older people. That's what was so wonderful in Paris. You'd hire a hall and do it and your friends would all play for you. That's what off-Broadway is.

I discover that my music publishers, my book publishers, a great many magazine editors are young men and I find them wonderful. I much prefer to deal with them than with my contemporaries, who are as nice as can be to publish me, but I know they're not going to be around too much longer and these young people are. They're interested in me; they're not afraid of paying high fees; they were brought up in a boom economy and they don't try to hold back. They're aware

Lincoln Center; Philharmonic Hall. Here is the newest supermarket for the production, distribution, and consumption of music.

The Metropole Café, Seventh Avenue north of Duffy Square. The owners don't mind giving it away to crowds on the sidewalk.

of both us *and* beatniks and they often have a high conception of what their intellectual obligations are.

And that means there is freedom, and amplitude, and I find New York a wonderful city right now. I realize these young people would put me right on the shelf or down the drain if they weren't interested in me, but since they are, they preserve and tolerate me, and even encourage me a little bit. They're making their way as we did. We loved the older people who encouraged us, naturally, but I do like to see young people take over. We did, and I never thought young people were any good if they didn't.

ROBERT SYLVESTER
A Broadway columnist for the New York Daily News

I'm from people who, on one side, were Connecticut farmers and canal people. The other side, we were whaling and seafaring. My father broke with that tradition and ended up tax collector of West Haven, Connecticut. In the middle Twenties, I was still in college and we'd come down and see the matinee at the Palace on Saturday. Christ, that seemed to me to be the greatest show business in the whole world. The only thing I was ever good at in school was English, history, literature,

Cooper Square; the Five Spot.
When the joint was torn down, the cats simply moved on to a new location.

and grammar, and I figured out then that the best racket for me would be something in the writing end – namely, newspapers. I think it was in '26 or '27 I wrote
a story called "Jazz Goes to Music School" – you can imagine how esoteric that
must have been – and I got on the train and brought it down to Nathan and
Mencken at the *American Mercury*. I didn't get to see them. I took the thing
down on my next trip and sold it to a magazine trying to imitate the *Mercury,
Plain Talk*. Twenty-five dollars. I was hooked. I got a summertime job on the
New Haven *Register* and from there made it down to the old New York *Post*.

I bought myself a cane and spats. I was working the lobster shift, and, of
course, I considered myself a great night owl. I had several things to learn. I used
to wear an ice cream suit, for example – with leather buttons. I was at Forty-
second and Fifth one day and a guy told me I looked all right and would I like to
buy an expensive diamond ring? He walked up to a plate-glass window, and,
with what I naïvely assumed to be the diamond, cut a gash that must have been
six inches long and an inch deep. I haggled and gave him eight dollars.

I'm too old to live through another depression, but it was the greatest fun period of our time. Everything was cheap. A landlord made any concession to get you; if you could hustle up enough booze, enough money for the rent and food, the whole town was a ball. We all borrowed from each other and lived off each other. It'd be impossible for a youngster today to live the way I did in a twelve-buck-a-week, two-room apartment in the West Seventies. They don't exist. In those days a boy or a girl from North Carolina would come up here, find a small apartment, write home; the next North Carolinian would come to the same building and pretty soon it was all North Carolina. The building next door might be New Hampshire.

The town was full of little rackets, which were amusing. Two girls would run a dance studio. There must have been thousands. They'd take the front room of a brownstone and clear out all the furniture except straight-backed chairs, because even with an easy chair, if you got nailed by a Vice Squad cop, it was a rap. The D.A. had a hard time with straight-backed chairs. So the girls would put a sign in the window, "Dolly and Folly, Private Dance Instruction." They'd take ads in the tabloids and the old lechers would arrive by the dozens. They'd dance real close and they'd come back until they tired of Dolly and Folly. Business would fall off; Dolly and Folly would dye their hair and get different gowns, another front room in another brownstone, open up as Margie and Chrissie, take the same ads, and the same old lechers'd be back.

I remember N.T.G.'s Hollywood Restaurant with the eight-by-ten glossy photos of the girls, showing them bare-busted. All such nonsense ended with that damned LaGuardia. In my book, he started the whole trend of making this town the square village it's almost become. All night life and so much entertainment have disappeared. A joint like Jack White's Club 18 couldn't possibly exist today. There's virtually no business in this town for anybody after twelve-thirty. You used to come out of Jack White's at four-thirty or five in the morning. Then, there were actors and musicians everywhere; the Capitol, the Rivoli, the Strand, the Paramount, the Music Hall, the Roxy, other theaters, had big pit bands and huge stage shows. Those actors and musicians lived in Broadway hotels, since they were transients, and they were the excuse for Lindy's staying open until four. It's only because of tradition that it doesn't close at midnight these nights.

Then the war. Here's what I found when I came back. A town that was making laughs when I left was just purely making big money when I came back. It was too busy for laughs. Everything since the war has been a drive to chase living people out and replace homes with vast office buildings. I point out to you that only five years ago Park Avenue was essentially a high-level living street. And the town's choked itself to death with traffic. It used to be, if you were bouncing, you could make three or four spots in a night. Now, getting just from dinner to the theater is a major operation.

A few years ago, if I could have made a score, I would have gone to Havana and lived outside the city there. It had the same kind of color, before Castro, the same kind of companionship I once found here, plus that wonderful Spanish side of life. But I didn't make the score, and, I suppose, if I had, I'd have been home by now. And, by now, I have so many personal and professional roots here that I couldn't live anywhere else. I guess I'm contented. I'm not happy, but I'm contented.

JEROME BRODY
President of Restaurant Associates, owners of the Four Seasons, the Forum of the
Twelve Caesars, Rikers, and other restaurants

Maybe we've succeeded, in a small way, in adding another color to the spectrum of this city, another sight, another tile of pleasure or gaiety. I think that in the case of the Four Seasons, specifically, we've tried to crystallize a picture of elegant New York as it is now; tried to say that New York is mature, has arrived, and is entitled to status in the world of the gourmet and the aesthete, as well as of the banker. A lot of the bohemian is gone from this city, a lot of the bizarre. The city is getting more sterile all the time, in some ways. The old, all-night night life is gone and what we've attempted is to fit into this new city, to be compatible with it, and, at the same time, to play a real role in it.

The Four Seasons Restaurant. The effect, so cunningly calculated, is of dining in a paradise designed by the Museum of Modern Art.

Opposite: Park Avenue; the Seagram Building and its neighbor to the north, the First National City Bank. Beauty had better be in the eye of the beholder.

Even though our reasoning was purely commercial, it was sound. From a business standpoint, we just couldn't exist in any other city. We could have the world's greatest restaurant in Kalamazoo, Michigan, but it would take a hell of a long time for people to find out about it. Here, in New York, you open, and, if you're right, it's like the floodgates have opened. When I was in Moscow a while back, I suggested they help us do a Russian restaurant in New York, and, conversely, that we do an American restaurant in Moscow. I was told, "In Moscow, we will have only our own restaurants," so nothing ever happened. I'm leading up to something. This may sound crazy, but part of our approach to La Fonda del Sol, which is Latin-American, was – you're free not to believe me – something of an attempt to fight a minority problem. We've had a recent wave of immigration from Puerto Rico and a lot of travel into Latin-American countries and where we could, we've indicated – in food, in décor – that these areas are cultivated and developed. We've tried to introduce New Yorkers to their cuisines and their backgrounds and to minimize negative things and differences – such as the mendacity of the approach that these people are bad because they don't speak English.

I can't make strong enough tribute to this city. I was born here. Ninety-nine per cent of the things that have happened to me came about because of it. I can't mourn the disappearance of a lot of old buildings. The city's beauty, such as it is, is increasing, not lessening. I seem to hear less noise; it strikes me the town is cleaner. So we lost some fairly attractive apartment buildings on Park Avenue. What have we got instead? A Seagram Building, a Union Carbide Building, a Lever House, a great Renaissance. We're off again; we're moving; we're alive, dynamic, virile. I guess I've got a little of my father's philosophy in me. He liked the idea that material and physical things wouldn't survive him. He would rather have seen them disappear in his lifetime.

ERNEST MARTIN
A theatrical producer

I believe I could make a living in show business in several other large cities of the United States and Europe. It's no particular credit to New York, but the fact is that the legitimate theater of America is concentrated here and I like working in the live theater. I'm sick of hearing this whole business about the theater dying. It's thriving more than it ever did in terms of quality; its economics are stupendous; its audiences are the best in the world. It would be cheating a little bit to allow anyone to assume that when I speak of New York audiences I mean they are made up of New Yorkers. They are made up of people from everywhere and, usually, the most discriminating people, at that. Whether New York gets the credit for it or not, the audiences you'd like to have at your shows do congregate in this city. Audiences in cities other than New York consist of people living in the immediate area.

There is no greater satisfaction to creative people than the knowledge that their work is going to be seen and heard by their peers or betters and, if they're lucky, even liked. That's the challenge. To misquote some quotes I read about Hemingway, you're in the ring with the champ when you take on a New York audience.

Rehearsal in a Broadway theater. Here – backstage – is where devotion is found.

Winning with an audience in any other city is never quite the same. Which leads me to an aspect of New York my partner, Cy Feuer, and I found out about as the result of a show we did in 1955 – *Silk Stockings*. It opened in Philadelphia a failure. Instead of bringing it to New York after three or four weeks' work, we kept on touring it for a total of thirteen weeks. Our difficulties became legendary.

We knew that the first-night audience here was aware that the show had been in trouble and we were terrified that they would come to it with brickbats in hand, ready to jump all over us. What we didn't know then was that, since all our previous shows had been successes, we were winners in the eyes of a New York audience and, because we had been winners, the audience came opening night to root for us, to see us keep on winning. We found out that New York likes the *over*dog, not the *under*dog. In that respect, it's different from all the rest of America. Anywhere else, it's un-American not to like the underdog. In that sense, New York is un-American.

The fact that it *is* un-American is another thing I like about it. It doesn't ask you to prove seven times a day that you're an American. It only asks you to survive. It's so busy with its own impossible problems of how to get somewhere in the heat and cold, how to find a place to eat lunch, how to deal with protecting

Khrushchev, Castro, or whoever, from being assassinated, that it doesn't have time to worry about any generic classifications. My partner and I deal professionally mostly with, we hope, comedy. To me, the best comedy is anti-authoritarian and so is New York. New York hates a cop. It hates pomposity and its only traditions are its dislike of traditions.

I spent half my life in Los Angeles, but it was only when my partner and I last stayed out there for any considerable length of time that I really came to understand the meaning of an old show-business saying – that Hollywood is double-Newark. Meaning, of course, that it's just a large small town, a city made up of suburbs with no city to hold them together. The feeling of life moving so slowly out there made it hard for us to think we were on anything but a vacation. It probably seems masochistic to say so, but the hardships of New York make it a better place to work. I enjoy the paradoxical combination of living in an area seething with culture and hardship at the same time. Out in Hollywood, I came to the realization, as well, that shrubbery couldn't compensate for people. New York provides a basic essence of life for people who, like myself, are of a nature to want to be away from nature. If I took a walk in Beverly Hills, a policeman would drive up and want to know what I was doing. Block after block and not a soul in sight. Here, I'm surrounded at all times by strangers, not necessarily attractive ones, often quite the opposite, but at least there is a feeling that I'm living in an inhabited area. Along that line, I think it was Proust's maternal grandfather who said something about a garden of a few square yards in Paris being more inviting than an estate in the country. Incidentally, the old man never slept away at night from his home in Paris. If he took a trip to the country, he insisted on returning home to sleep in his own bed in the city. I'm that way about New York. I love it.

THE SCRUTABLE CHINESE

CHAPTER **6**

If the Chinatown Fair, Inc., on Mott Street ("The Amusement Center of Chinatown. Win Beautiful Chinese and American Merchandise. Play Pokerino. Skee
Ball. Shooting Gallery – Real Bullets") is any criterion, then the Chinese are the
most scrutable people in New York, particularly on a Sunday, when they jam the
place and set their children to riding in the latest non-rising jet airplanes. Sunday
is the biggest day of the week in Chinatown, a fact which has not been lost on the
non-Chinese proprietors of the Fair, Inc., who put up a sign over the Pokerino lay-
out reading, "Confucius Say – Time Spent in Leisure – Like Money in Bank." The
pidgin English is an innocent slander on Confucius, who has had more things
attributed to him than Wilson Mizner or Dorothy Parker, and on the city's Chinese
in general, who, while both thrifty and aware of the uses of leisure time, speak
either perfect New Yorkese, one of five Chinese dialects, or Mandarin, which is
the official language of Chinese of the ruling classes and the government, the one
in Taiwan, at any rate.

Not many Chinese here mess with Mandarin. Most speak Cantonese, since
most of them are from Canton (the Third District of Kwangtung Province), and
it is taught in the Chinese public school. But it is possible to hear some Toysan
(Fourth District), Hakka (a word meaning foreigner), which is spoken by people
from Central or North China; Shanghai; and Amoy. Hakka and Amoy are the
common dialects of Taiwan. Cantonese can understand bits and pieces of Toysan,
but not the other dialects, and those who use the others can't understand any but
their own. In Chinatown there is an expression, "Not Three, not Four" – a reference to the dialects of the Third and Fourth districts – which means, interchangeably, *"Comme ci, comme ça,"* or "Much ado about nothing." A man accused of
indulging in "Not Three, not Four" is apt to be called a *jook sing,* which means
the hollow part of a bamboo shoot and hence "emptyhead." He might very well
retort with *jook kok,* which means the solid part of the same, or "knucklehead."
This is all Cantonese chitchat.

Such exchanges are invariably made in the greatest good humor and usually
among old friends who meet in Chinatown on Sundays. Upon greeting a man it is
customary to ask, *"Bin she fat choy?"* or "What are you prospering from?" and to
reply, *"Ngai sai gai,"* or "I am slaving through the world," which is, after all, just
about what Macy's tells Gimbel's. Among the younger and more raffish types, the
handshake may very well be accompanied by *"Hui nai yah ki dai?"* or "Where

173

Chinatown; clubrooms of a family association.
They include Chins, Lees, Wongs, Ngs, Leongs, Chus, Quons, Changs, and Moys.

174

you been, you old bastard?" the response being *"Mo chui hui,"* or "No place." After having greeted each other, inquired about friends and families, and conducted their business, they get down to discussing what has been on their minds ever since the damnable city improvers began destroying other neighborhoods: how soon will Chinatown disappear? In the past, they have seen schemes come and go, including one proposition to put up skyscraper apartment buildings with vaguely oriental pagoda tops. (The closest anything has come to that yet are the Telephone Company's golden street booths, which, in Chinatown, do have pagoda tops; tourists call them "cute," which is exactly what the telephone company had in mind.)

While, on the whole, Chinatown has no objection to being rehoused, it would hate to be dispersed. There are two hundred or so businesses that flourish there and that are, in effect, the focus of Chinese life in the metropolitan area. Should these be scattered, it is argued with complete justification, the Chinese community would experience almost insuperable difficulties in procuring many of the things it now gets in Chinatown. Furthermore, as the social thinkers have had pointed out to them repeatedly and to their distress and bewilderment, Chinatown, in its run-down tenements, lacking all green space (the kind of green space which gave juvenile street gangs in New York their greatest turfs for pitched battles) and similar doubtful amenities, has the lowest crime rate in the city and its families are models of family life. There are between 5000 and 7000 Chinese residents in the ten blocks that make up Chinatown and about 25,000 more elsewhere in the city, in New Jersey, Connecticut, and Long Island. A good many of them descend on what is unquestionably the most cohesive enclave in the city on Sunday, to visit families, friends, and *gung saws* (or associations – of which there are sixty-five – of a family, trade, district, or recreational nature), to shop for exotic groceries and mundane business supplies, to pay bills, pick up mail, get love letters and other missives written, translated, or interpreted, go to the doctor, eat at tiffin houses, coffee shops, or noodle shops, and go to the movies.

There are two movie houses in Chinatown, the New Voice and the Silver Star. The movies are as exotic as the groceries. At the New Voice, one may see such items as *Spring Comes Again,* which, like all Chinese movies shown here, was produced in Hong Kong. It is all about a man and a woman who fall in love and achieve eternal felicity, despite many obstacles. The dialogue is both straight-forward and poetic:

SHE: I have beauty
and I have money, too.
What more can I desire?
With my beauty I can attract anyone;
I can influence anyone.
How fortunate I am!

HE: I worship your beauty;
I admire your wealth.
Wonderful to possess both.
I worship your beauty;
I admire your wealth.

The movies get their big play late in the afternoon. The influx of visitors, however, gets under way at about eleven o'clock in the morning. As a rule, they will head for one of the tiffin houses for a late breakfast. There are four tiffin houses in Chinatown (there are at least seventy-five restaurants altogether) called the Pagoda, Lee's, Nom Wah, and Yuk Hing, and their specialty is steamed foods. (Most outlying Chinese eat fried foods all week long and like the tiffin houses for a change.) Late breakfast is not only late; it is extensive, and consists of, for example, *har gow* (shrimp dumpling), *sui gow* (meat and shrimp patties), *sui mei* (meat patties), *chun guen* (egg roll), *dow foo sui mei* (bean curd and meat patties), *char shu bow* (roast pork bun), *ju yim bow* (peanut butter bun), and *gum chin gai* (barbecued pork sandwich). A man may sip jasmine tea (*heong pin*), rose (*nui kwai*), chrysanthemum (*kuk fah*), narcissus (*sui sin*), or dragon well (*loong jing*). There is an impression abroad that coffee is alien to the Chinese. It is dead wrong. A good many Chinese will squeeze in a visit to the score or so of coffee shops in Chinatown on a Sunday. An educated guess is that each of these shops uses up 150 pounds of coffee a week. At 40 cups to the pound, this is 6000 a week per shop. (Another picture Occidentals have of the Chinese in New York is that they still sit around at banquets, gravely sipping rice wine. They sit around at banquets, all right, but they are not grave and they do not sip rice wine. They drink straight Scotch – the bottle is usually placed on the table – without water or ice – and they keep their heads; the sight of a drunken Chinese, indoors or out, is a rare one.) In the event that the Chinese appetite is a little finicking on a Sunday, the visitor may pass up both tiffin house and coffee shop for the noodle shops. There are about a dozen of these. One of them, on Mott Street, is open twenty-four hours a day and serves nothing but noodle dishes (better than a hundred different kinds) and soft drinks. Some Chinese eat with their families.

Replete, the Chinese then goes to his association. The outstanding family associations in Chinatown are those of the Chins, the Lees, the Wongs, the Ngs, the Leongs, the Chus, the Quons, the Changs, and the Moys. Chinese laundrymen turn up at the laundrymen's association. Players of the moon harp and similar esoteric instruments go to clubs that foster Chinese music and opera. The president of an association is known as the *gee jek* or head man. He is elected annually and gets into office on the basis of his venerability, wealth, intelligence, or public spirit. An indispensable adjunct of any association is the *choot farn*. For those Chinese who have difficulty with English, the *choot farn* is a trouble shooter, moderator, interpreter, and writer of letters, love and other kinds. He makes no charge, but it is seemly to give him anywhere from half a dollar to a twelve-course dinner, depending on whether he is knocking off a translation or assisting in the sale of a laundry or restaurant.

Some associations, like the On Leong and Hip Sing tongs, have quite elaborate headquarters, whose appointments range from television sets to Buddhist altars. The On Leongs and the Hip Sings used to be quite a terrifying bunch with pistols, knives, and hatchets back in the days when they ran Chinatown and parceled out the fantan gambling, opium and import-of-Chinese-maidens concessions. These are now defunct industries. The last tong war petered out back in 1926 and the two tongs are pretty much like Kiwanis and Rotary now. (There is even a Lions

Club in Chinatown, with a very Occidental outlook.) A good many of the associations maintain dormitories for bachelor Chinese. (There are some 2000 bachelors in Chinatown and Lord knows how many outside.) Chinatown's lurid past – it *was* pretty lurid, for all of the tourist fakery and stage-set opium dens rigged up early in the century by Chuck Connors, a Bowery character and the most blatant faker of all in Chinatown – comes to life palely out of the mouths of sight-seeing guides who take tourists through the area to look at the Rescue Mission, a Buddhist altar here and there, the curio shops, and, if there is time, one of the standard restaurants. The shops are full of the usual gimcracks, including plastic back-scratchers, but any well-heeled visitor with a discriminating eye can buy really precious jades or fine tapestries. The price will be high but right.

Among the supplies the visiting Chinese buy on Sundays, principally because they cannot get them anywhere else, are brown bean sauce, black bean sauce, dried ducks' feet, salted duck eggs, salted fish, dried shrimp, dried abalone, *fun*

Chinatown; The Bloody Angle of Doyers Street. The last tong war petered out in 1926 and the most lethal instrument on the angle now is too much egg roll.

she (rice noodles), and Chinese vegetables, all of which are grown on Long Island or in New Jersey. They also pick up soy sauce, thick sauce, plum sauce, and oyster sauce. They buy barbecued ducks, roast pork, and Chinese sausages in Chinatown's butcher shops – as delicacies – but whatever pork, poultry, or beef they need in their daily cooking (they don't eat much beef), they buy in their own neighborhoods. Laundrymen come in for laundry tickets and paper shirtbands; restaurant men for fortune cookies. No restaurant man ever attempts to get advance information out of a fortune cookie.

Sunday is the Chinese physician's busiest day (and the Chinese lawyer's, as well), because it is the only day a great many patients (or clients) can come in. There are ten Chinese physicians in and around Chinatown and their Chinese patients are remarkably faithful because the doctors not only know their business but also speak Chinese and understand their patients' personal problems much better, on the whole, than other doctors might. There are still plenty of Chinese who go in for their own kind of homeopathic medicine. At Lee Toy Kin's Quong Yuen Shing on Mott Street, a Chinese in the mood for it can purchase *ki she,*

Mulberry Street; the San Gennaro Festival. At this time, the Trinity is celebrated in sausage, calzone, *and* zeppoli.

a pale, mottled, venomous snake, which, dead and dried, is supposed to be great for rheumatism; or deer horn (in sliced sheets), at $40 to $125 for eight ounces, and dried sea horse at $200 a pound, both of which are fine for the blood. Rhinoceros horn, at $25 an ounce, will reduce boils. Another specific for rheumatism is *nam she tam,* the gall of a boa constrictor. High-quality sandalwood, a specific for asthma, retails at $80 a pound.

The younger generation goes to James Chu's Chinatown pharmacy, which is almost at the heart of Chinatown's Times Square (Mott and Pell streets), and does a big aspirin and prescription business, leaving the boa-constrictor gall and *ki she* trade to others. Chu also maintains a sort of neighborhood bulletin board in the front of the store, on which may be found such arcane notices as, "This note is on *blue* paper because the latest additions to the Chinese population are all HE BABIES to the following happy parents: Goldie and Freddie Chu; Marion and Douglas Ong; Alice and Jip Foo Chun."

Sundays in February and March, a lot of celebrating goes on in Chinatown and the newspapers never fail to write nauseatingly "cute" stories about the Chinese New Year and its, to them, outlandish name. At that time of the year, each of the associations holds a banquet and, on boards in association headquarters, strips of red paper, with black letters on them, may be seen. Each strip indicates the amount contributed to the funds of the association to keep it running. The strips are known as *heung you* or sweet oil, the oil part symbolic of the oil needed to keep the lamps of China burning and the sweet part signifying that it is always sweet to get money.

ALFRED H. BARR, JR.
Director of Collections, the Museum of Modern Art

The Museum of Modern Art was established in a paradoxical situation. New York prided itself on being the capital of modernity in this country, as well as the biggest and wealthiest city. This city, or, I should say, Manhattan, should have been a leader in the public patronage and presentation of modern art and yet it was well behind several others – Chicago, Buffalo, and Worcester – and, oddly enough, Brooklyn, a community reputedly more conservative than Manhattan.

The paradox was particularly surprising because the need for an adequate museum of modern art in New York was so obvious and so strong. We can look back to isolated events such as the Armory Show of 1913 and even earlier to the exhibitions presented by Alfred Stieglitz with the help of Edward Steichen, who sent Matisse and Picasso shows from Paris to the gallery at 291 Fifth Avenue. Katharine Dreier and Marcel Duchamp were given generous space in the Brooklyn Museum for their great Société Anonyme exhibition of 1927, a truly international avant-garde show. The Whitney Studio Club was active on behalf of non-academic New York painters. There was also Albert Gallatin's Paris-focused Gallery of Living Art. However, none of these brave but limited efforts had the resources or the program for an institution adequate to the needs of the richest city in the world.

One might have thought that the Metropolitan Museum would have followed the examples of Chicago or Brooklyn, but no, as the 1920s passed the Metropolitan manned its conservative bastions intrepidly. Its few curators interested in modern art were frustrated, and advanced collectors like Arthur B. Davies, Adolf Lewisohn, Lillie P. Bliss and, greatest of all, John Quinn, were not encouraged.

Thus, when the Modern Museum got under way in 1929, there was not a single canvas by Van Gogh or Seurat or Gauguin in the Metropolitan even though they'd been dead for thirty or forty years. This is not to mention Matisse or Picasso, and not even to think of Miró and Klee, both of whom had already produced some of their best work. There was only one Cézanne. There *were* three Matisse drawings and a mild Van Gogh water color, but they were usually hidden away in boxes.

New Yorkers older than I might be able to explain precisely why there was so little institutional concern with collecting and exhibiting works of art of our own time or, for that matter, of our fathers' and grandfathers' time. Looking back, it seems to me that the founders of the Museum of Modern Art were of the same general social and financial class as the trustees of the Metropolitan, but collectively their tastes were a full generation more advanced. One feels they even had a certain reluctance to start a new institution, but concluded there was no other way. Today we have not merely the Museum of Modern Art, but two others in Manhattan, the Whitney and the Guggenheim, all very much concerned with contemporary art, not to mention the Metropolitan itself, which now buys first-rate American paintings hot off the griddle.

There has been another remarkable change in the New York art world. Thirty-two years ago, New York artists were generally thought of as being overshadowed by the great Parisians. But, over the past dozen years, for the first time in history an American school of painting has taken the lead and has had a very considerable influence on painting throughout the non-Communist world. Granted that the New York School – specifically, the Abstract Expressionists and the painters sympathetically related to them – has had many men of enormous energy and talent. Nevertheless, it seems doubtful that they could have gone so far had it not been for the dozen or so painters who found refuge in New York during the Second World War. I am thinking especially of Mondrian, Duchamp, Matta, Masson, and Max Ernst, also the poet Breton, and the returned expatriate, Peggy Guggenheim, who, as a patron, did so much to foster the New York School in its infancy. The talent was there; the question was how to set fire to it and keep the fire burning. After the war, most of the Europeans and Peggy Guggenheim went back to Europe. But the fire was well kindled and there were a few dealers, critics, collectors, and museum people who, by 1950, were deeply involved.

Surprisingly enough, the two most powerful New York newspapers, the *Herald Tribune* and the *Times,* not only fought a losing critical battle against abstract expressionism but their editors, critics, and even their news columns have ignored to an extraordinary degree the international triumph of the school. Yet its success has been so great that it has tended to go to the heads of some of the artists and their supporters. Here and there one finds an almost chauvinistic insistence on the importance of the New York School. All the same, though, it *is* a highly novel and enjoyable situation in which one can worry even a little bit about excessive

Museum of Modern Art; Sculpture Garden.
The cooling winds of Fifty-fourth Street blow
only to soothe the fevers of the middlebrow.

Lower Broadway; a sculptor in his loft-studio-
home. Art may be sold on upper Madison
Avenue, but it is way downtown that it is
created, or, sometimes, forged.

enthusiasm over the virtues and international fame of a group of American artists. This is not to disparage the prestige of a number of individuals of the past, but none of them, from Benjamin West through Whistler, Feininger, Man Ray and our unique star of the Thirties, Sandy Calder, had the impact abroad which the phalanx of Abstract Expressionists and their colleagues have had in the last dozen years. And, thanks in part to their victory, it should be noted that the new generation, some of them in conscious reaction against their elders, are making their mark in Europe too.

There is a negative factor in the growth of the Museum of Modern Art that should be mentioned. The museum assumed whatever position it had at first almost by default and its almost embarrassing power and prestige in certain areas today is the result of a slow growth over better than three decades. I cannot over-emphasize the fact that the museum does not want to influence the course of painting and sculpture in this country or elsewhere, though at times it has attempted to do so in the arts of design. The public may think the museum influences art, but it simply follows as closely as it can what artists are doing. This would seem obvious, but to a great many it is not. They think we invented whatever kind of modern art they dislike. The truth is that, for the most part, we do like it; we believe in it; we think it's worth exhibiting and buying – but we do not make painting or sculpture or tell artists how or when or what.

I would like to insist that, as a matter of formal, conscious policy, we take very long chances in what we buy and show and we know we often make mistakes – not in terms of money, but in terms of quality and significance. The museum shows or buys something because it thinks it's good. Because we are an institution, the public is likely to feel that we know, in the absolute sense, what we are doing. This is not true. We have to feel our way through a very tricky minefield and we make many missteps. If some collectors and weak artists follow what they think is our lead, we cannot help it. Fortunately, we are convinced that there are enough strong and original artists and enough collectors of character and independence whose convictions we cannot affect. In them lies the vigor, the glory of the relation between the producer of art and the consumer.

WITNESS

RALPH WATKINS
Owner of Basin Street East and The Embers, night clubs

All the clubs I've had – Kelly's Stables, the Royal Roost, Bop City, Basin Street on the West Side, The Embers, and Basin Street East – were white elephants when I took them over. The Embers had fifteen operators prior to my getting in there. I don't say I made good with all the clubs. The move to Bop City from the Roost was a fatal one. I imagine it may have been greed on my part. I've got to be egotistical now, but in the café business, you separate the men from the boys. It's a sort of challenge to a café owner to be able to capture an out-of-town audience and also keep New Yorkers. Building a club is like building a skyscraper. You have to put in a good foundation first. That's why, I'd say, ninety of a hundred restaurants and cafés that open close. The survivors are very few.

I'd had my own band and then been in the theater-ticket business when I opened my first club – Kelly's – in 1939. I had a lot to learn. My first dealings were with, well, you know, people who were a little sharper than I was. I bought fifty per cent of the club not knowing the place was bankrupt, actually in the hands of the marshal. It lasted six months at the first location. We had a pretty good marshal – he got us loans to buy whisky. Then we reopened on Fifty-second Street. My God, the music. One band we put together included Bud Freeman, Eddie Condon, Artie Schutt, Pee Wee Russell, Brad Gowans, Maxie Kaminsky, Davie Tough, and Morty Stuhlbaker. Well, when Bop City closed down – I'd had three years of the war in the meantime and run the Roost, which was under the Latin Quarter – I decided to try the East Side of town and that was The Embers. The kind of music I was presenting on the West Side brought in quite a lot of East Side customers, only it had never been played on the East Side and I thought if I could combine good food and wonderful music it might go.

We opened with Joe Bushkin, Art Tatum, and Joe Mooney. Opening night, my wife came down to the kitchen and said, "The place is packed; I think it's going to be a success." I told her, "Better wait until I go upstairs and I'll let you know."

A Bowery saloon. On the Bowery, a man has, at last, arrived at his irreducible minimum.

I walked up, took a look at the audience, and the people were mostly strangers and then I knew it would be a success. Basin Street East I call the House that Benny Built. Benny Goodman. And Peggy – Peggy Lee – is the girl that kept it alive. Let me put it this way. You see a fighter in the ring and he feints an opponent but he doesn't let go with his right hand the first time. Well, everything up to Benny at Basin Street East was feinting. He came in November, 1959. Didn't want to play clubs any more, but I got him to do it. That night, people all stood up and cheered and I breathed a sigh of relief. I realized I had found the pattern to operate a big East Side club after a lot of feinting.

It's a terrible thing to say, I guess, but I don't like night clubs. Oh, I'll go occasionally when there's some talent in one I can enjoy. (That'll bail me out, I hope, with a lot of operators.) As a rule, the café man never has a chance to relax in his own place of business, but I do. I find my own two places the kind I like to go into to relax and you'll always find me hiding away in some corner of one of them. Take The Embers. It's a place where you can talk quietly and appreciate the music at the same time and where the food and service are wonderful. Sure, I'm boasting, but when I walk in there, I get the feeling of a customer. I hit it during the dinner hour, then I go back over to Basin Street – the feeling is the same there for me, only it's bigger – and then drop back around two A.M. and relax. I *act* like a customer. I'm enjoying the entertainment and the music I've bought for the other customers.

"GOOD NIGHT, BOOKS" CHAPTER 7

Until she died or became incapacitated or found what she was looking for, a small, elderly lady – it is the opinion of Dr. Gerald McDonald, the chief of the American History and Genealogy Division, that she was evidently a lady – visited the Local History and Genealogy Room (315G) of the Fifth Avenue Library several times a week for several years, very likely to retrace the begats of her family.

She was birdlike – bright-eyed and quick, cocking her head to one side at times, and capable of sitting quite still for long periods, like a sparrow on a telegraph wire. The only thing noteworthy about her was that when she left it was her habit to pause at the open stacks, decide what her favorite books had been that day, pat their spines and chirrup – it sounded so to Dr. McDonald, an anti-romantic – "Good night. Good night, books."

The main building of the New York Public Library, the marble Renaissance palace created by Carrère and Hastings (it is two blocks long, and, for a while, it

The New York Public Library; outside the main reading room. It is unquestionably the most versatile library in the world.

185

was the largest building of marble ever put up), was opened on May 23, 1911. President Taft, who came up from Washington, clearly felt the occasion warranted capitalizing rather than mere apostrophizing. "This day," he declared, "crowns a work of National Importance." Dr. McDonald's evanesced gentlewoman (materialized out of who knows what infinitely genteel order of brownstone, Tiffany glass, dark, polished armoires, and modest vinaigrettes – Murray Hill? Back Bay? Rittenhouse Square?) was, in her mildly eccentric, bluestocking way, symbolic of at least three characteristics of the library.

These are the unconstrained affection in which it is held by its users (very few of whom talk to books, but a good many of whom write them, and, more often than not, acknowledge the library's inestimable help in doing so); the liking the library has for its readers, in return; and the library's "little bit of a non-conformist" policy – the description is that of Harald Ostvold, who runs the entire Reference Department – of making "our services and collections available to almost all classes of people," something that is not usual in the most formidable of libraries elsewhere.

In fact, the library once said unequivocally of itself, in a voice surprisingly loud and clear for an institution accustomed to speaking in whispers, that it is "used by more persons for more purposes than any other library in the world"; it has not been contradicted.

Any day of the year – there is none on which at least the great Main Reading Room is not open – some 8300 people are likely to visit the library. It is estimated that an average of 700 questions a day are fired at the three librarians at telephones behind the information desk, a hollow square manned by a thin red line of twenty-one men and women. How many are asked of the valiant remainder who struggle under a saturation barrage at point-blank range (only the width of a counter separates asker from answerer), not even Archibald DeWeese, the Information Division's chief for eighteen years, is prepared to speculate. Six thousand or so letters a year, no less importunate in their demands for information, also reach his division.

The library's reference resources are so vast that the barest statistical cataloguing is staggering to contemplate:

Eighty miles of bookshelves on seven levels, exclusive of the reading rooms; 4,100,000 books (the first Gutenberg Bible to be brought to this country *and* Grace Metalious' *Return to Peyton Place*); 9,000,000 manuscript letters and documents; above 4,000,000 pictures; 3,000,000 broadsides, posters, photographs, and slides; more than 5,000,000 of what the library calls "ephemera" – permanent research files of clippings, pamphlets, pictures, maps, and so on; millions of other maps, of music scores, phonograph records, film and microfilm reels, fine prints, globes; Braille and recorded books, periodicals and music for the blind.

In all, it has a total of something like 28,000,000 items – and this does not include almost 3,000,000 books in the library's eighty-one branches in Manhattan, the Bronx, and Staten Island; Brooklyn and Queens have their own library systems. (Contrary to popular belief, the library is run on private money – endowment funds and contributions; the city pays only the operating costs of the branches and the circulation department of the Fifth Avenue Library plus part of that building's maintenance costs.)

The most important criterion governing the library's selection (or rejection) of material is: will it be as valuable for research and information in fifty years as it is today?

Toward that end, division chiefs and specialists regularly go over a thousand bibliographical aids – from book reviews to publishers' lists – obtained from every corner of the planet, and their selections are made on the basis of each chief's (and his specialists') judgment. When broader questions of policy come up – the addition, for example, of large bodies of material offered to the library, or of fringe or new subjects – they are decided by a Book Selection Committee, a group of division chiefs that meets monthly.

When items come into the library, they are examined once more. If it is then decided, on second thought, that they do not meet the criterion, they are used for exchange with other libraries. The library thus adds up to 100,000 books a year and hundred of thousands of other specimens. It never throws anything away.

The combinations and permutations of the human mind are intricated to infinity, but no sooner do they arise than the library takes note of them; acquires the evidence when it can, which despite a sore lack of money, is most of the time; catalogues them (the number of cards in the Main Reading Room is well over 7,000,000); and serves them forth with an air so lacking in triumph as to appear almost disingenuous, and a celerity that gives the effect of a conjuring trick. There are signs posted at the book desks that read, "If you do not receive your book within fifteen minutes, please notify the window attendant"; the average time is, however, less than ten minutes.

"This is an archival library," Ostvold once told a visitor. "We attempt to preserve everything forever." The thought made him smile faintly. "Oh, it's an ideal we can't hope to live up to," he went on, "but we do attempt to approximate it. And we're constantly testing our own premises.

"We can test them, first of all, by the use made of the library by scholars doing fundamental research. Secondly, we can test them by the use made of the materials – both materials from different parts of the world and from different periods of time – that aren't available anywhere else. It seems," he finished, spacing out each word cautiously, "the premises stand up. If the library didn't match up, we would know."

The testing of the library's premises is carried on unremittingly, year in and year out, in millions and millions of challenges from people representing every occupation and preoccupation known to man; for reasons that are sometimes frivolous; and with results that are often breathtaking, or, now and then, crucial to the welfare of the nation. (The number of people who visit the library merely to read, kill time, or settle odd bets is, in the opinion of the staff, no more than a tiny percentage of the daily 8300. With the exception of reference books on the open shelves, everything must be asked for – in writing – and waited for; and the supposition is that anyone who will request something in writing and hang around to look at it is not fooling.)

During the war, for example, a Japanese navy code was broken, for all practical purposes, in the library. Military intelligence had got as far as determining that the code was based on a Mexico City directory of a certain year. In all the non-Axis world – not excluding Mexico – only one copy of the directory was found – in the library, whose collection of city directories and telephone books is unequaled.

Allied fliers and ground soldiers learned an incalculable amount of what lay ahead of them in invasions – from topography to food to the state of mind of the inhabitants – from the library; primary materials were provided by it from which government chemists worked out dehydration procedures that saved fifty to ninety per cent of cargo-bottom space. Nor was the library overlooked in those secret years when the atom bomb was built, although to this day it has no idea how much it contributed.

Use is piled upon use. Three years were spent in the library by Eliezer Ben Yehuda in the course of putting together his definitive, sixteen-volume Hebrew dictionary. (The library caught him out in an error: in Volume 10, there is reproduced a letter from Ben Yehuda to another scholar, headed "Room 122, The New York Public Library, March 14, 1918." Ben Yehuda, who obviously had his mind on more important things, meant Room 221 in the Jewish collection. For the moment, he had forgotten that English, unlike Hebrew, is read from left to right.)

Another ardent patron of the collection was a man who had been interrupted in his daily reading of a historical serial by Saul Saphire, a popular Jewish writer, that had been published in one of the New York Yiddish newspapers. The man had been in alimony jail where, for some reason, he was unable to get his paper.

Some years ago, a husband-and-wife writing team sued a publisher, a book club, and a novelist, claiming a novel run up by the latter and distributed by the first two was a flagrant plagiarism of an earlier work of the couple. The pair said they had drawn on the library for many nineteenth-century government documents, original manuscripts, and so on. The defendant said he had used the same sources. The court took a long look at them, whereupon publisher, book club, and novelist settled out of court. It was obvious that the plaintiffs had been to the library and that the defendants had been only to the plaintiffs.

A few days after the last election, the New York *Times* called the library to identify a book President-elect Kennedy was holding in a photograph. Only the title showed. Information determined quickly that it was a pre-publication copy of Richard E. Neustadt's *Presidential Power*.

The research division of one of the largest meat-packing companies in the world wrote to the library that, having consulted all immediate sources, including the rare chemicals division of the Illinois Institute of Technology, it had been unable to find the chemical name of something it called "Roses of Lime." The company added that in the course of checking with other libraries it had "caused a great deal of interest on their part and at this point they all would like to know exactly what this Roses of Lime is."

The library racked its brain (it is in a position to do so in roughly 3000 languages, including up to 600 African dialects) and then wrote back, as tactfully as it could, that what he meat-packing people probably had in mind was Rose's Lime Juice.

Karl Kup's Prints Division was once greatly enlivened by a man who came in asking to see a baldachin. A baldachin is a sort of canopy supported by poles and much used in medieval times by the high and mighty and the clergy. Kup turned up just the thing for his visitor – the figure of an empress of the Holy Roman Empire under a baldachin, from an illustrated chronicle.

Some months later he received two tickets to the circus and went. "There was my baldachin," he said recently, with a good deal of cultivated enthusiasm. "It was above, I must say, a rather more scantily dressed lady riding on an elephant."

In Local History, a lawyer representing a builder found something he had been unable to find anywhere else: his client had put up a building near Lenox Avenue and 135th Street and then discovered it was being undermined by a spring. It was located in *Springs and Wells of Manhattan and the Bronx,* by James R. Smith, and ultimately sealed off.

These are accretions of years. But even on a single day in the library they could very nearly be duplicated. On one such day, the consul general of New Zealand was being shown about the place by Ostvold when the two men ran into Marchette Chute, the historical novelist, in the Main Reading Room. "I hope you realize," said Miss Chute, who has turned out more than one fine book in the library, "you are in the most fascinating and the most wonderful institution in the country."

The two men moved on and Ostvold said diffidently, "I know exactly what she meant. She's busy on another book."

In American History (Room 315A, Seat 828), a little, bald, bright-eyed man of fifty-five named William Frick, of Wallington, New Jersey, who works for a

Manhattan textile converter, was in his eleventh year of tracking down the burial places of all Civil War infantrymen, cavalrymen, and artillerymen from New Jersey, or most of the 60,000 Jersey men who fought in that war. He has located 11,000 and visited graves as far as Florida.

"I might as well be plain with you," Frick said, "I'm a nut." He laughed—decorously, as befitted his surroundings. "No, I'm not," he went on. "It's in the family." Frick said he had a grandfather, William Winter, who had been a corporal with Company F of the 131st New York Volunteers in the Civil War (he died in 1937) and who was wont to take him, as a boy, to decorate the graves of comrades.

"I don't know if I'll ever get finished," Frick said. "It's a gamble, but I'll have a nice record, finished or not."

In Seat 63 of the Main Reading Room (North Hall), Sister Mary Celeste of the Sisters of St. Joseph, Ogdensburg, New York, was working on a doctorate having to do, she said, with "general epic problems," and she was currently going through *A Catalogue of the Very Valuable and Extensive Library of the Late William Hayley, Esq.* Hayley was a poet and the author of an extensive essay on epic poetry.

In the Theater Collection (315 T), Curator George Freedley welcomed (by appointment) the Countess Bernadotte of Stockholm. She was looking for photographs of Eugene O'Neill for a biography (not written by her) of the playwright to be published in Sweden. She had been recommended to the library by, of all people, the proprietors of a Swedish glassware shop on Madison Avenue.

At the same time, in 315 T's Seat 335, Joseph P. Hudyma of Detroit, a retired cinematographer, was looking for material on the Russian motion picture director, Dovzhenko. Hudyma, it seems, had worked as a second cameraman under Dovzhenko in the Twenties (it was the time of the New Economic Policy, when the Soviets welcomed foreigners), had revisited the Soviet Union as a tourist last year, and had been asked for help here by two writers working on a biography of Dovzhenko.

A floor below, in Economics and Sociology (Room 228, Seat 42), an attractive red-haired actress named Anne Russell, who makes mostly television commercials (coffee, ginger ale, and cough drops, among others), was going through McKittrick's Agency List, a directory of advertising agencies. "I'm looking for *anyone* who might have a finger in casting," she said. "My agent should be doing it for me, I suppose," she added, "but—oh, well . . ."

In Seat 55, Miss Miriam Glickman, a retired teacher who once taught commercial subjects in a Philadelphia high school, set for herself (as she had been doing several days a week for a couple of years) problems in accounting as difficult as she could think up. "There's some psychological income," she insisted, "in doing tough problems and getting answers. I'm not terribly domestic. I had to give up tennis, golf, and swimming." Her voice trailed. "I never have a dull moment," she concluded. "I assure you."

Down the hall, in the Slavonic Collection (Room 216, no seat numbers), Igor Rubach, a clerk for an auctioneer of rare stamps, was reading—with every proof of sentimental satisfaction—*The Fifty Year Jubilee of the Law School in Petersburg; 1885.* "I have a law degree from that school," he said. He had left Russia in 1920, left Yugoslavia when communism arrived there, and made his way to this country eight years ago via Austria and Germany.

Across the hall, in Oriental (Room 219, no seat numbers), Professor Franz Rosenthal, the great authority on Semitic languages and author of *Ibn Khaldun The Muqaddimah,* was getting up a paper on "The Tale of Anthony the Hermit," a ninth-century Arabic work, to be presented at a meeting of the American Oriental Society.

Upstairs, in Manuscripts (Room 319, no seat numbers), Albert Fein, a young instructor in history at Long Island University, was inching ahead on a doctorate on Central Park. At the moment, he said, he was looking over the Bryant-Godwin letters. Parks Godwin was a co-editor of the New York *Evening Post* with his father-in-law, William Cullen Bryant. "Bryant is reputed to be one of the first to have advocated the park," Fein noted. "Indications are," he said, tapping the faded letters and betraying a certain scholarly elation, "his role has been considerably overplayed."

Two floors down, in Music (Room 84, Seat 33), Benjamin Feinbloom, the pit-band 'cellist for the musical comedy, *Wildcat,* was meticulously copying several bars from the score of Berlioz' "Damnation of Faust." Feinbloom collects stamps — musical stamps, stamps of composers and of famous instrumentalists who have played their works, and the like. He affixes each to a page, prints the music beneath that and a brief history of the composer as well. He said he had won prizes at stamp exhibitions for his hobby.

In the Dance Collection, separated from Feinbloom by a glass partition, sat Paul Frost, twenty-two (Seat 51), a graduate of the University of North Dakota and of military service. He was reading Doris Humphrey's *The Art of Making Dances*. "A girl I know," he said with some shyness, "goes to the University of Utah. She's studying dance and she said if I wanted to understand her, I should read this book."

Charles Bracelen Flood, a thirty-one-year-old novelist (*Tell Me, Stranger,* among others), emerged from the Frederick Lewis Allen Room, tucked away in the south wing on the main floor, late in the afternoon. The room was set up as a memorial to Allen. It accommodates a dozen or so writers in individual cubicles. Each gets a key to the room and the door is kept locked to outsiders.

Flood is a heavy-set man. He looked tired. He said he had been working in the room on a novel with a Revolutionary War background for a year and a half and was about done.

"I have a strong, strong sense of security here," he said. "This is my office, my place of work. And the exchange of ideas! No phony intellectualism of the kind you get at cocktail parties, but the real article. Why, here I was working on the Revolution and who was on one side of me? – James Flexner – and who was on the other? – Broadus Mitchell. Mitchell was doing Alexander Hamilton; Flexner was writing a history of American painting. They helped me greatly."

Two floors above, Karl Kup put on his coat and got ready to leave his domain – Art and Architecture and Prints – for the day. "What thrills me time and again," he said on the way down the marble stairs, "is –" and abruptly changed direction. "The satisfaction," he then went on, "does not come from the appreciation of the trustees – they take you on faith; it does not come from your friends – they, for polite reasons, praise you too much. The satisfaction comes from the use of the material by the scholar."

He said good night to the attendant at the Fifth Avenue door and marched sedately down the steps. "When I have answered a question satisfactorily," he said to the man who had walked out with him, "it's like having made a sale, and I sometimes even ring up the register. 'We have given you,' I may say, '$1600 worth of information,' and the response is usually a lovely smile." He smiled a librarian's smile and went on his way.

WITNESS

JAMES E. GAHAGAN, JR.
An Abstract Expressionist painter.

I know artists all over the country and they make a habit of using my studio as a sort of way station. We got into a discussion one night that didn't end until six the next morning and the things we argued about were: What is New York? What is a cultural center? What should an artist's relation to the city be? Is it necessary for him to be here? Their point of view was almost totally negative and I had no choice but to present to them the possibility that they were suffering from a second-city complex. It was very difficult for me to verbalize what the purpose of New York City was as a cultural center to an artist, one reason being that I just took it for granted they would acknowledge it. Eighty-five per cent of the artists in the nation are located in and around New York; it's the exhibition house of the United States.

The virtue of New York, especially for a painter or sculptor, is that he has immediate and direct communication with other working artists – in the broadest sense; people in the theater, writers, dancers, composers. There is an opportunity to respond to a constant flow of production in the arts, to accept or reject; new ideas, new views of old ideas. That just does not exist anywhere else in the country. On a purely practical level, one of the factors that makes New York so ideal for artists is that there has always been a tremendous availability of part-time work. A young artist can work at any number of things, support himself at least minimally, and still have ample time to paint.

It's difficult for me to feel hostile toward what at times is New York's grand callousness toward the individual when I realize that my continuing as an artist is so directly fed by the rich crumbs swept off this opulent city's table. At the same time, the breadth of individual freedom is fantastic – for the very reason non-New Yorkers criticize the city: the seeming unconcern one resident has for another. Your life is your own; other people do not want the responsibility for it. Your survival depends on your willingness to deal successfully with your personal problems. Yet, whenever an individual artist has had economic difficulties or become ill, his colleagues, for the most part, have helped him. It is on this kind of intimate sympathy and co-operation – given when it was needed absolutely – that many of us have survived. In the end, if you have faced up to it, what New York does is make you feel capable of lasting anywhere under any circumstances. You have already faced up to the highest competition in your profession. You have been forced to search yourself out. You have managed to get along economically. You have become the equal of the city and hence of any place in the world.

Visitors at the United Nations.
All are welcome, nay, sought after.

Greenwich Village; walkers on Greenwich Avenue near
Tenth Street. A woman is just a woman, but a good
cigar is a smoke.

Fire alarm box on the Lower East Side. The warning in Spanish against turning in false alarms is one of the gracious ways in which the city recognizes the existence of a large part of the population.

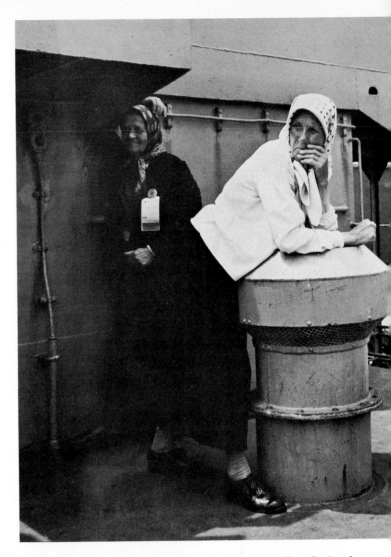

Immigration today; displaced persons arriving aboard a military transport. Even the natives are sometimes overwhelmed by the sheer bulk of their city.

East Houston Street on a Sunday. There are boccie courts, too, Katz's Delicatessen, and Yonah Shimmel's knishery.

JOHN I. ORTIZ, JR.

President of the Puerto Rican Journalists and Writers Association of New York City

For Puerto Ricans coming from the island, New York is a territory of hope. They know that in New York, if they persevere, if they work, if they go to school, if they are willing to toil and study, there are opportunities. The vast majority here suffer from everything it is possible for a minority group to suffer from, but suffering for Puerto Ricans is nothing new. Most who come here are, at the moment, clearly not people with a good education, because a well-educated person could do at least as well in Puerto Rico. No, they come here for work, because they cannot find jobs on the island. Most of them are twenty or over, with large families, and because they have to support those families, they have to work long hours at lousy jobs, at bad pay, and under the worst conditions. So that it is no wonder when they go home at night they don't feel like going to night school and learning English or a trade. On the other hand, the children of our families are being educated here a little better than their parents were and their future will be far brighter. These parents sacrifice their lives to send their children to school. That's where the change is going to come.

Let's talk about discrimination. To begin with, I don't have to tell you that the Puerto Rican constitutes an important part of the working class in New York – and the majority are in the lowest-paying jobs. You'd have no garment center, no restaurants, no light industry, no hospitals without them. Very well. They suffer from racketeering unions and from non-union shops. What good, may I ask, does it do for a Puerto Rican to pay $3.50 a month in dues to a union, to get $1.25 an hour when the federal government guarantees $1.25 in any business that's in interstate commerce? What about unions that make it difficult or impossible for a Puerto Rican to join? Furthermore, the benefits in some unions are only on paper.

Let's talk about police brutality. You see a cop beating a person – but how can you prove a cop beat up somebody? The policeman has booked him for assaulting a cop. He had to use force, he says, to subdue the man. Right? Puerto Ricans should account for a tenth of the crimes in New York, since they constitute a tenth of the population, but they do not. They have yet to form a Murder, Inc. They have very few numbers operators among them. Relations between the Puerto Ricans and the police have improved in recent years. A better, more favorable attitude on the part of the police commissioner; human relations courses which are given at the Police Academy. There is, of course, still plenty of room for improvement and responsible Puerto Rican civic and social groups are working with the Police Department to interpret the true role of the police among the Spanish-speaking people.

Let's talk about the Puerto Rican who can afford it and who is willing to pay for a good apartment. The owner says, "I just rented it to somebody else." What can he do? He can't prove it. How can you prove either that someone didn't give you a job because you're a Puerto Rican? There isn't any way. With what they do have to live in, Puerto Ricans do the best they can. We get tired of asking landlords to paint the premises. We paint ourselves; we kill the rats ourselves; we fix the windows ourselves. *And* we still pay the highest rents in the city of New York while earning the lowest wages.

Part of the discrimination comes from the newspapers. I don't know how many times it has to be repeated that crimes are committed by *people* and not by races or ethnic groups. I get mad and tired of seeing crime stories involving Negroes or Puerto Ricans that mention on purpose that they are Negroes, or, if they are Puerto Ricans, when they came up from the island and why – to get on relief, naturally. When a non-Puerto Rican commits a crime, the same newspaper doesn't bother to mention where he came from or whether he was born here. In the South, at least, the discrimination is open; they're honest about it; people know what to expect. Puerto Ricans aren't used to suffering from color discrimination on the island. When they come to New York, it's like coming to a reality they never dreamed could exist.

But even with all that, New York is a city of hope. I've figured this thing out well. There are over 300 Puerto Rican organizations – social, civic, home-town, sports – in this city now. They are healthy and active. We have about 160,000 kids in school. They'll be out and doing well within the next ten years. The papa'll retire; the mama'll retire. The children will know the language; they'll be integrated and not exclusively low-paid factory workers. From this 160,000, we're going to get some lawyers, some political leaders, some professional men. Then the children of that 160,000 will get out of school, and, by 1990 to 2000, there isn't going to be a so-called Puerto Rican problem in this city any more.

WITNESS

GEORGE DOWNS
A Negro businessman

As a child growing up in New York, I saw prejudice, naturally, but having grown up in a mixed neighborhood – Crown Heights, in Brooklyn; I was born in Smithtown, Long Island, and brought to the city as a kid – I wasn't very conscious of it. I had two experiences before I was eighteen, though, that I'll never forget. I went into a Chinese restaurant in Manhattan one day and the man at the door said, "No colored." *No colored!* In a Chinese restaurant. *That surprised me.* I'm putting it mildly. I didn't hear the word "nigger" used to me until I was sixteen. I was in Lincoln Terrace Park on the flying rings and there was this guy wanted to use them – all the others were taken – and he started shoving me. I didn't pay any attention at first. Then, he said, "Get off there, you goddamn nigger." I damn near killed him. I was furious at two things: one, I didn't like the guy, and two, I didn't like being called *anything,* let alone that.

My neighborhood being what it was, by the time I got home my grandfather had heard about it. He said, "You been fighting again. What happened?" I told him. He said, "Well, if you're going to be a nigger, be a good one. No matter what a man calls you, it's what you are and what you represent as a man that counts." His reasoning was that with dignity a man could walk anywhere, he could do anything and be respected. He felt it was the finest quality a man could

Housing development, Third Avenue and 101st Street. Between them, this is what the do-gooders and the developers thought up for people to live in.

have, where he walked as tall as if he were on stilts. Now I don't think it's important that being a "nigger" was brought home to me, but I think it *is* important what a Negro does with that consciousness, what a man from any minority does with being part of that minority. The idea is not to let it throw him. Other people will try to trip you with it; it's like a cop throwing a club between your legs – you've got to learn not to get your legs tangled in that club.

There have been marked changes in New York. Take the cop. When he stopped a Negro, his attitude was different than it was toward a white man. You were, first, a Negro, and then it was, "Why'd you do it?" Now it's more a case of just "What happened?" Of course, there are individual cops. There always will be. But policemen today are gentlemen by comparison with what they were when I was a kid forty years ago. I saw a man one day coming up out of the subway. He was white, he was drunk, his head was bleeding, and this cop was pushing him up against the wall. I said, "Don't push that man like that." He told me, "Mind your own goddamn business," and he was about to carry it further when I made a point of looking at his number and that stopped it. Recently I saw a Negro man lying in the street – I don't know whether he was sick or drunk – and, so help me God, I saw this cop leaning over him, saying, "Can I help you, buddy? Come on, get up, buddy." There was this Negro being treated as a human being.

Central Park South. And here are the pieds à l'air *for* les autres.

It's the white man's progression that's more important than the Negro's. Anyone in our world is going to grow in spite of being a part of a minority. How much has the white man grown in the direction of accepting the growth of the man he feels is not his equal? Some. I don't get people in the subway moving away from me any more. I don't hear the word *schwarzer,* the way Jews used to use it. It's seldom now I go into a theater or a movie and sit next to a white woman and she'll see I'm a Negro and move away. I can walk the streets and feel comfortable in any neighborhood. There was a time when walking in a predominantly white neighborhood late at night meant people would look at you strangely or the cops would stop you and ask what you were doing. I don't walk the streets as though I were a burglar any more. If it does happen, I'm not aware of it.

The other day, a white acquaintance of mine said to me, "You know, George,

I *approve* of what Martin Luther King, Jr., did down in Birmingham." I looked at him a good long while and then I said, "It doesn't make any difference whether you approve or you don't. He doesn't care. Approving or disapproving doesn't have anything to do with it any longer. These are the facts of life and as it happens they're highly moral facts." Of all cities in the United States, though, I believe New York is the best as far as Negroes are concerned. New York can only be just so vicious and no more, because every religion and every minority is so active. They've all been down and the biggest thing they're all trying to do is forget it.

A HOMOSEXUAL

The coming of the Mattachine Society into the New York homosexual life has given those who didn't care for cruising the parks or the bars or the baths a place where they could feel at ease with their own kind and, possibly, enable them to meet someone. The society started in Los Angeles in 1950, to further our legal and social rights, and, of course, to disseminate a wider understanding of what we are. The name comes from the Italian *mattacchione,* or jester. Court jesters were generally gay. And now, do you know, after six years in New York, we have just received our incorporation papers? But, Mattachine aside, I get the impression that there is sort of a better existence for homosexuals here than elsewhere. There's a kind of live-and-let-live attitude.

I have lived with a person for twenty years and we're respected in our neighborhood. It's not known that we are homosexuals. Indeed, what's interesting is this: I'm a Christian Scientist. He's not a member, but he accompanies me to church and the proof that people see us as a pair is that they are forever asking, "Will he join?" and saying, "How nice that you have a friend and are not alone." Since I don't drink, I always avoided gay bars and that sort of thing. I would go in parks or along the waterfronts. Where I met my friend was that hilly area between the George Washington Bridge and Dyckman Street. We call it "The Rocks." People would come up there on Sundays and cruise.

The police know all this, but it has always seemed to me that where the belles – the queens – had the worst experiences was not from the police but from rough trade who got to know this was one of our hangouts and came up there to beat them up and roll them. It was isolated and you could sunbathe or cruise on a Sunday and you left in the evening, of course, unless you were simply crazy. The police never bothered you during the day. Riverside Drive has its moments, too, and, yes, the Sailors and Soldiers Monument at Eighty-ninth Street and the Drive. We call it "The Wedding Cake." In fact, I wrote a gay song about it *called* "The Wedding Cake." And then there was Highbridge Park, along the Harlem, which was fine until the murder of a boy up there discouraged things. Homosexuals were not involved in that. They have a swimming pool and behind it was a dirt road and that's actually where I kind of "came out" – that was long before I met my friend.

Seventy-second Street on the West Side is kind of dead since the raids. Broadway in the lower Eighties and Central Park West are still active, and Lexington Avenue and Third in the Fifties. There's the Ramble in the park during the day

The red lighthouse beneath the George Washington Bridge. It is the kind of anachronism children are sapient enough to treasure.

and the Mall, after night concerts. I can remember when Bryant Park and Columbus Circle were something. And, naturally, the Village. There's what we call "The Meat Rack" on the south side of Washington Square. And the gay bars, although I am told there is a figure of something like $3500 you have to pay someone if you want to open a gay bar in the Village. But, do you know, I have seen a great many belles in Yorkville these days. They're certainly not German. It's all the new apartment houses they've put up that are driving them into Yorkville. The Germans can't afford them. You might say urban redevelopment is moving us on.

Another point that's interesting is that what we call drag shows – impersonation shows – have been having a great success in outlying boroughs. One opened in the Bronx and there are others in Ridgewood, in Brooklyn, and in Staten Island. Mariners Harbor, I think. They're local, and they don't have too much flair, but they *do* have *some* of the professionals and semi-professionals who used to work downtown around Second Avenue. Oh, but they're none of them like Francis Renault, whom I knew well. He's dead now. He was the last of the real great ones. I'm afraid he wore that famous feather headdress of his too long.

Riverside Drive at Eighty-ninth Street; the Soldiers and Sailors Monument. To homosexuals, it is known as "The Wedding Cake."

He'd come out in one of those night clubs with a low ceiling and say, "This is what I wore in the Ziegfeld *Follies*," and the ceiling would almost knock it off. He needed the space a stage could give him. Francis used to sing, "You're like flowers from an old bouquet," and toss out little artificial buds. Toward the end – it was really a shame – they were calling him the Florence Foster Jenkins of impersonators.

Another thing we have, which is possibly peculiar to New York. Amateur movies with homosexuals. The story line is always legitimate. Nothing pornographic. The man who makes them goes to quite a lot of expense. We've had, to name a few, *Speakeasy Queen,* a satirical two-reeler about the Roaring Twenties; *Fashions of the Twenties,* gay glimpses of what the girls wore in the Jazz Age, featuring a marvelous collection modeled by male mannequins; and *The Last of the Worthingtons,* which was two years in the making and is our first feature-length film. It was done on location in an old Brooklyn mansion. It's a comedy-drama, with an original piano score, about a vampire in the Gay Nineties. It's just full of laughs and thrills. Gay *pornographic* films are harder to come by. I'm not really interested in them, either.

Greenwich Village; basement of the Eighth Street Bookshop. The feast of reason has ten thousand courses.

THE PRECIOUS
SQUARE

It is noteworthy that nearly all of the few pitifully small and very likely in-conclusive victories won by ordinary citizens in New York after the Second World War over the loose but extremely powerful confederation of *condottiere* that runs the city – the faceless, essentially stateless bankers, landlords, manufacturers, and merchants; their political jackals and policemen; and their mealymouthed academic servants – were won in Greenwich Village. Elsewhere, the record of rapine is close to absolute. An exquisite section of Brooklyn Heights is saved by well-off middlebrows, lately persuaded by homosexual interior decorators of the *ton* of plush, ball fringe, and glazed pottery commodes; a piece of the adjoining Cobble Hill is, at last, recognized to be just as beautiful and it is agreed to retain part of it. The people who fought for the Heights and Cobble Hill are an undoubtedly worthy, earnest lot, but their vision is comically similar to that of Marie Antoinette playing peasant in the Petit Trianon and about as organic. The two areas will continue to exist as afterthoughts – Petit Trianons of a sort – to one side of what is known as the Brooklyn Civic Center. This is a collection of public and private buildings of a mediocrity easily paralleled, a graveyard of the spirit and a fitting agora for the lobbygows who legislated it into being. (They also furnished this necropolis with many new, expensive access highways to the Brooklyn and Manhattan bridges.)

There is an engaging paradox, a delicious irony, in Greenwich Village's tiny triumphs. In a section of New York thought of for half a century as the first refuge of the avant-garde, of dangerous radicals, icon-smashers, and feckless rebels of one description or another (usually against no more than regular em-ployment), the battles were led by individuals of unimpeachable bourgeois re-spectability and fought for the purpose not of changing but of preserving. Thus, the urban renewers and syndicate buzzards were kept out of a few streets near the Hudson River in the West Village, mainly by a determined architectural writer named Jane Jacobs and a mixed bag of intellectuals and humbler residents of the neighborhood. (The twentieth-century predators operate more subtly than, say, Commodore Vanderbilt. When he decreed a freight depot for his railroad, he simply got the complaisant city to condemn St. John's Park, to the south of the Village, and turn over to him whatever right of way he felt he needed for his railroad tracks. These once ran along Eleventh Avenue, which, because so many people were killed by New York Central locomotives, became known as

"Death Avenue." Today, planners make "surveys," invariably based on foregone conclusions; their piety toward the law is great, since the law rarely fails to confirm them.) On Bleecker Street, between Cornelia and Jones, one of the last of the city's outdoor pushcart markets – exactly nine pushcarts were involved – was preserved against the city's feverish desire to get rid of it so that the street could be turned into a through truck route.

If there is any part of the Village in which its history may be summarized, in which all the elements that went into making it what it is today are on display, it is in Washington Square. In the hundred and sixty-five years or so of its recognizable and sometimes precarious existence, the Square, a public park of fewer than nine acres, has served both the contentious quick and the acquiescent dead with a facility possibly unmatched in the history of any comparable number of square yards of earth in New York City. The body of the square – paved, poorly grassed, benched, playgrounded, sand-pitted, monkey-barred, comfort-stationed, fountained, railed and monumented – has been fought over again and again. A group of Villagers spent six exhausting years to have the Square closed to traffic over the terrible trumpetings of Robert Moses, who was then parks commissioner. (He had one of his customary axes to grind for some friends in the real-estate business – the developers of Washington Square Village, an architectural monstrosity thrown up southeast of the Square for luxury housing; they wanted wider roads through the park for their tenants' automobiles.) In the spring of 1961, Moses' otiose successor, Newbold Morris, tried to have the folk singers and guitarists – grave public menaces, destructive of morals and good order – eliminated from the park. He managed only, this bumbler of good family, to provoke a riot in which the police joyously beat dozens of passive and unarmed young people (some of whom had, significantly, beards) and hauled off to the station house, among others, an outraged novelist named Harold Humes who had the impudence to believe that he was defending his constitutional rights and those of the singers and players. After a couple of months of well-bred muttering and his usual ineffectual shilly-shallying, Morris gave in and the amateur performers were restored to their dangerous pastime: amusing themselves and others for all of three hours on a Sunday afternoon.

Once, Washington Square narrowly missed becoming the site of an armory and then of a federal courthouse. Men dueled on it and were hanged on it; they were buried under it by the tens of thousands during the yellow-fever epidemics that swept through New York in the late eighteenth and early nineteenth centuries; they rioted on it and the military that quelled them bivouacked on it. They have lived at its edges variously: in Victorian splendor behind the façades of red brick houses with Greek porticoes; in the middle-class anonymity of huge apartment buildings; in what is known alternatively and patronizingly as "bohemian freedom" or "picturesque squalor." They may still worship there, and they are still educated, housed, and fed there by New York University, which owns or controls better than eighty per cent of the land facing it. (As is evident from its ruthless policy of aggrandizement and its architectural treatment of the south side of the Square, the university preaches one thing in its classes in humanities and architecture and practices others in life.)

Artists informed with love have painted the Square. Musicians have composed

Greenwich Village; sidewalk tables at O. Henry's steak house. The customers work hard at being unself-conscious.

songs about it. ("I'm Rosie, the queen of the models./I used to live up in the Bronx/But I wander'd from there down to Washington Square/And bohemian honky tonks" is the lyric of Ballard MacDonald's and James F. Hanley's "Rose of Washington Square.") Poets have written verses about it. ("This is the end of the town that I love the best," wrote Richard Watson Gilder, the chill, conservative editor of the *Century* magazine.) Authors of the most notably disciplined nature have described it in terms of the frankest passion. (In *Washington Square,* Henry James, who was born on Washington Place, called it "the most delectable portion" of the city; he said also that it had "a riper, richer, more honorable look than any of the upper longitudinal thoroughfares — the look of having something of a social history." There is scarcely a guidebook on the Village that does not reproduce this little passage from James, and, in a way James could hardly have expected, it is still true.)

Union Square; subway kiosks. Year by year, there are fewer of these tiny, foolish, pursed mouths to the tunnels below.

Before Harry K. Thaw pistoled him to death on the roof of his own Madison Square Garden on June 25, 1906, the nation's best-known architect, Stanford White, had left his eclectic imprint on a good deal of the Square in the form of the Washington Arch (north), the Judson Memorial Baptist Church (south), and the Benedick (east), a hotel for bachelors in the past and now the university's Students' Building. (He also put up a wooden predecessor to the arch on the hundredth anniversary of Washington's inauguration; it stood where Washington Mews opens onto Fifth Avenue).

Greenwich Village; coffee-house interior. The life of the mind is often conducted in public.

Geographically, Washington Square is bounded by Waverly Place (named by the fashionable in a fever of admiration for the Waverley novels of Sir Walter Scott and persistently misspelled on all street signs and most maps since), Macdougal, West Fourth, and Wooster streets. Physically, it has undergone a steady, harsh, invariably purposeful attrition. The old, teeming warrens inhabited by artists (in all the arts) and loafers (of every and no philosophical persuasion) are gone. Only the lovely Old Row on the northeast, built for Rhinelanders, Goulds, Delanos, Stewarts, and Wanamakers in the 1830s, and a few like them on the northwest, are intact. But spiritually the Square is, as a man who has sat upon it in good times and bad has said, "the kindest enclave I know, an island of no pressure, a place to pull out for a while."

The fact is that, save for the harassment of the folk singers, there is a curious and pleasurable absence of violence, intellectual or physical, on the Square. It is an entity containing in itself elements of such places and cultures as the Boston Public Garden or Louisburg Square in that city, the Piazza San Marco, the Place des Vosges, and the *zóculo,* or public square, of Oaxaca. Chamber music and jazz have been played in it on stated nights and folk dancing has been done to the strings of a cornball band sponsored by a local bank. Art, all of it eager and most of it bad, is displayed twice a year (usually in June and September), for a month at a time, on its borders. On weekdays, it is dominated, without malevolence, by mothers and their children; by the university students, who use it as a campus; by those who work at night or on their own; by dog-walkers, the old, the unemployed, and the defeated. The mothers come twice daily from Village apartment houses (more of them high-rent than not) and superintend the children gravely at play in the sandpit on the north or the three small playgrounds elsewhere. The loudest noises are the rumble of roller skates, the spring squeak of baby carriages, and the exhausts of the buses.

A Sunday on the Square is an altogether different thing. On that day, the rigid difference of purpose that exists between the east side and the west side of the Square becomes evident. East is for quiet. West is the center of the social life of the Square. That life radiates out from the fountain, fifty feet in diameter (1870: mountain stone, artist unknown), to Macdougal Street, Waverly Place, and Washington Square South. In the basin of the fountain, the folk singers compete with each other and boys playing punch ball until the hot months when the sprays are turned on and the basin becomes the sole province of – it is strictly stipulated – children under twelve. A few of the musicians are professionals, or have made a record or two for some small company; the remainder are – nobody could mistake them for anything else – amateurs. All are, theoretically, required by the Department of Parks to have a permit to belt their guitars, banjos, mandolins, and washtub-broomstick basses. The police are aware that most of them do not have permits, but they now leave art alone – under orders.

The composition of the Square's population on a Sunday is reflective of the changes that have come over the Village. Slowly and inexorably, for example, the parochial Italians of the South Village have been assimilated by the sandals and beards, the toreador pants, the Roman shirts, and the middle class, that part of it, at any rate, which has moved downtown from Riverside Drive and West End Avenue. It is a nice paradox that better than half of those who use the Square on a Sunday come from elsewhere than Greenwich Village. It is impossible to identify them by either speech or dress: respectability has purified and gilded Bohemia; Bohemia has taught respectability not to shave on Sundays. The genuine bohemian lives in a cold-water flat deep in the Lower East Side. His cautious imitator, who buys high-class paperback books and stereo record players, looks and talks like him and lives uptown, in the Bronx or in Brooklyn. If he lives in the Village, it is in, for the most part, a luxury apartment house, and if he is a wealthy Villager, in a nineteenth-century red brick house or brownstone just off Fifth Avenue north of Eighth Street, for which he paid $50,000 and spent $100,000 more refurbishing. The upshot is that, more and more, the people who fled other parts of the city to live in the Village are living next door to the people they wanted to get away from in the first place.

There is no pride of place, however, on the Square itself. The fountain's rim is sat upon by anyone. The tourists gawp, but the indigenes remain tolerant; conversation curls upward like thin smoke. It is not particularly profound, and, while there are coterie silences, so to speak, there are no coterie conversations. Not even the sight of a pudgy young man in a self-conscious four-button suit playing, on an obviously expensive guitar, "Ain't Goin' Down That Mine No More" is provocative of sarcasm. Before sitting on the rim, it is a ritual requirement to take one circuit of the fountain, counterclockwise. Also, a quiet, genteel crane dance goes on for the benches. The chess and checker players on the south seem to have been in their seats for years.

It is this complex of folkways that causes periodic agitations over the Square, particularly over traffic. While there have been roads through the Square from time to time, only one could properly be labeled outrageous – or the first modern one – depending on the point of view of the historian. This was the work of William Marcy (Boss) Tweed, without doubt the most imaginative boodler New York City has ever known. Prior to 1827, there had been cart tracks running north and south and east and west through the Square, but in that year the city closed them off – forever, it thought – and fenced in the area. In April, 1870, however, Tweed got the state legislature to grant a home-rule charter for the city, the purpose of which was to enable him and his associates to operate without undue interference from Albany. He had himself appointed commissioner of public works and then ran a wide street and esplanade through the Square, linking up Fifth Avenue with what is now West Broadway. West Broadway was then known as Laurens Street, for Henry Laurens, a president of the Continental Congress and a negotiator of the peace with the British. Laurens Street was renamed South Fifth Avenue.

Eight years later, Tweed died in the Ludlow Street Jail, while his municipal heirs and assigns were maneuvering to have an armory built on the Square. (On

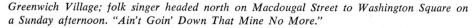

Greenwich Village; folk singer headed north on Macdougal Street to Washington Square on a Sunday afternoon. "Ain't Goin' Down That Mine No More."

its way to Greenwood Cemetery in Brooklyn, Tweed's funeral cortège passed down Fifth Avenue, but turned east at Washington Square, thus austerely denying him the use of the fine, broad road he had constructed for it.) Two men – Samuel Ruggles, an unusually civic-minded real-estate man and contractor, who created Gramercy Park and was instrumental in the laying out of Union Square, Irving Place, and Lexington Avenue, and Thomas Egleston, founder of Columbia University's School of Mines, organizer of the Public Parks Protective Association, and a householder on the Square – were instrumental in blocking the armory. The furor they aroused may be judged from the law passed by the state legislature on June 1, 1878. "The public park . . . known as Washington Square," it read, "shall . . . be used in perpetuity as one of the public parks . . . and for no other use or purpose whatsoever." Seventeen years after that, the reform administration of Mayor William L. Strong changed the name of South Fifth Avenue to West Broadway. A try at putting up a federal courthouse in the park was thwarted in the first decade of this century. The parallel between what Tweed did and what Robert Moses tried to do is obvious. Moses not only wanted Tweed's road bigger and better, he also proposed that West Broadway be renamed Fifth Avenue South. "The developers of the Washington Square Village apartments," he said without apology, "were formally, officially, and reliably promised under

Greenwich Village; the Bizarre, West Third Street near Sullivan. Frissons *for tourists, throw money for poets.*

the Slum Clearance Act a Fifth Avenue address and access for the large new population in multiple dwellings replacing warehouses." (Moses neglected to mention, as well, that the developers had originally promised to put up middle-income housing on the site. As a luxury project, Washington Square Village turned out to be a failure, so much so that the builders, who had planned another large excrescence on a superblock immediately to the south of it, gave up and quietly turned the land over to the university, which will build its own excrescences there.)

Aside from these politico-economic finaglings, the Square was the scene of what may very likely have been the gentlest and gayest of revolutions, staged by half a dozen political innocents, to secure it spiritually. The uprising of the innocents was held on a winter night in 1916 in the hollow, roomy entablature atop the Washington Arch, access to which was gained through a steel door and stairway in the western pillar. (It was one of Stanford White's boasts, characteristically American, that the whole affair was bigger than anything else of its kind. "No arch of antiquity containing but one opening has a span as great as that of New York," he wrote, "the nearest approach to it being the Arch at Aosta, which has a span of about 29 feet 8 inches." White's span is four inches wider.) A young and expansive Texas girl named Gertrude Drick, a pupil of the artist, John Sloan, flown in rhetoric at the Purple Pup near the west side of the Square, took it into her head to proclaim the independence of Greenwich Village and the Republic of Washington Square. (A little earlier, an editor of the old *Life* magazine had hit upon the same idea, tried it – inexplicably – in Central Park and been muted when the police arrived with machine guns.)

Miss Drick recruited Sloan, Marcel Duchamp, whose *Nude Descending a Staircase* had induced a terrible fright in the genteel at the Armory Show in 1913, two actors, and an actress. The six went up the arch fortified with food, wine, Japanese lanterns, candles, colored balloons, cap pistols, the declaration, and an iron bean pot, under which they lighted a fire. Miss Drick, whom a poet had called "The Golden Bird," read the declaration. The food was eaten, the wine drunk; the pistols were fired, the balloons and lanterns hung from the entablature, where they were discovered floating the next morning, hours after the revolutionaries had descended and dispersed. A year later, Sloan immortalized the coup in an etching, *Arch Conspirators*. (Three decades after that, a nameless bum with a reputation for being able to drink a fifth of whisky at a single, short sitting, lived in the entablature for almost seven months. The police got on to him because he fell into the habit of hanging his tattered bits of laundry over the side of the arch.)

Most of the eighteenth and nineteenth centuries is gone from the Square. The most nearly ancient object on it is an elm at the northwest corner, a hundred feet high and roughly a hundred and seventy-five years old. The oldest thing under the Square is Minetta Brook. The brook rises beneath the Flatiron Building, at Twenty-third Street, Broadway, and Fifth Avenue, flows under the Square, and makes its end in the North River. No one has been able to legislate it away, but it has had its uses. When the university dug for the foundations of its law center in 1950 (it destroyed a number of singularly beautiful houses in the process), 15,000 gallons a day of Minetta had to be pumped off. At the time, the city was in the grip of a drought and car washing was prohibited. A truck-rental firm, commendably unwilling to offer dirty machines to fastidious clients, arranged to cart away 6000 to 12,000 gallons daily until the foundations were put in. The brook bubbled up again when test borings were made for the Loeb Student Center late in 1956 (this is a glass shaft of less distinction than the meanest dumbbell flat of the nineteenth century), and the presence of the brook accounts for the circumstance that the swimming pool in Hayden Hall, the law school dormitory on Washington Square West, is nowhere more than five feet deep.

There is still a place in which it is permitted to be seen. Back in 1930, the Knott Hotels people, who started business with the old Holley Hotel on the west side of the Square, put up the adjoining Holley Chambers at the corner of Washington Place. (Both took their name from Alexander Lyman Holley, an engineer who developed the Bessemer steel process in this country; several engineering societies presented a bust of him to the city in 1889 and it was placed in the Square – for no particular reason, which is often the case with gifts of that kind. Holley was born in Connecticut, died in Brooklyn, and never lived on the Square.) At the suggestion of a former guest of the hotel, it was decided to let the brook memorialize itself in a fountain in the lobby. The Greenwich Village Historical Society entered into the affair with great antiquarian enthusiasm. A delicate bronze Pan was commissioned from the sculptor Gutzon Borglum. On December 3, 1930, with the egregious Grover Whalen presiding and Arthur Guiterman reading his own poem, "Minetta Water," written for the occasion, the fountain was dedicated in a broadcast over the seventy-four radio stations of the Columbia Broadcasting System. It remained there until a few years ago, when N.Y.U. tore down the hotel, put up Hayden Hall, and moved the fountain – round-bellied Pan and all – into what is now a small, pine-paneled faculty conference room. It has become the custom of both students and faculty to toss coins into it for luck, into the cast-stone basin beneath a lion's mouth out of which the brook's water trickles noiselessly, beneath a brass plate which says, ". . . the waters of Minetta again greet the light through this fountain as the spirit of Manhattan rising to greater glory." The university had fulfilled its civic obligation at small extra cost.

Like the brook, the Square may be altered, but it is somehow indestructible. "I that laugh shall rule at last,/When the massive walls decay,/When the towers to earth are cast," Guiterman declaimed in his dedicatory poem. Laughter, the decay of walls, and the casting to earth of towers (for the building of new ones) are endemic to the Square. The City's Common Council made a potter's field of Washington Square in 1797. More than 100,000 paupers and yellow-fever victims were buried there before the bodies were removed in 1823, taken first to the sites of Bryant Park and Madison Square and lastly to Wards Island. The editor of the *Evening Post* shot and fatally wounded the harbormaster of New York there in 1803. The two men had had political differences. (Half a century later, Edwin Forrest, the Shakespearean actor, severely caned the editor of the New York *Mirror* in the Square for discussing in print his pending suit for divorce.) Both gibbet and hanging elm stood in the Square, and in 1824 the Marquis de Lafayette witnessed the turning off of a dozen men.

The city set aside its potter's field in 1826 as the Washington Parade Ground. (A testy local historian named Charles Haswell remarked, in his *Reminiscences of an Octogenarian,* that "in the matter of public grounds, the necessities of the

Greenwich Village; looking north on Sullivan Street from West Third. "Ah, love, could you and I conspire to change this sorry scheme of things entire . . ."

poor have greatly ministered to the advantage of their more fortunate brethren. Washington Square, Union Square, Madison Square and Bryant Park all owing their existence as pleasure-grounds to prior use as pauper burial places.") New York University started to put up its Gothic main building in 1834 (it was torn down in 1894) and provoked a rich disorder. The university contracted for Sing Sing marble and the builder thought it would be handy to have the convicts up there cut it. The Stone-Cutters Guild rioted; the Twenty-seventh Regiment of the National Guard was called out, dispersed the protestants, and bivouacked for four days on the Square. (The Twenty-seventh camped there again during the Draft Riots in 1863.)

But it was in that building, a good many rooms of which were let out as lodgings, that Samuel Finley Breese Morse, a professor of painting at the university, perfected the telegraph (he complained of the leaky roof over him); Samuel Colt fiddled with his revolver; and such distinguished painters as Edwin Abbey, Winslow Homer, George Inness, and Eastman Johnson lived and worked. The number of toilers in the arts, the well-known, and the merely notorious who have lived on the Square in the last hundred years is beyond counting. At one time or another, a single building, 61 Washington Square South, known interchangeably as Katarina Branchard's rooming house and "The House of Genius," took in Stephen Crane, Floyd Dell, John Dos Passos, Maxwell Bodenheim, Art Young, John Reed, Eugene O'Neill, Guy Pène du Bois, Pierre Matisse, Adelina Patti, Alan Seeger, and Robert W. Chambers. (Madame Branchard died in 1927; the House of Genius was leveled in the summer of 1948 by the university; those who would like to, may read about it in the university's library.) Edward Hopper, Ernest Lawson, Rockwell Kent, and Walter Pach lived at No. 3 Washington Square North and No. 8 was once the official residence of the city's mayors. Washington Irving, Mark Twain, and Edgar Allan Poe lived near the Square and aired themselves in it.

None of these considerations has made a crucial difference to either the builders or the improvers. In the park, the Italian patriot, Garibaldi, his bronze figure in military uniform all verdigris (1888: G. Turini, placed by the Italians in America), endlessly grips the hilt of his scabbarded sword. There is a student joke to the effect that he draws it when a virgin passes. An opponent of anybody who wants to do anything to change anything in the Square observed once that, should the Square ever be materially changed or traffic again run through it, the great democrat would probably climb down from his pedestal and go somewhere else.

WITNESS   AN AFRICAN DIPLOMAT

When I came to represent my country here a couple of years ago, I knew, of course, that Negroes were regarded as inferior and I did not expect to be treated too differently, even in New York, which is supposed to be much more liberal than the rest of the country. Then I made an interesting discovery: as soon as I opened my mouth and people – whites – found out I was not an American Negro, I tended to get better treatment, to be less discriminated against. My color I certainly cannot escape; where I come from should have nothing to do with the matter. I feel a good many New Yorkers I have met cannot be sincere if they can have one attitude toward me and another for those of their fellow citizens who happen to be Negroes.

But if anything has disappointed me, it is the attitude of American Negroes toward those from Africa. Those who are wealthy or occupy more privileged positions are too busy making money or being superior to others to have any time for us. Those who are not either detest us in rebellion against their inferior economic or social status, or, on the other hand, believe us to be what they have been told we are – savages. In any case, I should not want to live in New York. The treatment of Negroes and other minorities apart, it is too much for the simple life Africans are used to. It is ironic, I find, that a city having so much to offer, intellectually and otherwise, should, at the same time, be so demanding that it becomes almost impossible to enjoy it.

The British delegation to the United Nations in cogitation. Within the enclave of the UN, all cats are gray; without, to be white is right, but to be black African is still better than to be black American.

The United Nations; early morning visitors. Peace is attractive at any hour.

Manhattan at night, from the Staten Island ferry.

A DRUG ADDICT

New York City, for junkies, is what Broadway is for actors. It's almost a *neces-sary* place to be. There's so much of it. That doesn't apply outside. I've seen old-time junkies in L.A. – sick, with money *and* connections – but there was no junk on the scene and they couldn't get straight. There's always junk on The Apple, just like there's always anything. You always know where to score somehow in New York City. I remember a panic in the Fifties. It was murder, police all over the place, but I still got straight. It may take awhile, anywhere from hours to a day, but no more than that, if you try hard in this city. And you do. When he starts hunting, a sick junkie can't stop until he's straight. Once you know you're hooked, you become like an invalid, and you don't leave New York too far behind.

I've seen junk grow into epidemic proportions in this city since I started using it in the mid-Forties, after I got out of the army. In my opinion, more people get turned on first here than anywhere else in the world – in terms of percentages, not just numbers. It's a port; the junk gets smuggled in; the racketeers control the docks. The question to all junkies, if they ever stop to think about it, is, How involved is the government with the racketeers? The flow increases all the time, like a good stock that keeps booming. Everyone has his own reasons for hating the head of the Narcotics Bureau. I suppose the majority hate him only because he puts junkies in jail without stopping the junk. My reason is that this cat and those above him refuse – for reasons of ego – to accept the fact that their drive has failed, is a failure, and will continue to be. When I started, you never heard about young kids using drugs for the simple reason that they didn't. Now you hear of them being hooked every day of the week and all of the things that go with being hooked, like stealing and family tragedies and suicide. How does the Narcotics guy explain the growth of the availability of drugs?

The drug problem of the United States couldn't have happened anywhere else but in New York City. And – this will kill you – I saw it exported. I saw a New York junk scene all over Europe. The whole style of behavior was New York, even the language. Do you know what they call heroin in Paris? The same as here: horse. You might think they'd call it *le cheval,* but no, it's horse. Horse and a fix and the scene and junk and getting straight and connecting and turning on and all the rest of it; in Stockholm and Berlin and London, too. Figure that out.

I got hooked through curiosity. When I came out of the army I started to drink. All I wanted was kicks or to lose consciousness. I'd always refused to smoke pot – marijuana – because I thought it was anti-social, evil, degenerate. But I did, finally, and I found it far more clean than drinking, more productive of euphoria, more stimulating, less expensive. I suppose jazz has to come into this somehow. We began to hear – my little group of bourgeois workers who smoked pot and liked jazz – a new kind of jazz that couldn't be rejected, just as, looking back, you couldn't reject Marlon Brando or the Abstract Expressionists. It had such vitality and energy. The people that were able to think and play and improvise it at such speeds, with the creativity and spontaneity that these musicians did, became heroes to us.

Then we began to hear that some of them were drug users – real drug users, heroin users. It was a contradiction and a confusion we were unprepared for. How could they play all this music and at the same time use drugs we had been taught to believe were used only by degenerates? At last I saw it right under my eyes. I saw somebody under the influence of heroin on Fifty-second Street and his behavior was summed up for me by his detachment. Later, I found out that the tensions of being so creative, so spontaneous, in public were such a drag and strain that only a powerful drug like heroin would permit these jazz musicians to concentrate on that inner music they felt. Now my emotions were always running away with me. I'd get excited, say things that weren't true; the line between fantasy and reality was a hard one for me to define. These musicians seemed to me to be totally removed from the confusion I knew and lived with. I didn't know how much I wanted to be rid of that confusion I knew and lived with. I didn't know how much I wanted to be rid of that confusion until I had my first shot. Nobody seduced me. As a matter of fact, I begged a guy I'd become friends with, a musician, to let me try it. He refused me a dozen times.

I watched him once at a wedding on the Upper East Side, the Gold Coast. He was on. I was very excited about something, I don't know what; underneath,

I may have been bored. But there he was, quite calm, very cordial, very gentlemanly, very much in control, exactly the way I wanted to be. Oh yes, he was very satisfied, too. I was introduced to the stage of being cool. Only a drug addict could have created that word "cool." No one can be cool, really, unless he's a mature older person, or unless he uses the powerful drug that heroin is. Otherwise, you're just normal and confused and bugged and happy and unhappy and all of the other things that go to make up life. No drug user takes them for any reason other than to repress some kind of pain. Well, I was in pain and so was the world in the Forties and there was no other release for me.

I thought it was some sort of magic, that if you took junk you became another kind of person. I was told I would become not only what I had been before, but fifty times more so. But I knew it, as the psychiatrists say, intellectually. Now I know it emotionally. To make a long story short, in his hotel room, this musician – he was white, by the way – said, "Okay, you son of a bitch" – it was more in a fit of temper than graciousness – "you want it, I'll give it to you." Let me make an aside. He warned me over and over, for one thing. For another, if he hadn't given it to me, I would have found it some place else. Every single one of my friends did. So he turned me on. Shot me. I say that to distinguish from sniffing. He gave me a good shot, right in the arm, which is like coming up to the major leagues your first year. Bang. No waiting; an instantaneous high. And that's where my troubles began, for a reason having nothing to do with drugs, but with me. When I felt that heroin, I felt that was it, what I had been looking for, the calming, maturing, controlled state of being I had always wanted. Once you feel that, though it may take years to get addicted technically, the fact is you're hooked, no matter what anyone says. Drugs aren't supposed to fulfill anyone the way they fulfill someone who becomes a junkie.

When I first got on, we used to score at 111th Street and Fifth Avenue. We'd walk into a little restaurant and there'd be four guys coming at you with caps – capsules – in their hands, saying, "Buy from me. Buy from me." We didn't worry much about the police then. The only way you could get busted was by accident. At that time the authorities, local and federal, were interested only in the pushers. A user might be caught redhanded and they might let him go, because what were they catching? Nothing. Somehow the police got involved and before you knew it, like overnight, we were being hunted. Suddenly your life was at stake. Instead of it being a private affair, you were in the ranks of the criminal. The scene shifted to midtown – for me, anyway. On the West Side, in the Fifties; in a cafeteria that used to be on Columbus Circle. I've even made a meet near the box office at Madison Square Garden. The midtown scene lasted a good five years. Then there was a Village scene and now the big scene is on the Lower East Side. For me, that is. You understand, of course, that you could always score all over. In Brooklyn, Queens, the Bronx, Manhattan, and even in Staten Island, although I never tried there. For a sick junkie, that ferry ride is a long trip.

Today, the quality for the rank-and-file junkie is much inferior to what it used to be. The big drag is, the people in charge of merchandising drugs in this town are non-users and don't understand the problem – or, rather, they do – and exploit the junkie.

BARNEY ROSSET
Publisher, Grove Press

Of course, this is the center of my life, of what I do – publishing – at least on the
surface. I say on the surface, because I find a vacant center; I can't quite locate
any center in a personal way. Recently, I returned to Chicago for a day – a long
one – and a night, and my feeling about New York was confirmed: at the end of
my day in Chicago, I had the rather pleasant notion that I had made real contacts
– some of them unfriendly, but nevertheless real; some with strangers, some not.
In New York, the feeling of connection should be great, but it isn't. People are
more tense, frightened, competitive, and hostile than I found them in Chicago. I
was born there, by the way. Somehow, each of us – even the same people, or the
same kind of people – is an atom in this city, wandering in a separate path, meeting other atoms only to conduct business and then separating.

What keeps me here is my own fractured life, publishing and bookselling, and
most of what I have in the way of friends. The major part of bookselling in
America is here. The island of Manhattan alone accounts for an incredibly large
part of the total number of books sold in this country. I get a great pleasure from

*The financial district; the floor
of the Stock Exchange. Money
screams, too, and waves its
arms.*

Harlem; a Salvation Army street meeting on 125th Street at Lexington Avenue. The white man's God has a tough row to hoe up there.

producing a book and then seeing the immediate result – the book being sold. I can't imagine living in Texas and publishing books; my state of depression would be constant. I came here in 1946 to do other things and when I got into publishing I found myself in a new, sullen world. To my amazement, I found that when a new company did things I felt certain some of the good older ones must think were fine efforts, worth while, yet no threat of any kind to their existence, no kind of encouragement was forthcoming. That has never ceased to astonish me. I have never met most of the heads of the companies that could be thought of as similar to mine. I've not only not met them, but worse, I have only heard stories about their trying to take our young writers away and downgrading us in general. It now seems naïve, even to me, but at first I expected that each new good book brought out would get some sort of friendly pat on the back from my seniors. Instead, there was only a stony silence or underground rumors.

WITNESS

MOHANJEET GREWAL
A Sikh girl, of Lahore, Pakistan

The only reason to return to New York is to renew oneself in a work way and that is what I have done in the last month and a half; I feel I have gathered enough momentum here to last me quite some time. Being in New York is like being in touch with a part of the world which is moving far ahead of everything else – in politics, in economics, in almost everything. But not in living. It was either your Henry James or your Henry Adams who said that one needs two kinds of education: one to make a living and one to live. New York is a place to make a living. I was studying for my doctorate in political science at the University of California in Los Angeles when I talked to Krishna Menon. That was in 1955. He said to me, "What are you doing on the West Coast? You must come East."

New York meant a new beginning. I spent almost four years here after talking to him. It was here I started to work. I found a whole world of opportunity; nothing stood in the way of it. Things would not have been so open to me in London, Paris, Rome, or Berlin, as I have since found out. At the same time, I could not escape from this city. It never leaves one. I used to try to do this in Central Park – everybody said it was unwise – but even there the sound of the city was overwhelming, overbearing; it bore me down. I sat, but I was never away from the city. It roared around me and I did not like that because I love silence and peace.

People also, in New York, though they are very available, are not with you. They tend, in a way, to take on the character of the city, in the sense that they are only background, a loud sound, something you can get to but that is not with you. The city does not intimidate me, nor the people; they only make me feel a little unprepared for them. I like to work for six or seven days with fullness and feeling and then not for another seven days. I want to do nothing but sit on a balcony or walk aimlessly before shops – never in them, I hate going into shops. But I neither can nor want to do that here. They are all alike. Not only are they all alike, but so many other things are all alike. The shops are like the restaurants, the restaurants like the petrol stations, the petrol stations like the motels, the motels like the hotels, and the hotels like office buildings. Other places in the world are places to live. I make my home in Paris now.

The Statue of Liberty.

Julie Harris lunching on Forty-second Street west of Seventh Avenue. Sarah Bernhardt would have been appalled at this Actor's Studio style of dining.

THE ONLY WHEEL IN TOWN

CHAPTER 9

In 1952, Richard Maney, a theatrical press agent whose appreciation of the picturesque megalomania of his clients – a race as inbred as a cage of ranch mink, as provincial as a settlement of Jackson Whites, and as full of special reference as the Quantum Theory – is matched only by his firmness in putting it down, delivered himself of a mordantly affectionate rescript on the New York theater. "It is a curious confusion of art and honky tonk," Maney said. "At its best, I suppose, it reflects what cultural facets there are in American life. At its worst, it's a clip joint. It's a hell of a season that sees even two or three good plays. And yet, in it is concentrated the best of the amusement life of America. If you're outside of New York, you might as well be camping out. You take a guy from Euclid Avenue, Cleveland. If he paid $7.00 for a theater ticket to a broker in his home town, he'd scream. He comes to New York and gets scalped $100 for a pair and he boasts about it." In 1962, by then the survivor of forty years of *jihad* on Broadway, Maney could see no reason to change his mind, save for such minor emendations as that Clevelanders could brag they were being taken for as much as $150 to $200 a pair.

Asked why he chose to continue as a *muezzin* in so rickety a mosque, Maney replied, "After so many years of exposure to its princes, paupers, and maniacs, I'm a little touched, too. My long association with and admiration for them has disqualified me for any other profession or vice." In this mingling of a fierce parochialism (Maney's was such that he dismissed off-Broadway as the "coolie offshoot of the theater") with pride, disenchantment, repulsion, and, most appealing of all, the inability to disengage himself, Maney's attitude is quite typical of virtually everybody bound up in the institution. Elsewhere, it is clearly recognized that the theater serves New York only in an ancillary way and art only fitfully. It is a tourist attraction, an outlet for expense accounts, a means of gaining status (the price paid for scarce seats is the gauge among the crass; among the barely less crass, proof of elevated sensibilities is attained through the earliest possible attendance at a hit), and a come-on for business in general. When the actors struck for ten days in June, 1960, and shut down the theater, as much concern was expressed over the financial losses incurred by hotels, restaurants, night clubs, department stores, renters of limousines, and owners of taxicab fleets as over those of the theater. (To describe as coincidence the fact that two of the theater's most important figures, Roger L. Stevens and Robert W. Dowling, are primarily real estate men and bankers would be, without impugning their motives, to outrage credulity.) The question of the strike's effect on the theater itself was held to be irrelevant and it was raised only by boors and theater people.

The decline of the theater has been documented with as much fidelity and in as many words as are devoted to fallings-off in the Gross National Product. The organization of producers, The League of New York Theatres, Inc., even went so far as to commission a professor of economics from Yale, Glenn O. Saxon, to do a study of theater economics. The substance of it was that the number of productions dropped from 264 in 1928 to 57 in 1960 and the number of legitimate theaters from 66 in 1931 to 33 in 1960. Not to put too fine a point on it, the League acknowledged the existence of motion pictures, radio, and television but put most of the blame on "the cost-price squeeze" and taxes. (The League, of course, had nothing to say about off-Broadway. Off-Broadway began as such on the eve of the Fifties. Little theater, from Bulter Davenport's Free Theater to Eva Le Gallienne's Civic Repertory, has existed in the city from time to time but never reached sizable proportions. Off-Broadway rose from nothing to roughly a hundred productions a season in thirty-odd theaters. It has experienced the same cost-price squeeze of which Broadway complains; the same percentage of failures and proportion of financial loss; with exceptions, naturally, the same diminution in inventiveness; and it also serves, in its lesser way, the interests of non-theatrical business and intellectual climbers.)

The New York Ticket Brokers, Inc., issued a pamphlet blaming everything on maldistribution of tickets. In nineteen pages of special pleading, the brokers argued that things would be fine if they got larger allotments of tickets. In one week in 1961 the New York *Times* published eight front-page articles – roughly 20,000 words – on the current condition of the theater. They were meticulously researched and written by the entire staff of the newspaper's drama department, in addition to its labor expert; they were enormously authoritative in presenting every possible and conflicting point of view – so much so that readers discovered everybody was to blame for everything and one *Times* man, evidently in a state of controlled bafflement, wrote, "It flouts every law of good sense," an indisputable conclusion. In an interview with the Fund for the Republic, however, Walter Kerr, drama critic of the New York *Herald Tribune,* said sensibly that "We could analyze the historical causes of the theater's problem forever. We've talked about three or four. We could talk about six more and then try to establish a relationship between them. But that would mean splitting hairs, trying to establish when this element came in and when that element came in, which element was more harmful, which less harmful."

He then made his point with admirable brevity. "I would merely summarize the situation," Kerr said, "by saying the potential audience for the theater is bored not only with the theater it sometimes goes to but with the thought of going to the theater. This could be because in some way the theater is boring in itself, its premises are wrong. Or we could bypass that and simply say that its premises may have been all right for the time in which they appeared but that they are now stale. I prefer to start with the simple fact of boredom. People are no longer excited by the theater. It doesn't give them any thrill." Something that seems to

Greenwich Village; the Premise.
The hippest gig on the scene is an
import from Chicago.

have been overlooked by commentators on the theater is that, for all of its surface anarchy, it has simply undergone the same rationalization as industry in general: fewer but larger manufacturers, processors, and distributors of theater; mass production of standard brands; cheaper ingredients in bigger packages for the widest market; and fewer choices for the buyer, discriminating or not. If the analogies are short of perfect, the reason is that the creative process and the temperaments of theater people are still – regrettably, from the point of view of cybernetics – erratic and sometimes almost intractable. The adherence of these people to the theater, whatever their motives (usually more honorable in the instance of performers, musicians, writers, and craftsmen than in that of a good many producers), is an act of laudable and impressive unreason invariably reflected in their behavior; they may very well constitute the last sizable repository of eccentricity in this country.

About as instructive, not to say bleak, an insight into Broadway as exists – aside from a matchless skill in maintaining an almost unbroken continuity of dogs, cats, and musical comedies – is afforded by the employment record of Miss Julie Harris. This might be described as skimpy but is probably best characterized as bizarre, since she has been acclaimed repeatedly as one of the two or three finest actresses of her generation and privately held to be one of the most malleable;

nor is she anywhere nearly as expensive to hire as, say, Ethel Merman or Lucille Ball. Nevertheless, in nearly five and a half years – between June 2, 1956, when she closed in *The Lark,* and October of 1961 when she opened in *A Shot in the Dark,* a trifle adapted from the French by Harry Kurnitz, which became a hit – Miss Harris had been on Broadway a total of 152 times in, to gloss matters over, three highly exiguous productions. She was the rule rather than the exception, and she made her living in television. But some idea of the love and terror the theater churns up in those who work in it may be found in something she said shortly after *A Shot in the Dark* opened.

"I've been upset for a long time," Miss Harris said, "and I've thought I had better give up acting. Period. Who cares about Broadway and the state of the theater? *I can't act.*" (She had overwhelmingly refuted this estimate of herself ever since walking on a stage professionally; moreover, *A Shot in the Dark* was, if not the antithesis of everything else she had ever done, certainly light-years removed.) "I didn't even want to take this play," she continued. "It demands so much freedom, good humor, and relaxation. I was really crazy to take such a part if I thought I would fail at it. Well, the first day of rehearsal came and we read the play and that night I went home and I said, 'Get me out of this; I'll fail, get me out of it; you'll have to find some way – I'll be sick, I'll be something.' That whole first week, for the first time in my life, I was late to rehearsals. I have got into this terrible situation where I feel I can and I can't. I don't feel I'm absolutely lost; there *are* times when I have confidence – in rehearsal. But it's in the execution. . . . Where have I fallen short? Where have I failed?" She wept. Her husband, Manning Gurian, who was listening, closed his eyes and rubbed the bridge of his nose with a thumb and forefinger.

"I can't trust myself," she went on. "I know what I do in rehearsal. I know how full I can be and, because I get afraid, I restrain myself. The fear. It's not, you see, that I shake or that my voice shakes. Ah, no. It's a feeling as though something had a clamp on your heart and you can't really allow yourself to feel anything and I keep saying to myself, 'It's going by, it's going by and it'll never come again and you're not feeling anything.' It's beaten me down. I try to save myself. I try to exercise some control over it. I think, for one thing, if you don't get too fatigued . . . ; fatigue hinders me from doing my best work." Her voice trailed off and she wiped her eyes. "It was a great shock in *A Shot in the Dark,*" she said finally, almost in a whisper, "on opening night and I heard them laugh. 'My God,' I thought – right in the middle of everything – 'they find it *amusing!*' That helped me a lot."

For all of the flickerings of madness that light up rehearsals and tryouts (these are frequently productive of lifelong enmities, which in the theater may last as long as two weeks), it is on opening night that the nature of the theater worker is exposed fully and shamelessly. A playwright, a man with a conspicuously Gothic outlook, a fairly long list of successes, and a gift for free association, once remarked that a Broadway opening was an apocalyptic experience. He even thought that the sensation could be raised to the level of a general principle. "Nothing at all to do with the Bible or revelation," he said, raising his right hand in a somber wave of dismissal. "When I was about six my mother, for reasons she has yet to account to me for, took me with her to see Valentino in *The Four Horsemen of*

Central Park; Shakespeare in performance. The Merchant of Venice *is the play.*

the Apocalypse. Follow me? As I remember it, the damned thing opened in a tinted belch of flame and smoke, with that ghastly quartet of jockeys riding their selling platers right at me in a dead heat." He drew in his breath at the memory. "I started to quake and squeak," he said. "I ducked under my seat, comatose, and the old lady finally got me out of there. I was a mess. The trauma has remained with me, although I have sublimated it. The only thing I have riding at me today is seven unhorsed critics. I get drunk, however, and I am still a mess."

The opening-night syndrome of playwrights varies from individual to individual, but with few exceptions a single dreary pattern can be picked out. It is compounded of a tearing sensation of vivid anxiety on the one hand and an enthralled numbness on the other. In its ambivalence, it is accompanied by symptoms of irritability, resentment, fear, and the sense of both *déjà vu* and *jamais vu;* restlessness, temporary aphasia, and a spiraling garrulousness; acute depression and elation; flights into and from reality; the invocation of magic, and a pressing need either to make or to avoid contact. Some years ago, a playwright who felt he had experienced all but one of the symptoms satisfactorily covered the remaining ground (making human contact) by hitting his wife between the acts.

Playwrights create and are subject to innumerable fantasies connected with their first nights. Through the exercise of yoga, Ben Hecht has made theaters vanish. "I try to remember a favorite relative," he has said. "One or two aunts I join up with. Or I get in a historical mood where nothing matters of small consequence like an opening. Sometimes I find myself in Mexico – Taxco, say. Opening night has the effect of a mugging. It's a social art, like getting kicked out of a restaurant. Once I thought I was pretty calm. Someone bumped into me and I fell over. I remember saving Charlie MacArthur's life at the opening of *The Front Page.* He started to lean against a door in the balcony. Only it wasn't there." More latterly, Hecht stays backstage. "Actors are charming and calming," he says, "and I might as well be executed in good company."

Toward the end of the second act of *The Rainmaker,* N. Richard Nash, who walks the streets for the greater part of an opening night, got the distinct impression that he was listening to a play that he might very well have written but that had never been staged. "I got to wondering where the producer got hold of it," he said. "I was on the verge of asking what happened, but I couldn't bring myself to." Horton Foote is assailed by the feeling that everything is being done in slow motion; that the laughs come at several removes from the lines and that the audience is responding far too late. Abe Burrows, a victim of the same delusion, stands at the back of the house, attempting to speed things up by exercising body English, and George Axelrod's vapors were so egregious that they were translated into a television script called *Confessions of a Nervous Man,* which was well received by the critics.

The late Moss Hart was twice overcome by a species of amnesia. He entered his bathroom prior to dressing for an opening, switched on the light over a shaving mirror, put his hands under it, and waited for the water to run. "I thought in some irritation," he recalled, " 'Of all the nights to have the water fail.' " Another time, having already dressed, he went into his bedroom to remove a new satin spread from a bed on which he planned later to have his guests at a post-opening party throw their coats. Hart carefully folded the spread, removed his dinner jacket, and hung it away, similarly disposed of the rest of his clothes, slipped into a pair of pajamas, and climbed into the bed.

Such trips out of the real world are, at most, an inconvenience. Robert E. Sherwood, in his lifetime, went to greater lengths than Hart. On the day in 1940 that *There Shall Be No Night* was to open, he rose at 3 A.M., dressed, packed a suitcase, and took a cab to the Pennsylvania Station. There he boarded a train for Washington. "By the time I got there," he said, "I thought, 'What the hell did I do that for?' I was just worked up. It was a disgraceful piece of escapism, I concluded. I had a glass of orange juice and a cup of coffee and sent a telegram to my wife which said, 'For some reason, I have gone to Washington and will be back at noon.' " Harry Kurnitz, a writer who was hardened in Hollywood, or believed he was, spent most of the first night of his first Broadway play, *Reclining Figure,* in the ladies' lounge of the Lyceum Theater, in the company of Abe Burrows, who directed it, both men thoughtfully leaving only at intermissions. Bella Spewack also favors the ladies' lounge and reads motion picture fan magazines. Edward Chodorov sits in the balcony; John Patrick behind a closed door in any room of a theater; Robert Anderson on the stairs; Arthur Miller walks out when a scene he is doubtful of is being played.

S. N. Behrman is unquestionably a special case. He stays home. He has·attended only one New York opening of the score or so of his plays that reached Broadway. This was one called *The Second Man.* It opened on April 11, 1927. "I know the date better than the Battle of Hastings," Behrman said. "I got a bad headache – I'm subject to them, anyway – and I figured I don't have to go to openings to get a headache. I don't understand why anyone goes. I stay home. It saves me headaches and the compulsive politeness of my friends. They all say it was a wonderful evening in the theater, when what they mean is that it was an evening in the theater. Opening nights are a combination of sadism and barbarism. What is always absorbing to me is how the most casehardened succumb to the insincerities of their friends on opening night." While all playwrights are made more or less uneasy or worse by opening nights, Burrows reserves a particular detestation for the parties that follow them, not for the parties per se, but for the people who insist on reading notices aloud at them. "I've warned guys about that," he said. "Good or bad. These people become the bearers of ill tidings. You know, in history, the bearer of ill tidings was killed."

Of all the macabre rites rehearsed by Broadway for its own immolation, the party given doggedly upon the opening of a new play is probably the one most closely approximating the fourth Lord Chesterfield's description of an eighteenth-century wake. "When the lower sort of Irish, in the most uncivilized parts of Ireland, attend the funeral of a deceased friend or neighbor," wrote Chesterfield, "before they give the last parting howl, they expostulate with the dead body, and reproach him with having died, notwithstanding that he had an excellent wife, a milch cow, seven fine children, and a competency of potatoes."

The reasons for the resemblance are quantitative and qualitative. The competency of potatoes in the living theater is far lower than the incidence of demises and the expectation of a quick closing in most of the celebrants at first-night routs is as conspicuous as a wen on the Witch of Endor. "In the theater," a man who has borne with its powerful frailties for upward of three decades once observed, "nothing enrages like success. At these damnable parties, every table is a bier populated by a handful of people whose lives are hanging in the balance and a lot of other people hoping for their finish." He cited the extreme case of an investor in *Reclining Figure*. This individual had put up $1000. When the reviews were read – they were generally poor – he was overheard to murmur gratefully to the lady on his right, "Thank God, it's not a hit," only later remembering in some confusion that he had money in the show.

No such vulgar conflict rove a principal backer of an expensive musical for which great things had been foretold. He gave the post-opening party in his Park Avenue apartment. He arranged with the play's press agent to telephone him first with the reviews, intending to retail them to his guests himself. He was busily accepting the interim admiration of a group of the latter when he was summoned to the telephone – in another room – and learned that the reviews were, in fact, obituaries. The backer returned to his gala (in his head was the pounding of guns; Napoleon's troops were retreating from Moscow) where he was buttonholed before he could open his mouth by a close friend who wistfully expressed regret that he had not bought a piece of the show. "Tell you what, I'll sell you half of mine," offered the backer, no man to throw away his entire equity; the off-chance existed that the show would run. The commitment was made; it was also honored quickly, or roughly about the time the play closed.

Some first-night parties are held in restaurants, notably Sardi's, a shrine in which the outlines of disaster may be perceived with terrible clarity and unparalleled speed; some are given in the public rooms of hotels. A majority take place in private residences. They are given by producers – novice producers with the confidence of the callow, and old, smart producers transfixed in autohypnosis; by rich backers whose casting standards for the party are more exacting than for the play; occasionally by a star, a director, or an author. Regardless of where they are held, or by whom, or for what ostensible purpose (the word "celebration" is employed brazenly), they reek of much the same atmosphere to be found among sailors wet and huddled on a raft in an engulfing sea; the need for communion, even the communion of spite, is felt thickly.

Whether limp with humiliation, edgy with anxiety, or, after the fact, drunk with power, the behavior of participants, including those whose only involvement consists of wishing a production ill, is apt to be strange. There is an authenticated instance of a playwright and a director who, upon learning that their efforts had been poorly received, left a party together after midnight, stumbled into a drugstore, entered adjacent telephone booths, and got their psychoanalysts out of bed for some supportive therapy. The actress, Doe Avedon, had her analyst accompany her following the opening of *The Young and Fair,* and was thus spared the necessity of waking anybody up. By comparison with Kim Stanley, however, Miss Avedon was downright slipshod. On the night she opened in *A Touch of the Poet,* Miss Stanley whipped in her analyst, her internist, and her obstetrician, although for reasons of gratitude rather than necessity.

Another salient feature of these overwrought affairs is the opportunities they offer for the renewal of ancient feuds and the exchange of recriminations. At the Stork Club, on the night of the opening of *Don Juan in Hell,* Charles Laughton expansively hailed Lee Shubert as an "old son of a bitch," to which Charles

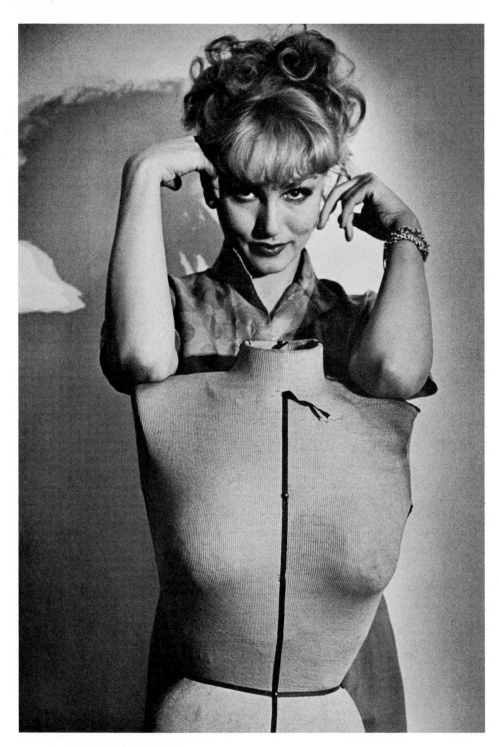

Julie Newmar, an actress. "I want the best of everything and the best of everything is in New York."

Boyer raised his glass of beer and Shubert graciously inclined his head. There was no crucial misunderstanding among the three. Jed Harris, an irascible man at his mildest, took the opportunity at a party for the people involved with *The Crucible,* which he directed, to call the producer, Kermit Bloomgarden, "a bookkeeper and an accountant," an insult for which there is no ready equivalent outside the theater. Another producer, having been given the bad news *before* any festivities, went on morosely but dutifully to the home of the man who had arranged them. He headed at once for the buffet on which a ham and a turkey had been tastefully laid out. A flush of rage spread over the producer's otherwise livid face and he turned on his host. "You did that on purpose," he shouted. "You never liked the play, anyway."

Neither friends, husbands and wives, nor fathers and sons are immune to the virus. At the party for Lillian Hellman's *Days to Come,* in 1936, a play uniformly disliked by the critics, Miss Hellman asked Dashiell Hammett, an old and valued friend, "Didn't you tell me yesterday this was the best script you'd ever read?" "Yes, I did," Hammett admitted. "But I saw it tonight and changed my mind." The producer of another play, all anticipation, called out, "Dad," as his father entered Sardi's soon after the third-act curtain fell. "Son," said the father adjusting his hearing aid, "that was about the worst damned play I ever saw in my life."

A definitive portrait of the opening-night party at its grisliest has been put together by Robert L. Joseph, a producer who has managed, with some results, to match every success with a failure of esteem, or at least a failure. Joseph also sketched in, like the background in a nineteenth-century genre painting, a defense of his trade. "All a producer has to do," he said, "is get a script, raise money, find a theater, sign up a name director and two stars, not lose too much money on the road, get seventy-five theater parties before opening, and, once he opens, start talking actors into staying on for the summer and it's a cinch. The odd thing is that all the others connected with his production treat him as a creative talent while he's pulling everything together. Once that's been achieved, they instinctively create a *front populaire* against him. It is his function to be the common enemy. It may not be believed, but his sufferings at an opening-night party are – and not solely for the money in it – as scarifying as anybody else's.

"The consolation speech," he continued with reminiscent, if rueful, relish, "is what everybody comes prepared with. They're dying to make it. All right, let's say you've got a flop. You'll hear, 'Don't quit, kid, you got to fight 'em. It's a great audience show.' Or, 'If the critics had suffered the way we have – but, of course, they just didn't understand the play,' and 'I don't care what they say, *I* just loved it,' and 'It's criminal, the work and money that went into this.'

"Meantime, someone's booking your theater for a musical a table away; the actors' agents are ordering them to pick up a new script in the morning, and the director has plane tickets to Hollywood, anyway. And there is the producer sitting at a table buried in half-eaten *smorgasbord* – the cigarettes are sticking up from it like grave markers – with his mother and the assistant stage manager and his loyal secretary. His secretary – his little, loyal secretary – looks at him with those big brown eyes and says, 'You want me in the office tomorrow?' Does he want her in the office tomorrow!

"You have a hit? *That* is The Picture of Dorian Gray. When they hear the notices for a hit, a deadly silence sweeps over the room for a moment. Then the make-up starts to peel off the women; the men's dinner jackets seem to fall off; their voices crack, they all flake away and the naked envy shows. These things – I won't call them parties – are one long line of meatballs and Chinese food. I will never have another opening-night party," he concluded positively, "and you're invited."

Opening nights on Broadway and the *brouhaha* accompanying them are, by comparison with off-Broadway, not so much vulgar or blatant as merely less subtle. It is not even necessary to attend an off-Broadway opening; in fact, it is chic to wait awhile. In his relentless, hot-eyed pursuit of cachet, man has, at one time or another, fallen maddened on the Mission Oak sideboard, the bongo drum, the tourmaline knob for an Alfa Romeo floor gearshift, and the forked beard. One of the cheapest, outside of the beard, is going off-Broadway. It is simultaneously as purifying as morris dancing, as stimulating as wheat germ, and as avant-garde as a dollar-and-a-quarter paperback containing a play by Jean Genet within and an abstract drawing without. Indeed, the paperback usually contains the text of the very play the devotee is on his way to see and is carried, bulging carefully, from the right-hand pocket of a well-tailored suit, to the theater, which may be a whitewashed basement next door to a Turkish bath on the Lower East Side.

A number of disciplines are observed in attending a play off-Broadway, whatever the age, sex, or station in life of the postulant. The most crucial of these is literary, or the appearance of it, on several of what are called "levels." Thus,

Rehearsal in a Broadway theater. Here is the only place in which an actor toes the mark.

while it is no novelty for drunks to show up on or off-Broadway, the off-Broadway drunk must look like J. M. Kerrigan; wear a heather shawl roguishly around his neck (over his overcoat, a shapeless bundle); affect a persistent, lilting Irish brogue; and claim intimate acquaintance with Brendan Behan, proving it with two or three unsubstantiated anecdotes. Should the play be staged in a former church, the drunk may adopt a Welsh accent, quote lines freely and inaccurately from Dylan Thomas, and trumpet defiantly to the young woman sitting behind an old table used as a box office that he came to sleep and not to pray. However, such bravura demonstrations are thought by serious off-Broadway theatergoers to be excessive, if not debilitating, and the demonstrator is likely to be set down simply as an anti-Philistine Philistine. It is much more appropriate, for one thing, to laugh *before* the actors read their putatively funny lines – this shows undeniable familiarity with the play – or even to interject titters, chuckles, or thigh slaps at junctures where the author *should* have had laughs.

This must be reinforced by suitable lobby behavior. When a lady off-Broadway playgoer meets a male one in the lobby (not uncommonly, it is adjacent to the garbage cans in a tenement basement; the vestry of an old church; the spavined landing in a loft; or the corridor of a skyscraper), it is required that the pair first stroll up and back in glum silence before the exhibition of paintings, sculpture, or photographs set up in conjunction with the show and furnished either by the scenic designer or by the art student who shares a cold-water flat with him on Avenue D and has had a three-line poem published in *Mandrake,* which is not only a little magazine but a tiny one. Having come to rest, finally, the gentleman says to the lady: "Vajda," to which she responds tenderly, "Ionesco." A murmurous colloquy follows, consisting mainly of "Von Hofmannsthal" and "Hauptmann"; "Alfieri" and "Pirandello"; "Wedekind" and "Sudermann"; "Congreve" and "Wycherly." If the two stand on the dangerous edge of contemporaneity, "Sartre" and "Camus" will do.

Just as Broadway is not without its out-of-town buyer, so is off-Broadway not without its gaunt primitive: a man once sat through a full act of *The Man with the Golden Arm* at the Cherry Lane in the fixed belief that he was watching *The Threepenny Opera* at the Theatre de Lys. Another, having observed that an advertisement for *The Iceman Cometh* at Circle-in-the-Square stated that theater parties could be arranged, asked the box-office people to arrange one for twelve to *My Fair Lady.* The display of literacy is, of course, paramount, but there are subsidiary attitudes that need sedulous cultivation. The off-Broadway patron must affect to believe that all of the theaters are (a) hard to find and (b) easily confused with each other. This is sometimes the case and is always provocative of some piquant rallying before going. (An off-Broadway house may be said to have arrived when a Good Humor truck parks near it during the summer and a cab line forms there during the winter.)

The off-Broadway playgoer makes a point, at intermissions, of not dashing across the street for a drink, the principal reason being that the nearest bar is usually a block or two away, but of hunting up a neighborhood candy store and ordering an egg cream. An egg cream is a soft drink containing neither eggs nor cream; it is simply a chocolate soda without ice cream, but with milk. A piece of chocolate-covered halvah is eaten with an egg cream and small, nostalgic jokes

Gramercy Park; the statue of Edwin Booth. It is a beautiful, green square, but private and locked; keys are held only by the privileged handful who live on its borders

are made about how the price of both has gone up. A second procedure is to remain gravely in the lobby. It is not incorrect to smoke, but it is wrong to talk about anything other than the play, or to look anywhere but at the listener's face, all the time making one's point by tapping him gently on the shoulder with a rolled-up copy of *France-Amérique* or *Aufbau,* the *Observer* or *Le Monde.*

The audiences tend to fall into types. Possibly the most easily recognizable are Europeans, who may be picked out by their tight blue suits, black slouch hats, the reiterated conviction that Piscator did it better in Berlin in the Twenties, and silent wives. Hard upon their heels tread the intellectuals, the men in hairy sports jackets, the women in hammered-silver earrings, both in glasses with heavy rims. They are followed by the sober middle class—the readers of Spock, opera librettos, and *Partisan Review*—husbands one night, wives the next because of the baby-sitter problem. The college group resembles its intellectual elders, save only that it is neither lined nor furrowed. The slummers from uptown are always surprised to find padded seats, and professional theater people can be distinguished mostly by the fact that they go on Sunday night, which is an off night on Broadway. All display faces that shine with the consciousness of doing a good deed in a naughty world for relatively little money. "They're cleansed," a man who has watched them closely once said. "They've been sitting under a hair drier of beautiful thoughts for a couple of hours."

ADA LOUISE HUXTABLE
An architectural historian

On this bloody, fishy street—Front Street down in Fulton Market—behind a pile of wooden crates were two authentic Georgian buildings, unseen, unloved, unappreciated, uncared for. The only ones who cared were the cats who lived in them. They're coming down. Then, in that redevelopment around Park Row, there are some small brick buildings with that demolition stencil already on them. There, there they are—the original slate steps, rough slate, and the most beautiful doorways. Such fine, beautiful woodwork, the fluted columns, the delicate fanlights. The very paint that obscured the columns with its thickness had even worn off. And it will all be gone. And nobody knows or cares.

I'll tell you what bothers me about New York. I know it's overspecialized, but even so, the *blindness* of New Yorkers . . . They live in a city they don't even see. They never look up. New York's is a story in building you will find nowhere else in the world. Begin with the block-long rows of four- and five-story red brick buildings early in the nineteenth century. Then, in the Fifties and Sixties, you have the beginnings of the commercial palaces—stone and marble and cast iron. We took an Italian architect, Ignazio Gardella, on a tour of New York. Over on Worth Street, between Broadway and Church, where the manufacturers fixed up a whole row of cast-iron buildings, painted, put in flower boxes and so on. Gardella gasped. "Of course," he said to my husband, "all this is protected by your government." He found it very difficult to grasp that *nothing,* or almost nothing, was government-protected. And those, too, are gone now.

South Street; gargoyle on the Seamen's Church Institute. It is a ridiculous piece of folderol of the architecture of the Twenties, but somehow it has more meaning than curtain walls.

You know, of course, that Louis Sullivan has one building in New York – the Condict Building or the Bayard Building, on Bleecker Street, east of Broadway. Look at that building and then let your eye wander to others in the neighborhood of similar size and scale. You just can't escape the fact that it's a masterpiece. The beautiful relationship of ornament to structure, the way it both emphasizes and reveals the frame of the skyscraper. I'll tell you an anecdote. The Community Trust felt the building was such an important landmark, it offered the owners one of the first commemorative plaques it ever gave out. It was refused. The reason was obvious, even if nobody said anything. Nobody wants a building singled out as a landmark which will take it out of the realm of speculative commercial real estate.

The Woolworth Building. For almost two decades, Cass Gilbert's Gothic cathedral to the five-and-ten was the tallest building in the world.

The Flatiron Building, at the junction of Broadway, Fifth Avenue, and Twenty-third Street. What made it world famous was its shape.

Gramercy Park South; gas lamp in front of the Players' Club. For a few, it is more illuminating than the harshest of mercury-vapor standards.

Grant's Tomb and the Riverside Church. Child's riddle: Who is buried in Grant's Tomb?

Fulton Fish Market. "Begin New York with the block-long rows of four- and five-story red-brick buildings early in the nineteenth century."

Power shovel at work in the West Fifties. By definition, progress.

I say also that until our planners have a combination of historical knowledge and aesthetic sensitivity to equal their good intentions, planning is a lost cause in this city. None of them show any signs of it as far as I am concerned. It hasn't been part of their training. Have you ever seen a planner enchanted by a map on a drawing board? It's so easy to do on paper, to develop some grand scheme. Very commendable. But they destroy the values they should be preserving. Let them put up their drawing boards on a street corner and look at these buildings and see to it at the same time that they are trained enough to know what they are looking at. I care very deeply about New York. There are more people who do than you would think.

AN APARTMENT BUILDING SUPERINTENDENT

You learn a lot about people being a superintendent. It's the type of job that's on a par with any where you have to cater to the public. There's none of them's easy. One conclusion I've come to is the attitude of the person has a whole lot to do with their financial status. They try to be more impressive the less they have. The attitude of the average tenant is that you're just – what? – one step under them, would you say? It shows in the requests they make that aren't my responsibility. I don't feel any way inferior to them whatever. I might not have the responsibility of the jobs they have, but I still feel as though I'm their equal. Besides, I think a lot of them are living in my particular building for prestige purposes. They don't tip or give gratuities because they are not in a position to financially. They're skimping themselves out of this or that. Why, I know of one particular tenant wears the same clothes day in and day out, Sundays, holidays, or work days, just for the purpose of having what you call a fashionable address.

I don't have to get annoyed by tenants giving me secondhand things, the way they do in most buildings, because I have a fairly big crew of men and the tenants give their things to them. But I'll never forget the time a man dropped dead around Christmastime. His wife packaged up his ties and a pair of shoes, real nice, in four separate packages, and gave them to the elevator man and the handy man. The handy man didn't waste any time dropping the shoes in the garbage. He'd seen those shoes before. "I wouldn't wear 'em," he said to me. "I'm liable to die with 'em on." I don't recall what two of the operators did with the ties, but the third man didn't even open his package. He laid it on a table in the lobby, hoping someone would steal it. They didn't. "Boy," he told me, "we got a lot of honest people in this building." He dumped his in the garbage eventually, too.

A super never knows what to expect when he's called to open a door or there's an emergency. I've seen four dead in my time. Once, a doctor calls me in when one of the tenants died. The man'd been sitting in an armchair. Natural causes. The doctor wanted him straightened out before rigor mortis set in. I picked him up, put him on the bed, pushed his knees down, closed his eyes, pushed his mouth together, and folded his hands in front of him. "Where in hell did you learn that?" the doctor wanted to know. I explained I used to hang around with an undertaker in Connecticut. I wasn't kidding.

Bowling Green and Broadway from the Custom House. A name, a patch of park, and the statue of Abraham de Peyster.

WITNESS

JANE JACOBS
Critic of architecture and author of The Death and Life of Great American Cities

I came here from Scranton when I was eighteen. For quite a few years I thought of Scranton as my home. I know the very night I changed. I was living on Morton Street in Greenwich Village and I used to travel on the Ninth Avenue El, from Christopher Street to Fiftieth. The day came when they closed down the El. That El belonged to me and I felt some gesture was necessary. I suggested to my sister that we take the last ride on it. We rode uptown. It was about eleven o'clock at night and the weather was chilly. I had thought it would be a very gay ride and

The Custom House (1907) and No. 2 Broadway (1960). The aluminum module is cheaper than marble and grandeur is measured in square feet of rentable space.

The Third Avenue El; Fourteenth Street station. It disappeared with the Second, the Sixth and the Ninth.

crammed with riders, but it wasn't. It had a lot of odds and ends of people – we were sort of odds and ends ourselves – and there was nobody singing or anything like that. In fact, there were people walking up and down the cars taking out light bulbs. They were rather considerate, though, they left one bulb in each car. It became very dim and a little grim. Others were pulling down cardboard advertising signs. The whole thing was very weird and not at all what we expected; we'd thought it might be like a Girl Scout sleigh ride – all full of jollity – but still we enjoyed ourselves. I know *we* were excited and giggling and waving out the windows to anybody who could see us in the apartment houses.

Distinctly, that was the time I realized this was my city and not Scranton – it came to me with great force – and that I would no longer go there on weekends and holidays and think I was going home. The fact that the El was going to be gone *meant* something to me, even the people taking the light bulbs. I wasn't an outsider, even among them; I wasn't taking bulbs myself, but I felt they were fellow citizens suddenly, not strange, alien creatures.

New York is a little like having a dangerous pet. You never know when it will turn around and scratch you and throw you out. It isn't quite as simple as that, though. I have the feeling that I'm partly responsible for it now, that I'm partly its trainer. I guess what I'm trying to say is that it is alive and, like any living thing, you have to be just a little wary and very respectful of it, even if you love it. It's a *presence*. Even the things that are bad about it and dangerous are important things that are bad and dangerous in our world and there's no use trying to run away from them. I wouldn't want to live in a place where everything was artificially solved or arbitrarily eliminated. I'd feel I'd been gypped of my time in history. You live in a certain time by chance and you might just as well live fully in it. That means coming to grips with what's wrong with it, as well as enjoying what's right. New York isn't artificial. It gives you lots of opportunity, but it doesn't shelter you or protect you or wrap you in cotton batting.

I feel a great temptation to despair sometimes and to wash my hands of it. Then I come to the conclusion that if you're in despair with New York you're in despair about our life and times, because New York is the essence of them. Most of the time, though, I feel hopeful. I may get to thinking things are going to hell in a handbasket and then I'll go to a Board of Estimate meeting on some housing row and hear people, ordinary people – not the Board – saying such sensible things and caring so much. They're quite *extra*ordinary. Yes, there're still enough of them who know what city life is and can be, who don't regard such horrible, subhuman projects as Penn Station South as normal. You know the way weeds will grow in a railroad track if it's not used, or spring up in a path? Well, people are just as dogged about life. Given just a little encouragement, they can grow over such places and turn them into living things again.

You get your life and times telegraphed to you here; they don't come by slow mail. And a lot of these surprises are very disturbing. One of them that came to me sharply was that so many institutions that are supposed to be the helpers and friends of the people and of society have been evolving into creatures that are not that at all. They are becoming the subhumanizers of the city. I mean, for example, the universities, the churches, and a great many of the settlement houses. They are taking decisions into their hands which the people they are supposed to serve oppose – and oppose with good reason. These institutions, instead of working in concert with ordinary people, are working with profiteering real-estate land-grabbers, city eaters, and dictatorial city officials. They sponsor projects that victimize the very people they should be protecting. Worst of all, they do this and still pretend to represent ordinary people. If what's happening in New York is a forecast of what's happening in our society generally, then maybe we *do* have reason to be frightened.

St. James Place near Oliver Street; the first cemetery of Congregation Shearith Israel. It is also the oldest burying ground in Manhattan.

WHITE NIGHTS AND WAN GENTILITY chapter 10

By comparison with the fine, noisy state of affairs that once obtained, night life in New York has taken on a kind of wan gentility and assumed early hours, so that it is now possible to walk into a night club at two or three o'clock in the morning and fire a cannon without hitting anything, or shoot reindeer, or get snowblind from the tablecloths, which are old rounders' sayings, not unlike the homely sentiments to be found on wall samplers. During prohibition there were an estimated 30,000 speakeasies in New York and a minimum of 70 first-class night clubs, in which it was usual to meet gangsters. The latter would occasionally murder or maim each other. It was customary then to dine in a speakeasy, go to the theater, attend a night club where there was a reasonable certainty that there

Harlem; a bar on 125th Street. The 'fays make the scene, all right, but the ghetto doesn't swing with them.

would be no gunplay, and wind up in Harlem at four o'clock in the morning to eat fried chicken and listen to Cab Calloway or Ethel Waters sing. This regimen was not greatly diminished by repeal and was nicely stimulated by the Second World War. On the whole, though, no one makes the kind of splash in night clubs now that, for example, the rich and extroverted Tommy Manville did on a white night in 1940 when, in full evening dress, he unhitched an aged white horse from a hansom cab, mounted, and spurred the sagging animal forthrightly into Leon & Eddie's, a congenial deadfall on Fifty-second Street, a few doors west of Twenty-one, a fashionable restaurant that is about the only relict of the great block between Fifth and Sixth avenues.

Ornette Coleman at the Village Vanguard. More jazz can be heard in New York than anywhere else in the world.

"Today, night life is a stale road company of the real thing," a retired member of the outgoing generation that flourished during prohibition and for some years more has said. Trapped in reminiscence, he delivered himself of a long elegy on the subject. "I've had the real thing," he said. "That's why I hang around in poolrooms now. They're the only place I can find all *my* people – boosters, touts, hoodlums, three-time losers, guys who know what six, two and even means." The very slang he used had about it a faint, yellowed *moyen âge* tinge to it. "So it makes me a guy who likes thieves," he continued, a bit defiantly. "That's the way I am. Those days, we used to wind up at the Club Argonne – Texas Guinan was there then; it's Al & Dick's, a music-business restaurant now. Up on Fifty-fourth. Or we'd hit the Club Richman on Fifty-sixth or the old Dizzy Club upstairs from that and we'd all go up to Harlem. There were fifteen good places – the Ubangi Club, Ye Old Nest, the Clam House, Dickie Wells, Clarence Robinson's, Yeah Man, Small's Paradise, the Breakfast Club. It was a dollar a drink – everything was a dollar a drink. The liquor was, of course, real rotgut. Gladys Bentley'd sing 'The Boy in the Boat.' How many people, you think, have any idea what the title means? It's too dirty even for today.

"And the hoodlums. In those days they were playboys and spenders. Today they're businessmen. It *was* an exciting era. We had a mayor with a broad. He ran out of liquor and Dutch Schultz brought him a bottle over to his table at the Central Park Casino. When Leo Reisman, I think it was, was the bandleader up there, he had a line. He'd say before playing, 'It's going to be a long, cold winter, folks, so shake your ashes.' I got no knock on the Little Flower, but he put an end to all that, just like he did to burlesque. We had district attorneys then were all pieces of raisin cake. If a man made a threat, it was something to worry about. Today, you spit in his eye. There were always fights. Now you don't see a decent fight. About five, six o'clock in the morning, we'd get back downtown to Dave's Blue Room. There's a Chinese restaurant there now. Seventh Avenue, the low Fifties. More girls, club owners, hoodlums, and also a million fights. One night, I remember, Joe E. Lewis made a crack about one of a certain hoodlum's fighters. The remark didn't set well with him. There was a picture of Joe E. in Dave's. This hood made it so that everybody came in one morning had to throw something at Lewis' picture. He paid for all the damage. Dave made himself a couple of hundred bucks.

"We had one real law-and-order guy in those days, Johnny Broderick. He really dumped hoodlums, but only if they got out of line. There was Pretty Amberg. He wound up in quicklime. Those days, he was going with a girl from the

Manhattan at night, looking south from the Tower Suite in the Time-Life Building. What is the sum of all the events framed in each square of light?

Harlem; the Apollo Theater. You don't swing if you haven't played the Apollo.

old Paradise. He heard she was going around with another guy and he stuck his false teeth in a glass of water and made her drink it. Broderick found out about it and he went over to the Kings Terrace where Amberg was that night. He sent in a message, 'Tell Amberg I want to see him.' Amberg wouldn't come out. Broderick went in and grabbed him by the hair, dragged him out, and Amberg went to Polyclinic for three months. Those days, the password was, 'Take him to Polyclinic.' Even after repeal, it was still good for a while. I recall an opening night at the downtown Cotton Club in 1937. Bill Robinson, the Nicholas Brothers, Ethel Waters, Cab Calloway, and Ada Ward. J. Edgar Hoover was there with Clyde Tolson and Winchell; Dietrich with Cole Porter and Erich Maria Remarque; Ed Wynn, Ozzie Nelson and Harriet Hilliard, Tony and Renée de Marco, Jim Barton, Milton Berle, Franklin Roosevelt, Jr. – and our best hoodlums. *They* sat in the boxes. When the show was over, Dan Healy, the mayor of Broadway, introduced the celebrities. He got them all out on the floor and he said, 'Let's all follow Bill in a soft shoe dance.' Where do you see that kind of thing today?"

Like the art of Gustave Moreau or the novels of J. K. Huysmans, this picture is somewhat overdrawn, a little bloodshot and rather luridly lighted. Nevertheless, even after the haze of sentimentality is dispelled from it and the drippings of bathos are wiped away, there is enough objective evidence around to prove that the night life of which the retired rounder spoke was, if no more extensive than it is now, certainly less pinched spiritually. To go back to the lobster palaces of the first decade of the twentieth century, to ragtime and *thé dansants;* to Reisenweber's (wonderfully, the building that housed it still stands on the west side of Eighth Avenue between Fifty-seventh and Fifty-eighth streets), Shanley's, Mouquin's, the old Waldorf, the Knickerbocker on Times Square (it stands, hacked up into

offices; its Maxfield Parrish mural of Old King Cole is in the bar of the St. Regis),
the Fifth Avenue Hotel and the Hoffman House on Madison Square, Ada Rehan,
the young Sophie Tucker, whoever or whatever, is, at best, an exercise in history;
at worst, it is a fake nostalgia for the young and a futile one for the old. A contemporary example is at hand of the destruction of a way of doing things at night
that was without parallel: the passing of Fifty-second Street.

The street – nobody but a publicity man ever called it "Swing Street" – was a
strenuous block between Fifth and Sixth avenues that survived, and even encouraged, thirty-two speakeasies, jazz of several varieties, burlesque, and a general
casting away of inhibition; it declined spectacularly, in five colors of neon tubing,
and the wreckers hauled it away, piece by piece, like a musical comedy heading
for a theatrical warehouse after a long run. The first phthisic intimation of its
mortality came when Rockefeller Center put up the Esso Building in the Forties,
causing a damp limestone chill to fall over the street, and its end arrived when
Jimmy Ryan's, the last jazz club on the block, was pulled down to make way for

*The Metropolitan Opera House; curtain time. Neither Belmonts nor Vanderbilts could have
foreseen that the opera would move north to Lincoln Center.*

the new Columbia Broadcasting System office building in 1962. Until the early Twenties, the five-story brownstones housed Rhinelanders, Iselins, Wagstaffs, Mrs. S. Stanwood Menken, and Bernard M. Baruch. They were followed by some of the most outstanding speakeasies in America, including Leon & Eddie's and Twenty-one, which people used to call Jack and Charlie's, and which began life on Forty-ninth Street as the Puncheon Grotto. Jack and Charlie's was often looked upon as an annex of the Ivy League colleges and its owners, the numerous Kriendler family and their partner, Charles Berns, were highly thought of. In an interview on shipboard upon his return from Europe in 1932, the late George Jean Nathan, the drama critic, declared, "Jack and Charlie of my favorite speakeasy would make the best President and Vice-President. The speakeasy makes money and the customers and owners are happy. In what other business is that true?"

Twenty-one cultivates a proud, quiet reserve with what amounts to passion and its standards may be said to be a sort of lamination of those imposed by the late Ward McAllister, Lucius Beebe, show business on good behavior, horsy people from Virginia, smooth-grained account executives from the big advertising agencies, and the less raffish (and better-heeled) creative minds from magazines, newspapers, television, and radio. The impression is created with the very façade of the restaurant, its wrought-iron gates and balcony. Spaced at intervals along the balcony and an unused outside stairway are twenty-eight hitching posts in the shape of little Negro boys dressed in the racing silks of leading stables, some of them no longer in existence. Until the police made them take it away, the proprietors had a traffic sign outside that read, "No Parking Here, Not Even Buicks." A legend of Twenty-one's inaccessibility to hoi polloi grew over the years; it is not entirely unjustified, although the people who run it insist that anyone in a decently tailored suit, with a reservation or the approval of two suave but bulky men who work the door, can get in.

Actually, Twenty-one is more than a restaurant. The Kriendlers have lent their customers money – some $20,000 during the Roosevelt bank holiday in 1933 – found them apartments and tickets to the theater; bailed them out when they got thrown in jail occasionally; and chartered planes for them when the need arose. It is one of the rare restaurants ever to memorialize a customer. That was the late Robert Benchley. Over a table in the bar, where Benchley used to sit, is a small bronze plaque that reads: "Robert Benchley, His Corner, 1889–1945." There is an inclination to forget that Twenty-one once was nothing more than a pleasant speakeasy. It wasn't even the first on the block. The first was opened, as far as can be determined, in 1926, by a man named Jean Billia, and Twenty-one, which opened on January 27, 1930, was third, after Billia and Leon & Eddie's. Most of the speakeasies arranged with federal agents and the police to be raided, with great fidelity and few casualties, every two or three months, but Twenty-one went to extraordinary lengths not to submit even to ritual indignities. The restaurant devised a system which included four push buttons in the vestibule. There were four so that the doorman could be sure of reaching one, no matter how muscular the agents became. When the alarm rang, all drinks were placed on the bar. Another button was pushed and the whole bar tipped back into a wall recess. Everything went down a chute into the sewers. On the day that repeal took effect, Twenty-one's customers poured *en masse* into the street in the late afternoon to assist the help in carting indoors the first legal shipment of liquor.

But it was hot music, as much as anything else, that gave the street its fine flavor. A short while after the end of prohibition, there were at least seven jazz parlors in operation on the block and the names of some of them have entered the hagiography of the idiom: the Onyx, the Three Deuces, the Famous Door, and Jimmy Ryan's. The birth of modern jazz took place at Minton's, in Harlem, but it was nourished on Fifty-second Street. The Dixieland, or moldy fig, tradition was maintained sturdily only by Ryan, an ex-hoofer and lifeguard and an outstandingly permissive man where Dixieland musicians were concerned. It was in Ryan's one night that Georg Brunis, a powerful trombonist who dropped *e's* in his first and last names on the advice of a numerologist, rose from his chair during a rendition of "High Society," waved at the band, and marched with band and audience out into Fifty-second Street, leaving only the piano, drums, and bass on the stand. The parade stopped traffic and ended with an eight-bar rideout in the powder room, the tone of which may be judged from the fact that it was run by the mother of a well-known piano player. The next night the police confined the parade to Ryan's.

Jazz is a chancy business at best, so that it was probably inevitable that its place would be usurped by the strip joints that were almost the last pleasure domes on the block. They were long, low, narrow rooms decorated in a sort of bastard *art nouveau* style. Their individual décors are rather difficult to describe, since they opened and closed like accordions, changing paint, policy, performers, names, and owners with refreshing regularity; they were constantly having their licenses suspended by the State Liquor Authority for, as the disarming legal word went, "suffering" indecent performances and exhibitions. Not long after her place of business had been shut down for several weeks, a talented peeler observed moodily to a friend, "They're slapping us to death with suspensions." She went on to say, "It's such a little, lousy street. Why can't they leave us alone? They're putting a lot of people out of work. People want flesh shows. If we didn't have them, these joints'd have to stay closed for good." Hers was the immemorial complaint of the crofter being displaced by the machines of the Industrial Revolution. Whatever is left of the stripping business in New York may be found on West Third Street, in Greenwich Village, hemmed in by coffeehouses, Italian restaurants, and garages, and it is a shabby remnant: a good many of the tinted pictures displayed outside are of girls long since flabby and departed.

What has happened to night life in New York is that, by and large, it has come to be conducted in an atmosphere of furious rectitude and intellectual uplift. About as good an index of this, aside from a brief outbreak of poetry readings in solemn jazz clubs on the Bowery and Hudson Street, was the wildly improbable appearance of John Cage, the Dada Daddy of serious composers, in a night club, the Village Vanguard. (The Vanguard had previously presented Jack Kerouac, the avatar of the Beat Generation, reciting, or rather mumbling, something he appeared to have made up on the spot; on the night of his debut, Kerouac was backed at the piano by Steve Allen, a patron of the arts; the two later made a recording together.) Cage became well known, or notorious, for his experiments

Upstairs at the Downstairs; the intimate night club. The formula is infinitely more difficult than is supposed.

with what he calls the "prepared piano," the strings of which he blocks off with wood and metal so that the instrument makes sounds like "gunk" and "clook." Now and then he closes the keyboard and thumps tenderly on the wood. Sometimes he writes a work without a score, explaining that "the conductor, like the players, has his own part. He represents a chronometer of variable speed. Each performance can be different, since each individual independently makes his own time-program from the material supplied him. Harmonious fusion of sound is not here an objective. . . ."

At the Vanguard, before an audience of reedy partisans and a handful of stunned but dead-game neutrals, Cage offered the world première of his "Concert for Piano, Voice and Four Instruments." The voice was furnished by an imposing blonde contralto named Arline Carman, whose general conformation bore a throbbingly vivid resemblance to that of the splendid female who once travestied the quartet from *Rigoletto* with the late Willie and Eugene Howard. The text of the piece, thoughtfully passed out on mimeographed sheets, read:

U, LI, 10, IJ, mud-luscious*, IU, E-H, Glory', W, Shem⋇, In Feld und Wald″, sur le feu avec du beurre°, erfreuen sich″, the cold ashes@, water@, A, fickle, freckled (who knows how?)', A, a Naga, or a Nagi, or a Yaksha, or a Yakshi, or an Asura, or an Asuri, or a Garuda, or a Garudi, or a Kinnara, or a Kinnari, or a Mahoraga, or a Mahoragi, or a Gandharva, or a Gandharvi, or a Bhuta, or a Bhuti, or a Kumbhanda, or a Kumbhandi, or a Pisara, or a Pisaci, or an Austaraka or an Austaraki, or an Apasmara, or an Aupasmari, or a Rakehasa, or a Rakshasi, or a Daka, or a Dakini, or an Aujohara, or an Aujohari, or a Kataputana, or a Kataputani, or an Amanushya, or an Amanushyi**, Why@, far and wee *, unhemmed as it is uneven!⋇, hoppy on akkant of his joyicity⋇, Die Voglein schweigen im Walde%, letting go as I do@, OE, (W) D, Er steht′′′, UB, intricate imperfect various*, U, LNL, Tell me, tell me, tell me, elm!⋇

*	e. e. cummings
'	Gerard Manley Hopkins
⋇	James Joyce
″	Friedrich Schnack
°	L. Dufour
@	Huang-Po Doctrine of Universal Mind
**	Lankavatara Sutra
%	Johann Wolfgang von Goethe
′′′	Anon

written in response)
to a request for)   instantaneous   and unpredictable
a manifesto, 1952)

nothing is accomplished by writing a piece of music) our ears are
″ ″ ″ ″ hearing ″ ″ ″ ″) now
″ ″ ″ ″ playing ″ ″ ″ ″) in excellent condition

When it was all over, Cage remarked that the surest indication of how far along music had come was that, whereas formerly a composition of his had required fifty to sixty rehearsals, that night's needed only one. Max Gordon, the owner of the Vanguard and of the Blue Angel uptown, a tiny, natural-shoulder man with a monklike fringe of gray hair, who has put up with any number of peculiar professionals since he opened the Vanguard in 1934, murmured to no one in particular, "My God."

The principal shorings under public night life in New York are out-of-towners, a group cosseted so assiduously that one night club waiter captain has devised a system for identifying them, sectionally at any rate, by their teeth. It has been the experience of this man, who works for the Copacabana, and whose blanket designation for all non-New Yorkers is "hoops," that the teeth of Westerners are large, square, and white; that those of Midwesterners are somewhat darker and a little more equine, although not buck. He found Southerners to have teeth that were both smaller and rather more tarnished than those of Midwesterners. He had no line, he said, on New Englanders, "because they rarely open their mouths," and he declared of New Yorkers that "their teeth are like their clothes – worked on. They have Brooks Brothers teeth."

Whatever the state of their dentition, or even of their finances, out-of-towners account for up to seventy-five per cent of the trade of New York's night clubs

Times Square; the Latin Quarter. One of the last of the old-fashioned night clubs, it looks like the inside of a box of Turkish delight.

and they are cultivated with a tenderness formerly reserved only for celebrities, moneyed hoodlums, and the late James J. Walker. The steady rise of the non-New Yorker in the ephemeral estimation of cabaret owners and headwaiters is the result of a number of things, one of which may be termed the factor of ironic democratization: taxes have decimated the ranks of local big spenders; despite restrictions, expense accounts make it possible for non-residents to tarry at the fleshpots. While a good many New Yorkers have expense accounts, too, they use them, in the main, to entertain out-of-towners, thereby producing not much more than a grave exchange of economical amenities at high prices paid by other people.

Greek café on the West Side. The belly dancers came from the Piraeus until the strippers from Brooklyn caught on.

Any real money possessed by a New Yorker, after he has paid his taxes, furnished his home, and sent his children to school, is apt to be spent on a vacation. He never spends his vacation in New York night clubs, if only because he has a television set which will give him far more expensive entertainment for nothing. The out-of-towner is equally harried by taxes and comforted by television, but he is either drawn to New York or forced to visit it on business, and, as a respected cabaret owner has observed, "He comes here to find what he hasn't got in his home town. *And,* if he had it in his own town, he wouldn't patronize it. It isn't for real unless he's seen it in New York and can tell folks back home about it. It is," he concluded, "a good thing for us he feels that way."

The leveling-off process has been profound. The sightseeing-bus people, for example, who once shuttled resolutely between Grant's Tomb and Chinatown, and whose customers, although worthy and from out of town, were hardly regarded as the mainstay of the cabaret business, have added a carefully frenetic slice of night life to their itineraries. Tour 8 of the Gray Line runs the gamut for $14.75 per person and "There Is Nothing More to Pay." It includes "Cocktail and Full Course Dinner" at the Copa at 6:45 P.M.; "One Drink of Choice" at Sammy's Bowery Follies, a downtown institution in which the presumed flavor of other days has been carefully reconstructed over sawdust, at 10:30 P.M.; and another "Drink of Choice" in the Hotel Lexington's Hawaiian Room at midnight, to say nothing of floor shows in all three places. The tour breaks up at 1 A.M. In urging its patrons to "Get Set for Your Liveliest and Smartest 'Night Out' in New York City," the company adds in its brochure: "Unescorted ladies are of course welcome to join our night life party. (GENTLEMEN WILL WEAR COATS AND TIES)" Gray's closest competition is Times Square Sightseeing Lines, Inc., which by a coincidence also has a Tour 8. This is, however, really only an extension of its No. 7. No. 7 is a two-hour trip through the Bowery ("The Street of Forgotten Men"), Greenwich Village ("Nite Clubs and Artist Colony"), and the Lower East Side ("The most congested streets in New York"). In making No. 8 out of No. 7, the line added an after-dark visit to the RCA observation tower and the Latin Quarter. At the Latin Quarter the visitor, says the folder, "is regaled by the eye-filling floor show of the famous 'Latin Quarter.' A full course chicken (or fish) dinner is served," and, as far as the company is concerned, clients can hang around the club as long as they like. The price is $12.95, tip and tax in tab.

The severe reorientation of night life has left out-of-towners with only four large clubs to patronize, and a generous but shifting clutch of small, dark ones of the kind known in *Variety,* the house organ of show biz, as "smalleries" or "intimeries," because they are small and intimate. The big ones are the International and the Latin Quarter on Broadway, the Copacabana on Sixtieth Street, just east of Fifth Avenue, and Basin Street East on East Fiftieth Street, which is really an oversized and highly successful outlet for non-controversial jazz and popular singers. The International is competition of a kind for the Latin Quarter. The Quarter, which has become as institutionalized as the New York Public Library, resembles the inside of a box of Turkish Delight, its furnishings running to red plush and plaster cartouches, as well as a score and a half or so of chorus girls, production singers, specialty dancers, and show girls; two bands and anywhere from five to a dozen acts. Farther north, the Copa still strikes a judicious balance between Broadway and Hollywood on the one hand and the rest of the United States on the other. For years it provided customers who thought themselves knowledgeable with a delicious thrill: the frequent presence of Frank Costello, an unfortunate gangster, and the rumor that Costello was one of the owners of the place. The rumor has never been substantiated. Early in 1962, however, the Copa's clients were treated to an unscheduled bit of entertainment: the reputed mouthpiece for a group of Brooklyn gangsters was, inexplicably, punched in the mouth by persons unidentified, of course.

The most enduring smalleries are the Blue Angel, which is on the East Side, and Downstairs at the Upstairs on the West, both of which demand a certain amount of cerebration from their clients. The Greek cabarets on the West Side, in Chelsea, have been in existence since the early Forties but, upon being discovered all over again in the late Fifties, have proliferated. They feature belly dancers, the majority of whom used to be imported from the Piraeus, the port of Athens, but the better part of whom are now imported from around the Port of New York. The girls writhe equably to the squeak and screech of clarinets and Middle Eastern stringed instruments (*bouzouki* and *oud*) and the banging of peculiarly shaped tambourines of Turkish origin (*terbouka*). The customers tuck folding money into the ample valley of their brassières or at the summit of their sketchy girdles. Often as not, male Greek customers will bound from their seats and dance a maddened, sinuous *zembekiko, sheftitele, sirte,* or *kalamatiano,* either alone, with the girls, or with each other. They are usually very graceful and half drunk.

Despite the demise of Fifty-second Street, more jazz can be heard in New York than anywhere else in the country. The cave of Birdland is on Broadway and the Hickory House a couple of blocks east of it on Fifty-second near Seventh Avenue. Around the corner and down Seventh Avenue a way is the Metropole, which, since it always keeps its doors open, gets as many non-paying customers on the sidewalk as it does paying ones inside. Eddie Condon no longer plays at Eddie Condon's on East Fifty-sixth Street, but his heirs and assigns – the New York-Chicago-neo-Dixieland musicians who came to the city with him in the late Thirties – do. Aside from Birdland, jazz is most advanced and gets taken with the greatest seriousness at a couple of transmogrified saloons downtown. These are the Five Spot, which moved up the Bowery, from south of Cooper Union, when its premises, well over a century old, were torn down, and the Half Note which is in a cluttered, grimy, and run-down manufacturing neighborhood on Hudson Street near the river. The Five Spot is run by an amiable man named Joe Termini, with his brother Ignatius, and it became what it is absentmindedly, so to say. The painters who have studios in the neighborhood got into some sort of internecine dispute with the owners of another gin mill they frequented and began to drop into the Five Spot, sharing the bar with a raggle-taggle of Bowery bums. They began making plans for Termini and these resulted in the importation of jazz into the Five Spot. As is always the case with a growth industry, so was it with the Five Spot. Prices went up, the bums were either ejected or were unable to afford the place, and it became a hangout for serious jazz fans and slumming Medicis from uptown. Actually, the bums did very nicely, panhandling outside and drinking elsewhere. As for Termini and his brother, they still seemed a little dazed years afterward by what had been wreaked upon them.

The chances are that in terms of concentration, vigor, and sheer exuberance – an exuberance quite often matched by quality – the night life of Greenwich Village is unequaled by anything uptown and is cheaper, although not as inexpensive as tourists like to think. It is conducted in a small area whose north-south Axis is Macdougal Street from West Third south almost to Houston and whose east-west axis is Bleecker from West Broadway to Sixth Avenue. The *quartier* is a tangled proliferation of night clubs, to which it is veritably impossible to attach any kind of description, since they change policy erratically; coffeehouses, bars, restaurants, pizza stands, a delicatessen, Italian bakeries, off-Broadway theaters, a movie house specializing in the old and avant-garde, and, of all things, two undertaking parlors and a rifle club. The night clubs include what is probably the only genuine *café-concert* in New York – the Village Gate; the Premise, which originated in Chicago, made an art of improvised satire and then imported itself to New York; the Second City, which is, in fact, a second Premise; the Bitter End; and Gerde's Folk City, which is, as it were, the Carnegie Hall of folk singers.

One other kind of night life has been taken up in New York by the young, ardent, and relatively impoverished. This is attendance at art movies, as far uptown as the New Yorker Theater on upper Broadway and as far down as the Charles on Avenue B. It is felt to be chic for a group of no more than eight, one of whom at least must have a beard and another of whom must wear a checkered cap with a short peak (women may come in stretch pants and ballet

First Avenue; public bath. Soap and towels cost two cents. There are few left; for the most part, the proletariat has achieved indoor plumbing, however foul.

slippers), to meet at exactly 9:30 P.M. in a queue in front of the house, where, while waiting, they will engage in a spirited discussion of, say, the theology of Paul Tillich or Martin Buber or the return to respectability of representational painting. At 9:45 P.M. the group, having been admitted to the theater, will repair to the lounge, there to drink a lukewarm demitasse furnished by the management and also to murmur brokenly over an exhibition of lukewarm abstract photographs furnished by a friend of the management. Nobody goes upstairs before the last complete show, which is scheduled for ten o'clock. A man who once did so was accused of being a parvenu in search of a seat and was not asked out again.

The show always includes an esoteric short subject, which won *second* prize at the Cannes Film Festival, and a French, Swedish, or Italian picture with English titles. The titles are sedulously ignored by the group, all of whom profess to speak French, Swedish, and Italian, or bits of them, and laugh or nudge each other knowingly in the right places. When the picture is over, it is *de rigueur* for everyone to drift languidly over to a dimly lighted espresso joint and to talk only about the director of the picture or about the short subject. In the coffeehouse, the participants order many different kinds of coffee, some with cinnamon sticks in it, some with chocolate. All of it is said to be of Balkan, Turkish, or Russian origin. They also eat small, unidentifiable sandwiches. By then the picture has been dropped and everybody is making intimate revelations. Of the eight, seven are, as the saying goes, "in analysis"; four are six weeks behind in their payments; the eighth has stopped going and has begun to sneer at the others. Everybody says that everybody else is "hostile," "aggressive," or "projecting," "failing to relate to" or just plain "sick." At 1:30 A.M. the eight have gone to bed, all of them inexpressibly depressed and with plenty of fresh material for what they no longer call the "headshrinker," but the "coach." The eighth man, of course, is now "well" and has to endure his misery by himself.

WITNESS

ERNEST NAGEL
John Dewey professor of philosophy, Columbia University

I think it could be said that there is an identifiable school of philosophy of New York, just as, for example, there is at Oxford. New York is probably unique in that respect in the United States. There's something called naturalism. I suppose one of its distinctive features is that it is secular. In one sense, it is materialistic in that it doesn't subscribe to the view that there are non-material agencies operating in the world. It also subscribes to the conception that standards of the good life are to be obtained, not from transcendental sources, but from a kind of consideration of what actual living interests are. In short, to the extent that naturalism is a general attitude, I think most of the people I know at institutions in New York – this would not hold true for Fordham, which is a Catholic university – all share this.

Let me amend that. It would not be correct to say that all New York philosophers adhere to a common conception as to what philosophy ought to be, nor are their

Lunch in the graveyard of Trinity Church. The air is tonic in the canyons of Wall Street; the headstones are décor.

Central Park; chess players. The clock never runs out on them.

standards uniform. In my own department, some of us differ very seriously on how philosophy, in detail, ought to be done; how rigorous one ought to be in one's analysis and so on. Some of my colleagues have an outook that is more like philosophy in the grand manner, in which one offers a total survey of the world. Others of us, however, feel that this isn't quite the way it should be done, because there is a great danger then that one will come forth with truisms dressed up in high-sounding language. Make your analysis, they will say, always in the context of some very concrete problem.

But, by and large, all of us in New York have a sense that if you're going to make philosophy just a specialty cultivated by specialists then (a) the vitality of philosophy and (b) its historical mission as a clarifier of ideas will be gone. All of us do, in some way, feel that we don't want to have students who will go into philosophy and that's all; that we're simply training a future group of professional philosophers. We like to believe the students we have will acquire a perspective which will be of some relevance to what they're doing, even if they go into some scientific specialty, or law, or administration, or what not. This, I believe, does distinguish a group that can be called New York philosophers.

The sort of concentration one finds in Oxford is probably impossible to achieve here. At Oxford, something like sixty people teach philosophy and since theirs is a relatively small community, they can meet frequently to carry on. One would think, *a priori,* that in a large place like New York the opportunity for frequent and intensive philosophical discussion would be very great. I do not find it to be so. Everybody is too busy; one takes on a variety of obligations that in a small place, perhaps, would not be attempted; there are too many demands on our time, too many chores. In that sense, I think, New York may have less to offer than a smaller place. But if a man's conception of the task of philosophy includes contributing to the clarification of the ideas of people other than philosophers, then it seems to me that being in a city like New York has some advantages that offset the advantages of a smaller city.

As I say, my particular interest is in seeing philosophy not as a highly specialized discipline, with its own limited problems, but as a much wider one. I'm interested in the philosophy of science. I find it rewarding to engage in serious discussion with people in the physical, biological, and social sciences and to learn something valuable at first hand from them. I'm interested in the philosophy of law and I have the opportunity both to teach it and to participate in a joint seminar with a specialist in the law. It's not likely I could do this even at many of the larger universities elsewhere. Columbia makes it possible for a man like myself, whose concern in philosophy is to establish some sort of bridge between one discipline and another.

To what extent New York, with its heavy concentration of the arts and sciences, influences a philosopher, I don't know, but it's not impossible that it does. I do know this, for example: New York, being the center of a good many of the larger trade unions, influenced the direction a number of serious philosophers took in the Thirties. Also, the existence here of movements which attempt to supply a need that, in many cases, traditional religious institutions provide – without their theological commitments – has influenced the course of certain New York philosophers.

An attorney

I suppose it's wrong to talk in terms of size, but there's a fairly substantial group of lawyers in New York who have no interest in the law other than to earn as much money from it as they possibly can. They make it from the settlement or referral of negligence cases, but to me they are agents and businessmen, and their involvement in the law is no greater than that of a textile merchant selling goods made by others. They get cases and have other lawyers try them. I hardly think of them as practicing law. Apart from these, however, I feel that you will, by and large, find more dedicated lawyers in New York than in the majority of cities. Oddly, they are not held in as high esteem, nor do they esteem themselves as highly. The lawyer is less unique in New York than he is in a small town and for that reason less respected.

There's another thing that's different about practice in New York as opposed to, let us say, Columbus, Ohio. There, lawyers trust each other completely. One will call up another and make agreements that are never recorded. Each remembers an agreement and lives up to it. In New York everything is recorded and signed – we make stipulations, as the phrase goes – indicating a lack of trust. I will add

The Garment Center; a dress house. Only because of Seventh Avenue have American women a thing to wear.

The Lower East Side; lawyer's office. "I feel that you will, by and large, find more dedicated lawyers in New York than in the majority of cities." – Ephraim S. London

The United States Post Office. The service is not nearly as imposing as the building.

that, whenever I deal with a lawyer I don't know here, I require signed confirmations of everything agreed to. I won't do it with one I know well, unless I know him not to be a man of his word. I'd say that, of those I do know, I can trust more than half. In Columbus, I could trust them all. Also, in Columbus, if a lawyer gets the reputation of not being a man of his word, he couldn't survive. Here lots do and do well, even though other lawyers know they are not to be trusted.

One thing about New York practice is bad. Some time ago I addressed the Bar Association in Paterson, New Jersey. I got talking to some of the Paterson people and I found that the lawyers who were assigned to defend indigent criminals were the really experienced ones, men who also had the highest incomes. This has not been true in New York. The practice here has always been to take lawyers just out of school and assign criminal cases to them. Or there are hangers-on in the criminal courts who get such cases by assignment and then somehow get the defendant's family to fork over a hundred dollars or so. If they get a couple of these a week, they're doing fine. It's only in murder cases that the state pays anything – $1500 for a defense, $1500 for an appeal – but these go to political hacks for the most part.

My complaint is that the better lawyers just do not volunteer to take on these cases or to help with them in any way. The result is that the majority of indigent criminal defendants are badly represented. The thing can be licked. I'll tell you a story to exemplify it. It concerns a federal judge, a man I have nothing but reverence for, but the lesson applies to the state courts just as well. This man had a criminal case before him – I won't particularize – involving several penniless defendants. He asked them if there was any lawyer they'd like assigned. Yes, they said, one especially, but they wouldn't dream of asking him to work for nothing in a trial that might take, so far as they knew, months. The judge called this lawyer in. "There's nothing in the world I'd rather do," this man said, "but you know I've got a wife and two kids and, with my kind of neighborhood practice, I make about $6000 a year. It would be an awful chunk to have to give up that practice for two or three months."

"I think I can solve the problem," the judge told him. He then summoned three leaders of the New York bar, all of whom, he knew, had incomes well over $200,000 a year. "Gentlemen," he said, "I have this case" – which he described – "and I have to assign a lawyer. I have decided to name a man of real competence. As a result, I have singled out you three and I will name one or two of you to try the case." They became apoplectic. "It'll make little or no difference to you," the judge told them. "Suppose you *were* to lose some income for two months? How much would that be out of your lives? I think these men are entitled to first-rate representation."

Suddenly one of these men recalled that he had a heart condition and the other two found themselves with impossibly crowded schedules. "Well, there *is* a solution," the judge said. "If you were to go to your friends, tell them about the case and let them know that it would be possible to employ adequate counsel, provided a way were found to raise the money, *and* if such a fund were raised, I think I could hire a lawyer who would be satisfactory to these defendants." Do you know what happened? They raised $15,000 in no time at all – out of their

The New York Times *at edition time. Its stature is such that among news-papers there is nothing to compare it with.*

own pockets. Rather than be assigned. The judge turned the money over to the young lawyer. He got more for a relatively short period of work than he would have earned normally in a year, to say nothing of funds for investigation and so on.

These were topflight lawyers, I point out again, really good minds. And they were appalled at the thought of being assigned a criminal case. They think criminal cases are dirty and they feel they lose status if they defend them. This is a terrible weakness in the administration of justice here. The brahmins of the Association of the Bar of New York are scared stiff at the idea of doing anything formally that would resemble what the judge did. They would be appalled merely to hear the subject brought up. They would call it "socialized law."

In the final analysis, I don't want to seem to condemn my profession. I have more respect for lawyers than I do for businessmen. But there are very few law firms of any stature that contribute their time to such things. Doctors, bastards though you may think they are, *have* to spend a lot of time in clinics and they do a good job. Lawyers will raise money for charities or children with multiple sclerosis or anything else, but they have no time or stomach for this thing. *This* is the debt we lawyers are not paying. The law is not regarded as a humanitarian profession as is medicine. It should be. I don't expect much of a merchant. I have a right to expect it, though, of a lawyer.

COLLEEN DEWHURST
An actress

I've seen New York from a number of different vantage points. I saw it as a typical suburban child, living in Crestwood, and New York was where my mother brought me once a year to Radio City and John Wanamaker at Christmastime to hear the carol singing and to buy clothes for school. It meant only that it was exciting and that I would see my father at his office and go to the Automat. When I moved to the Midwest my mother kept the city alive for me, she loved it so. Then, when I came back to go to the American Academy of Dramatic Arts, I had a kind of finishing-school period – nice clothes, seeing organ grinders on the street, flowers being sold in subway stations, and I thought the city was very romantic. When I left the Academy, I more or less left my mother's household and support, and entered on my profession. Now, New York looked very different to me. It was overwhelming.

It has never frightened me, though. I have never felt oppressed by it. I *have* felt anger at not being able to have everything from the city I wanted, a tremendous yearning and a tremendous desire. I can remember, in the early days, walking on Fifth Avenue at Easter in whatever one good outfit I had and thinking that New York belonged only to successful people, that it was not really a city of joy, except to those who were successful. By then the city had become a succession of apartments with overstuffed furniture that wasn't mine, and bedbugs and windows that looked into air shafts. It's amazing how, wherever you

Central Park; the Conservatory Gardens, Fifth Avenue at 105th Street. The group is a gift to the children of New York in the name of Frances Hodgson Burnett, the author of Little Lord Fauntleroy.

Old-fashioned rooftop in the mid-Eighties on the East Side and sunbathers.

Fifth Avenue and Fifty-ninth Street; the Pulitzer Fountain in winter.

live in New York, a single place can become your whole existence – the bus stop a half block from your building; the job you have to hold to keep alive. What always sustained me was that I knew it was not going to stay that way.

I found all the clichéd things about theatrical agents being tough to be true and I went through the years of working at a reducing salon, working as a receptionist, working for the Telephone Company, working at Macy's as a demonstrator, but I think all of those things, without my knowing it at the time, and much as I hated them, made me very much a part of New York. I guess all the really tough, grimy, repulsive things that were happening to me, too, were a kind of love affair, possibly a kind of marriage with New York. I suppose it's like living

Rockefeller Plaza rink and skaters. For some, New York is once a year—an hour on the ice, three more in the Music Hall.

with a person – when everything's hearts and flowers, you don't know whether you really love him; it's when the tension starts and the going gets rough that you find out. At one time I thought New York was where I had to be because here was where my career was. But I love it now and I always will. It will always be the first city for me.

I wouldn't change the dreadful thirteen years I had at first for anything, because whatever came out of me, whatever made me the human being I am, is the result of those thirteen bad years. I've learned this city can belong to nobody. It belongs to itself. It is very much like a human relationship. Whatever you give it, you will get back; what you choose to see in it, you will see. I

The Empire State Building, looking south. The Waldorf-Astoria moved north.

never thought I would have a life where I would go to Central Park in the morning with my children and hear carrousel music or see my husband play in actors' baseball games. It's become a softer city for me, a city I had never seen.

New York has done me damage, too. How could it not? I think that, just as it took me away from many stultifying influences, so it also gave me a false sense of release, and for a period there was a blunting of moral standards in me. I found it a little easier to do certain things; I was in a profession that puts no set limits on behavior; I had no one, therefore, to answer to, except myself. I lost my religious aspirations – not out of any desire to find other truths – but simply because it was easy; they didn't seem to fit in. And so, in a way, I *did* conform to the city. But, as I go on, I find that I want to return to a good deal of what I believed.

The city has been wonderful for me, but, like very good friends or people you love, you have to get out of it. When I return, even when I return on the worst possible day, I can find it in me to love it. I can remember George and me coming across the George Washington Bridge on one of the hottest days in history – we had driven all across the country – and my saying, "God, it's so *good* to be back," and the two of us ending up roaring with laughter, because, obviously, we were entering a hell of a place at just that moment.

Central Park; the Zoo. In the jungle of New York, the tiger is safer than the child.

The statue of Justice atop City Hall.
She may not be blind, but she is often mute.

THE DEAD STAR CHAPTER 11

I am an urban man of amorphous or, rather, poorly focused longings, disorderly habits, and a vast, badly concealed sentimentality in certain areas. I have raised three sons on a medley of "East Side, West Side," "A Bicycle Built for Two," "Take Me Out to the Ball Game" and "And the Band Played On." For all of my slipshodness in many other matters, the sequence never varied. In their bedrooms at night, on swings and seesaws on a weekend afternoon in one of the city's gratuitously hideous asphalt and concrete playgrounds, I sang the songs to the boys for years after any necessity to do so existed, indeed, after they had repeatedly made it plain they were bored with them. When that happened, I was taken aback; these songs had the power – stupidly – to bring tears to my eyes and I realized at last that it was to myself I had been singing them all the time.

Aside from their simple-minded melodies and lyrics, which are so appealing, what they had in common for me was that they were, I thought, true New York City songs. They were almost the first I learned or that I remembered and they were as unavoidably a part of the love I felt for the city in which I was born as anything I could summon up. I find that they still run through my head – bidden or unbidden, it is hardly important – whenever I am most nearly happy, which is not very often the condition of a city man. At best, a dweller in New York can be anesthetized in his undefined but pervasive unhappiness.

But over the years a curious and, to me, a shocking thing has happened. These songs, these criteria (I thought) of New York, have occurred to me less and less often in my city and more and more often elsewhere – in such unexpected places as the Boulevard Magenta in Paris, which is really no more than a secondhand street, or on the Buttes Chaumont; on Pioneer Square, the Skid Row of Seattle; in Louisburg Square or back of Faneuil Hall or along Commonwealth Avenue in Boston; in a grassed square in Charleston, South Carolina; almost anywhere east of Sixth Street and south of Walnut in Philadelphia. There is no need for me to be any more tendentious about it than I have been.

What this phenomenon showed me, to my infinite chagrin, was that I am an anachronism and a willed one at that, not even an old man left alive untimely. The apartment in which this was written stands on the southwest corner of Bleecker Street and Broadway. (I have not overlooked the irony that the building is a modern one and its rooms are air-conditioned.) It was on Bleecker Street that the last horsecar line in New York operated until sometime in July of 1917. My apartment is a block south of the Broadway Central Hotel, in which Ned Stokes shot Jim Fisk to death over Josie Mansfield and in which major-league baseball was organized. (A plaque in the lobby commemorates only the latter.)

Fishing below the George Washington Bridge. The pastime is more ritualistic and therapeutic than productive.

A short block to the east, at Crosby Street, is the only building by which Louis Sullivan is represented in New York, the Bayard Building. A block south of it, on Crosby at Houston, is a vacant lot, but I know that on that lot once stood the notorious saloon and dance hall run by Harry Hill, in which, of all things, the Salvation Army held its first public meeting in America.

Greene Street, which is two blocks to the west of me, was once an almost unbroken string of brothels from Canal Street north to what is now Eighth Street and the old Haughwout Store, in which Otis installed the first really workable passenger elevator, still stands at the northeast corner of Broadway and Broome Street. On Fourth, just east of Lafayette, is a modest museum of the early nineteenth century, the Old Merchant's House, but how many are there who know or, knowing, care that it was *lived in* – lived in amid the terrible decay of what was once the most fashionable neighborhood in New York – until 1933, by an admirable spinster who died in the bed in which she had been born ninety-three years earlier?

Splinter Beach, an East River pier. "Boys and girls together,/ Me and Mamie O'Rourke . . ."

Splinter Beach No. 2, an East River pier. ". . . We'll trip the light fantastic/On the sidewalks of New York."

Beneath an arch of the Brooklyn Bridge. The arch of course remains, but the buildings have been torn down and with them the small mysteries of a crooked street.

A part of LaGrange Terrace, originally nine marble, colonnaded dwellings of an inordinate grandeur, built in 1831 and occupied by, among others, Astors and Delanos, remains on the west side of Lafayette south of Astor Place. Across the street from it is the Hebrew Immigrant Aid Society that uses the buildings of the great Astor Library, which stands on the site of the Vauxhall Gardens, a sort of innocent amusement park. Half a block south of Houston Street, on the west side of Mercer, dwarfed by huge and ugly loft buildings, stands the brownstone Firemen's Hall of 1854. It is used as an ordinary firehouse now; it has been stripped of its decoration and the statue of the fireman on the roof, but it is there.

I yearn for whatever is left of this tangle of past generations and mourn whatever of the little that is left is made away with. In the spring of 1962 there was destroyed a small mystery which I had never had any desire to see dispelled. The mystery was the presence of Hague Street, a tiny thoroughfare no more

Hilton and Americana hotels. They contain the biggest of, the most of, and the newest of.

than, say, sixty feet long, running into an arch of the Brooklyn Bridge, on its north side. Incredibly, there was an apartment house on Hague Street in which people lived; there were doorbells and names above them. I could not bear to ask these people who they were. Mine would have been, I believed, the most egregious invasion. I was wrong, however; that was performed by the bulldozers and when I walked down to Hague Street one day to show a friend this hidden Street it was gone – gone save for a fire hydrant and the lamppost on which, like a dead hand, the street sign still hung. I do not walk there any longer.

In the fall of 1962 two tiny houses, a hundred and twenty-five years old or more, with steeply pitched roofs and dormer windows, on the west side of Broadway between Washington Place and West Fourth Street, were torn down to make a parking lot. On many of these old buildings, the floors and walls were braced with iron rods and the rods bolted to the outside walls with threaded iron ornaments. The wreckers let me have half a dozen – on these buildings, they were five-pointed stars about a foot in diameter and weighing above ten pounds apiece. And so I now own some fragments of New York. But no sooner had I got them home than I knew I had again deceived myself: the stars were dead; they had no function and supported nothing.

Hans Andersen in Central Park. His bronze nose is shiny from all the loving tweaks it gets.

The stars have no function; the songs about New York have no meaning. I am oppressed by the glass-curtain walls of Third Avenue, Park Avenue, and Sixth Avenue; appalled by dun-colored housing projects twenty stories high; always aware of how cold it is in a supermarket and of how little a supermarket resembles anything peculiar to New York. There are almost no neighborhoods left. Man is not the measure of anything in this city. There was a time when – no matter what the historians say – he was. Whatever the city did to him, it did it to him as a man. Now, he is acted upon as a number, as an account, in a computer.

And yet, the most astonishing thing is that for all I hate what has happened to New York, for all I believe it to have lost the qualities that made it uniquely New York, I am unable to live anywhere else. I am uneasy in other cities and miserable in suburbs. My city angers me now and frustrates me and makes me bitter. It has become very nearly impossible for me to live in New York, but it has also become impossible for me not to. I am in no better and no worse case than any other New Yorker.

A view of the Pan Am Building from West Forty-fourth Street. The motives of such architects as Emery Roth & Sons are perfectly comprehensible but what excuse have Gropius and Belluschi to offer?

Battery Park; commemorative pylons for members of the armed forces dead in Atlantic coastal waters during the Second World War. Here, too, Jenny Lind was adored.

INDEX

Page references to pictures are in italics.